BLACK AND QUEER ON CAMPUS

BLACK AND QUEER ON CAMPUS

MICHAEL P. JEFFRIES

NEW YORK UNIVERSITY PRESS
NEW YORK

NEW YORK UNIVERSITY PRESS
New York
www.nyupress.org

Please contact the Library of Congress for Cataloging-in-Publication data.
ISBN: 9781479803910 (hardback)
ISBN: 9781479803941 (paperback)
ISBN: 9781479803972 (library ebook)
ISBN: 9781479803965 (consumer ebook)

New York University Press books are printed on acid-free paper, and their binding materials
are chosen for strength and durability. We strive to use environmentally responsible
suppliers and materials to the greatest extent possible in publishing our books.

Manufactured in the United States of America

10 9 8 7 6 5 4 3 2 1

Also available as an ebook

To my family, with love,
and to the students quoted in this book.

CONTENTS

INTRODUCTION

Kamala Harris is not only the first Black and South Asian woman to serve as vice president; she was the first sitting vice president to march in a Pride parade. On June 12, 2021, she used her platform at Capitol Pride in Washington, DC, to reaffirm the Biden administration's commitment to LGBTQ+ rights and commemorate those killed in the Pulse nightclub shooting five years earlier on June 12, 2016. After highlighting the transgender community and young LGBTQ+ people as groups in need of more protection, she affirmed, "There is so much more work to do, and I know we are committed."[1]

Harris's commitment to LGBTQ+ rights dates back to her time as an elected official in California, where she began as San Francisco district attorney before becoming California attorney general and eventually United States senator. She spoke out against the ban on same-sex marriage resulting from the passage of Proposition 8 in 2008, and officiated California's first such marriage once the right to wed was restored in 2013. She began strategizing ways to end the use of gay and transgender panic as a defense in court in 2006,[2] and California banned the practice in 2014, becoming the first state to do so. And when she was selected as Democratic presidential nominee Joe Biden's running mate, she appointed Karine Jean-Pierre as her chief of staff. Jean-Pierre thus became the first Black person, Black woman, and Black lesbian to serve in the role. Harris is not immune to criticism from those disappointed in several aspects of her record on LGBTQ+ rights. During the presidential campaign, advocates pointed out that Harris's stance towards sex workers as California attorney general had a disproportionate impact on LGBTQ+ people, who are overrepresented in the industry. Her office also filed court briefs arguing against providing transgender surgery for inmates in the California prison system. Still, when Biden selected Harris as his running mate, Human Rights Campaign president Alphonso David affirmed, "It's clear the Biden-Harris ticket marks our nation's most pro-equality ticket in history."[3]

No doubt, Harris's values were shaped by her upbringing in the San Francisco Bay Area, long considered one of the most hospitable regions in the country for LGBTQ+ people. But looking back on all the forces that molded her, Harris says, "There are two things in particular that made me who I am today: An incredibly strong mother and a family that nurtured me, and Howard University."[4] In discussing her time at Howard, Harris talks about how it helped her understand her mother's reminder that she did not just "fall off the coconut tree"; she was part of a chain, a legacy of people that predates and will outlive her. She is running a race that started long ago, and the question of her life is, "What will you do with the baton during the time you have to carry it?" The strength in numbers and the diversity of Black life on campus also showed Harris that she could be anything she wanted to be, and the college would support her in realizing her full potential.

In 2013, seven years before Harris was elected, President Barack Obama gave the commencement address at another storied historically Black college or university (HBCU), Morehouse College. Obama hit all the expected notes in a symphonic performance of Black respectability, emphasizing the legacy of Morehouse alumni, and urging students to aim for a higher standard of manhood. One chord he struck rang awkwardly. After telling the story of a graduate in attendance named Frederick, who enrolled at Morehouse to remain close to his girlfriend and their child, he implored each graduate to "be the best husband to your wife," and paused for effect. The crowd was silent as Obama continued, "Or your boyfriend, or your partner," dipping his head and raising his brow, for emphasis. Obama paused for effect once again, and this time the silence was broken by murmuring and laughter, which Obama responded to by lifting a finger, signaling that it was no laughing matter. Without missing a beat, he continued, "Be the best father you can be to your children." He transitioned from these commands to addressing the mythic "cycle" of Black fatherlessness, soothing the sting of queerness with the salve of hetero-patriarchal respectability politics.

Obama had broken ground highlighting LGBTQ+ people in other spaces. His victory address in Chicago the night of the 2008 presidential election was the first that featured a president-elect explicitly naming queerness as part of the American body politic and his core constituency. "To anyone who still questions the power of our democracy, tonight is your answer," he said. "It's the answer spoken by young and old, rich and poor, Democrat and Republican, Black, white, Hispanic, Asian, Native American, gay, straight, disabled and not disabled."

Just as LGBTQ+ people heard their voices and contributions echo through the public sphere on election night, LGBTQ+ people at Morehouse heard theirs echo through the Black public sphere. Obama's somewhat chastising conservatism notwithstanding, members of the Morehouse community saw it as a watershed moment. As Jafari Allen wrote, "It was a simple recognition of the humanity of queers, but it was nonetheless profoundly significant, especially at this time, and in that setting, where, until recently, we had remained unacknowledged from pulpits of power, and where queer students and their allies have been working for at least a generation to receive just that sort of acknowledgment of their belonging at Morehouse and in Black communities."[5]

Harris and Obama are the two most visible and powerful Black elected officials in United States history. Harris is HBCU educated and had arguably the strongest record of support for LGBTQ+ rights of any member of the executive branch at the time she assumed the vice presidency. Obama's presidency brought about the restoration of marriage rights, the end of Don't Ask Don't Tell, and a collection of unprecedented public statements by a president affirming the dignity and belonging of LGBTQ+ people in all spaces, including Black spaces like Morehouse. Harris's and Obama's public affirmation of LGBTQ+ rights and dignity cannot be separated from their racial identities and embeddedness in Black communities. And in parsing these identities and the places they visited to build and maintain the bonds of Black siblinghood, we find HBCUs at the core.

Black and Queer on Campus is the first research-based book about Black lesbian, gay, bisexual, transgender, and queer (LGBTQ+) college students. I draw on in-depth interviews with forty Black LGBTQ+ students from nine different HBCUs, and another twenty-five Black students from seven predominantly white institutions (PWIs), in order to bring their compelling stories to life.[6] I decided to prioritize HBCUs for two reasons. First, I want to engage with the stereotype that Black people and Black institutions are more homophobic than white ones. Views on marriage equality are often presented as evidence for this belief. Though a majority of Black Americans now support marriage equality, public opinion data suggest that Black American attitudes towards gay marriage and homosexuality are less favorable than white attitudes.[7] These data are often hastily offered in the service of an argument that Black people stand in the way of LGBTQ+ rights. This is distortion and scapegoating. It ignores the diversity of views about LGBTQ+ rights among Black people and implies that Black LGBTQ+ people either do not exist or are too small in number to matter. This explanation also pits Black people against LGBTQ+ people, as critics suggest that Black folks should be able to see similarities between their civil rights struggle and that of their LGBTQ+ siblings. It suggests that the root causes of LGBTQ+ suffering are the attitudes of Black people rather than the long and ongoing institutionalized discrimination and violence LGBTQ+ folk are subject to.

Still, Black people's values, beliefs, and practices—the building blocks of Black culture—must have some effect on the lived experiences of Black LGBTQ+ people. There is no static and monolithic "Black culture of homophobia." Though the stereotype is wrong, we cannot ignore the particular formations of homophobia and transphobia that emerge in Black spaces. Because HBCUs are spaces where Black culture flourishes, Black campuses are excellent sites for exploring these issues.

The second reason I prioritize HBCUs is to disrupt the pattern of treating HBCUs as afterthoughts in higher education. Discussions about "elite" higher education routinely ignore the most prestigious HBCUs and the life outcomes of HBCU graduates. When we talk about "the typical Black college student," we are frequently led to imagine a Black college student on a white campus. In this book, the value of HBCUs is beyond dispute, with or without a comparison to PWIs. It is impossible to describe Black experiences in college without focusing on HBCUs.

Long before I decided to write this book, several Black LGBTQ+ students at the PWI where I work told me they felt there was little space for them on campus. In queer social spaces, they said, they could not be fully Black. As Trent, a student I interviewed for this book, told me, "Within, like, the Black community, there's a lot of homophobia, and within the queer community, there's a lot of racism. So it's, like, kind of having to build this community by yourself, like with other queer and trans people of color, 'cause you kind of don't fit in anywhere else." Students like Trent who attend PWIs feel pressure to code switch and temper discussions of racism and criticisms of their non-Black peers. In Black social spaces, they often feel pressure to minimize their nonconforming gender identity and/or sexual orientation, or hide them altogether, in order to be accepted.[8] So I had suspicions about Black LGBTQ+ student experiences at both PWIs and HBCUs. The students I interviewed both confirmed and confounded what I thought I might find.

I set out with three main questions: What are the day-to-day experiences of Black LGBTQ+ college students? What roles do LGBTQ+ student organizations play on campus? How do the experiences and beliefs of Black LGBTQ+ students at HBCUs compare with those of their peers at PWIs?

FABULOUS, FLY, AND QUEERTIDIAN

The first two decades of the twenty-first century have brought about unprecedented Black queer visibility in American popular culture. There is a burgeoning market for narratives and representations of Black LGBTQ+ people, evidenced by the success of films like *Pariah* (2011), *I Am Not Your Negro* (2016), and *Moonlight* (2016), and television shows such as *RuPaul's Drag Race*, *The Wire*, *Orange Is the New Black*, *How to Get Away with Murder*, and *Pose*. The Black LGBTQ+ actors, directors, and writers who produce the shows and play many of the characters are increasingly willing to tell their own stories, fusing artistry with advocacy. In publishing, Black LGTBQ+ activists and writers like Charlene Carruthers, Darnell Moore, Patrisse Khan-Cullors, Michael Arceneaux, Jacqueline Woodson, Saeed Jones, Janet Mock, and Charles Blow have built on the foundation laid by James Baldwin, Audre Lorde, and others, enriching the canon of first-person accounts of Black queerness. These are not commercially inflated characters or caricatures packaged for consumption. This is a new generation of stars and change makers, and Black LGBTQ+ college students are their audience and interlocutors.

Many, though not all, of these artists and advocates embrace colorful Black queer fabulousness as part of their self-presentation and politics. Madison Moore outlines the defining features of the phenomenon in his book *Fabulous: The Rise of the Beautiful Eccentric* (2018), explaining that fabulousness as a queer political aesthetic does not require celebrity or wealth in order to be enacted. He also insists,

> Fabulousness is dangerous, political, confrontational, risky, and largely (but certainly not only) practiced by queer, trans, and transfeminine people of color and other marginalized groups . . . It's about making a spectacle of yourself not merely to be seen but because your body is constantly suppressed and undervalued. . . . It's also a form of protest, a revolt against the norms and systems that oppress and torture us all every day, things like white supremacy, misogyny, transmisogyny, patriarchy, toxic masculinity, gender policing, and racism. . . . The style and presence you're commenting on is the direct result of all sorts of trauma, depression, and anxiety, not to mention verbal and physical street violence.[9]

It is not hard to understand why fabulousness is enacted as a radical, self-affirming reaction to the violence and silence imposed on queer Black people.[10] Nor is it difficult to understand why Black queer fabulousness is so useful and attractive to the entertainment industry; it is, by definition, captivating and spectacular. Moore's characterization was never meant to be a comprehensive description of Black queer life or Black LGBTQ+ people. But I want to describe the great merit and potential limitations of fabulousness to set up the central idea of this book, which I call the "Black queer mundane," or the "Black queertidian."[11]

Let us begin with the value of fabulousness. Moore's summation is essential because it explains a tradition of affirmation and freedom in the face of condemnation. I want to push this to argue that queer fabulousness is actually *more inclusive than it appears* at first glance. Queer fabulousness may seem somewhat restrictive, in part because "queer" is not an unquestionably inclusive term. Political scientist Cathy Cohen, for example, has written about how "queer" identity does not suit her. In the 1990s, "queer" implied a politics, and a politics of race, that was not a good fit for her life as a Black lesbian or for the lives of gay, lesbian, and bisexual Black folk more broadly.[12] A 2020 study found that people who identify as queer rather than gay, lesbian, or bisexual "are overwhelmingly cisgender women and genderqueer/nonbinary (GQNB), younger, and more highly educated than other groups."[13] And of course, many transgender people do not identify as queer.

Despite these qualifiers, "queer" has become an expansive term that is frequently used as a substitute for all the identities indicated by "LGBTQ+." Many of the students referred to themselves as both "gay" and "queer" at different points during my interviews with them. They are comfortable using "queer" and "LGBTQ+" as categories even if they have a more specific identity than the umbrella term "queer" could capture.

Moore is careful about all of this, as he recognizes that "queer" has specific connotations. He uses "queer" to describe the folks who practice fabulousness, but is also attentive in his foregrounding of femme and transfeminine people. "Femme" connotes an intentional and queer embrace and performance of femininity that does not abide by the standards of cisgender womanhood. The specificity matters, because the fabulous and fierce aesthetic Moore describes is most often associated with Black and brown femmes and transfeminine people, rather than masc-of-center, butch/stud/aggressive, and transmasculine folk. Even within queer communities, femininity is often devalued and treated with suspicion and disdain,[14] so Moore's affirmation of femmes and transfemininity pushes back against transmisogyny and the devaluing of femininity across heteronormative and queer spaces.

So we have acknowledged that not all LGBTQ+ people call themselves "queer," that not all LGBTQ+ people proclaim themselves to be fabulous, and that we need to emphasize and celebrate spectacular queer femininity because it is the basis of fabulousness and so frequently disparaged. Without diminishing this emphasis on queer femininity, I want to suggest that some of the features and implications of fabulousness are connected to other forms of prideful LGBTQ+ self-presentation. Masculine-of-center (masc-of-center) and nonbinary queer folk may not embody femme-queer-fabulousness, but they also share in such a history.

Like "femme," "masc" is a queer embodiment of masculinity that does not aspire to cisgender straight masculinity. Masc queer folks may embrace a prideful and intentional style and performance that may not be spectacular the way fabulousness is, but is no less striking or powerful. One example of such an embrace is a style that M. Shelley Connor describes as a "dapper" queer aesthetic, with roots more than one hundred years old among masc-of-center Black queer women. Connor explains, "Speaking for myself, I enjoy the look and feel of how my particular womanhood expresses itself through this style of dress. It isn't manhood or maleness, but masculinity—a trait most associated with men but not exclusive to them—that I present as a dapper woman."[15]

Creating a taxonomy of Black queer styles is an impossible task; even worse would be to suggest that each Black queer person chooses one style and sticks with it. What I want to seize on is the impact of Black queer styles when they foreground the effort, intention, and pride of gender performance. Is Janelle Monáe's trademark outfit—the immaculate Black and white suit and tie—spectacular and fabulous? Not in the exact same way as RuPaul's couture. Monáe's suit is not femme, and it signals and plays with gender differently, so perhaps we should call it "fly" instead. Further, the material risks of performing femininity and femmeness are demonstrably different from those of performing masculinity and mascness, especially for Black folk. But we still can perceive the connection between dapper queer Black women and their fabulous femme and transfeminine siblings who imaginatively, beautifully, and intentionally cultivate their style and self-presentation. So this is the value of fabulousness I want to trumpet: it is a liberating and spectacular practice derived from the practices of queer, femme, and transfeminine Black people. But its impetus and spirit—prideful affirmation of gender queerness and intention—are not exclusive to Black LGBTQ+ people with those specific gender identities and expressions. To signal its expansiveness while preserving the gendered implications of the concept, I will reframe it as "fabulous/fly," a perhaps unsatisfactory hybrid that is meant to hold space for other captivating Black queer styles and affects that lie beyond the dualism.

Having affirmed this value, let me turn to the potential distortion and dangers of unhinged commercial celebration of the Black queer fabulous/fly, especially by those who do not belong to Black LGBTQ+ communities. First, there are questions of impact and power. Eye-catching Black queer art and performances are commercially successful and critically acclaimed. Fabulous/fly Black queer celebrity-activists have taken up the mantle of leadership with unprecedented visibility. None of this acclaim and celebration, however, has reversed the harrowing trends of homelessness among LGBTQ+ youth of color, or halted the rampant killings of Black trans women. I am not arguing that Black queer fabulousness/flyness *causes* Black queer suffering, or that Black queer people are responsible for their own oppression. I am pointing out that the forces aligned against Black LGBTQ+ life and liberation may, in some respects, be strengthening or growing more dangerous as Black queer spectacle and political celebrity become increasingly common.

On this point, Carly Thomsen warns against championing visibility as a precondition for LGBTQ+ liberation, highlighting the links among visibility, the presumed illegibility of rural queer people, postraciality, and capitalism.[16] In her memoir, Black Youth Project 100 founder and Black queer activist Charlene Carruthers cautions readers not to assume that one form of progress or visibility begets another as she considers the true impact of President Obama's rise. Despite Obama's status as a Black role model and ally to LGBTQ+ people, Carruthers laments, "The Obama administration did not lead the advancement of radical Black politics in the 21st century," and in many ways solidified the politics of imperialism.[17] Things certainly did not improve during the Trump presidency. It is wrong to say that the continued precariousness of Black LGBTQ+ life is proof that Black queer fabulousness is ineffective resistance. I am not arguing that fabulous/fly Black queer practices are politically nonserious or immature. Without this tradition, the history and imagination of Black politics and Black queer politics would be impoverished, and the broader queer liberation movement would be stripped of many of its founders and most important contributors. Still, we should not mistake the Black, and especially white, American *pop-cultural* rise of Black queer fabulousness/flyness for *political* power. Cultural politics is a form of politics, in that cultural creations give life meaning, and in that there is no material political action without meaningful motivation. But "political" is used here in a more limited sense: the distribution of rights and resources continues to disadvantage and harm Black LGBTQ+ people even as Black queer fabulousness occupies ever more space in the zeitgeist.

The second danger hidden in exalting the Black queer fabulous/fly pertains to expectation and responsibility. One might read Moore's argument about fabulousness and conclude that Black LGBTQ+ people are, by virtue of their life experiences, more qualified and better positioned than others to analyze injustice and act against it. The precarious state of Black queer life is one of many dangers that contributes to a sense of urgency that we need in order to meet this political moment. Black queer people, it seems, are destined to take up the mantle of resistance because they are spectacular, radical, and courageous *by nature*. Ava, another student at Birch University, believes queer folk have a unique understanding of the possibility of change: "That's why a lot of people, a lot of activists, a lot of people who make change or who are change makers, a lot of organizers are also queer. Whether it's outwardly or not, it's because we understand that fluidity is at the center of our cause, and it's at the center of our existence as humans in general."

Given this interpretation, why shouldn't we expect Black LGBTQ+ people to assume their rightful position as leaders of Black freedom movements? After all, they have been doing it for decades without proper recognition.

There is little question that Black social movements would be more ethical and just if straight cisgender men more consistently followed the lead of Black women and Black LGBTQ+ people. Nor is there any question that the imagination and insight of Black queer folk are essential for Black liberation. This does not mean that Black LGBTQ+ people are, or should be, primarily responsible for Black politics. It is not their duty to lead us to freedom. Placing such onus on Black queer folk is an abdication of responsibility. Assuming that fabulousness/flyness and political virtuosity are inevitable adaptations to the violence of racism, sexism, homo- and transphobia, and postcolonial capitalism romanticizes Black queer suffering and erases the cost and labor of Black queer eccentricity. Fabulousness and flyness are beautiful and, for many, necessary modes of being. They are not the only ways that Black LGBTQ+ people survive, thrive, and go about their days.

When people marked by others for suffering love themselves and each other, love is a radical act. As musician Siena Liggins affirms, "I believe it's important to remember that every day I walk outside of my house as a Black, gay woman that it is an act of protest and that's the case for any BIPOC and/or any LGBTQIA+ person as long as there are still blatant attacks on our communities, our rights, and our peace of mind on this earth. Our existence is activism."[18] But Black LGBTQ+ people's courageous commitment to self-love does not guarantee that they all think of themselves as unrelentingly fabulous/fly or politically radical. Most of the students interviewed for this book do not describe themselves as eccentric or radical, and they do not spend all their time talking about politics or engaging in activism. Even if they affirm the political power of their existence, most of these students do not experience each moment of each day as a political act or affirmation.

Instead, many students describe their lives in mundane ways. They chose their college for many of the same reasons as straight students: affordability, geography, and comfort on campus (I am not implying that these are morally acceptable criteria because straight people use them too, just that they are commonplace). Their average day entails going to class, studying, working, and chilling with friends. They strive to maintain their health and wellness, learn as much as they can, earn their degrees, and get jobs once they graduate. They struggle with "adulting": paying bills, making career decisions, and maintaining relationships with friends and family. Their lives are often unglamorous and quotidian.

But the Black collegiate quotidian is queer for Black LGBTQ+ students. So many college students ride the waves of romance and friendship formed when young adults are squeezed into cramped dormitories and apartments beyond their parents' and guardians' gaze. These arrangements often reveal queer possibilities that could not be spoken, let alone explored, by young LGBTQ+ people prior to college. Maintaining mental health can be challenging for all college students, but it is especially daunting when Blackness is viewed as suspect, queerness is viewed as illness, and there is little access to healthcare professionals who specialize in the issues Black queer students face. Finances cannot be managed without considering family support and obligations. When relationships within birth and home families are unpredictable or hostile for LGBTQ+ students, calculations change. Career choices are shaped by training and mentorship, but instructional and professional relationships depend on trust between mentor and mentee. Such trust and mirroring are hard to find on campuses and in workplaces where disclosures and affirmations of Black queerness are shamed, so Black queer college students often turn to each other.

In this way, common student concerns, as well as common indulgences and delights, are transformed. The Black quotidian becomes the *Black queertidian*, undeniably mundane, but inflected and enhanced. It is ordinariness with "an open mesh of possibilities, gaps, overlaps, dissonances and resonances, lapses and excesses of meaning," as Eve Sedgwick's explication of queerness suggests.[19] These possibilities include Black queer mundane pride and contentedness. This book positions the Black queertidian beside the fabulous/fly, and attends to the mundane dimensions of Black LGBTQ+ students' lives.

QUEER COLLEGE STUDENTS OF COLOR

In 1966, students at Columbia University formed the Student Homophile League, which is widely considered the first gay college student organization in the United States. The political climate and culture of New York City provided context for student activism. Harlem and Greenwich Village were home to thriving gay social scenes, and in 1963 New York mayor Robert Wagner began a campaign to rid the city of gay people in advance of the 1964–1965 World's Fair. Wagner's primary tactics were revoking the liquor licenses of known gay bars and using police officers to entrap suspected gay men and charge them with solicitation. Restaurants and bars in New York openly discriminated against gay customers at the time, so when members of an organized crime family transformed the Stonewall Inn into a bar that catered to gay customers in 1966, they knew there would be plenty of patrons. The police raid that sparked the Stonewall Uprising occurred in June of 1969, and reverberations of the rebellion continued into the next calendar year. In June of 1970, activists in New York, Los Angeles, and Chicago marked the one-year anniversary of the uprisings in what would become the first Gay Pride marches in United States history. Also in 1970, the Student Homophile League changed its name to Gay People at Columbia, and by 1971, they had established a gay student lounge on campus in Furnald Hall.

The Stonewall Uprising was led by Black and brown queer folk like Marsha P. Johnson and Silvia Rivera. As Roderick Ferguson argues, LGBTQ+ politics was and is inseparable from racial and class politics, and the late-twentieth-century turn towards a deracialized (white) rights-focused gay rights movement in America is a betrayal of those radical roots.[20] One of the crosswinds that shaped LGBTQ+ student activism in the late 1960s was student activism focused on ethnic studies. In 1968 and 1969, the Black Student Union at San Francisco State University led a coalition of activists in a movement designed to redress discrimination against people of color within their university and across higher education. Their actions led to the founding of the first ethnic studies department and curriculum in the country, inspiring like-minded students to undertake similar protests on their campuses throughout the United States. Again, Ferguson's work is instructive, as he explains how those protests led college and university administrators to both accommodate and undermine the students' agenda. On one hand, Black studies and ethnic studies were institutionalized in ways they had never been before, and more robust support systems for students of color were put in place. On the other hand, university leaders dramatically increased the presence and reach of on-campus police, and "diversity and inclusion" offices and initiatives were created as a means to manage student protest and radicalism.[21]

People of color are frequently omitted from the most widely accessible histories of the Stonewall Uprising and founding of Pride, and queer students are rarely the focus of the historical accounts of the ethnic studies movement of the late 1960s and 1970s, largely because queer students across racial categories were ignored in higher education research through most of the twentieth century. The invisibility of LGBTQ+ students on campus began to be addressed by researchers in the late 1980s and early 1990s, as Kristen Renn notes that three distinct fields of higher education research were evident by the turn of the century: "(a) visibility of LGBT people, (b) campus climate for LGBT people, and (c) LGBT student identities and experiences."[22] Renn has pushed the field forward herself by focusing specifically on LGBTQ+ student activist leaders. Her 2007 study found that "increased leadership led to increased public LGBT identity and a merged gender/sexual orientation and leadership identity."[23]

The stakes and meaning of "public LGBTQ identity" are shaped by race and racism. In 2019, Antonio Duran published an invaluable literature review on the state of the field of queer people of color (QPOC) student studies.[24] Poring over books, articles, and doctoral dissertations, Duran found that the research points to four main themes, all of which are addressed in this book. First, scholarship on QPOC collegians focuses on coming out and sources of support. Duran notes that the idea and process of coming out are not uniform across racial groups, and Black queer studies challenges conventional understandings of coming out and LGBTQ+ identity development on both theoretical and empirical grounds.[25] Still, research shows that the process of publicly claiming an LGBTQ+ identity is a central concern for QPOC on campus, and support systems built on relationships with students, faculty, and nonacademic organizations are essential to students' well-being.

The second major theme is campus climate, as studies focus on the social and academic dimensions of student life to demonstrate how class, race, and gender inequities prohibit QPOC from maximizing their time on campus. Renn describes campus climate as an established genre in the late-twentieth-century academic research on LGBTQ+ students, and Duran confirms that this focus has expanded to QPOC students in the early twenty-first century. Duran notes, however, that campus climate studies almost always focus on QPOC on PWI campuses rather than at HBCUs.

Third, Duran draws on Harper, Wedell, and McGuire's characterization of the "complex individuality" of QPOC students. This theme might just as easily be called "intersectionality," as it calls attention to religion, gender, citizenship status, and other factors that influence QPOC experiences and identity development. The final theme is simple enough: QPOC at both HBCUs and PWIs suffer from a lack of resources and representation on campus. There are few visible groups with administrative and financial power dedicated to supporting QPOC college students, and few prominent people on campus who identify as LGBTQ+ and are viewed as reliable advocates and mentors. In addition, groups designed to address student needs beyond those related to gender equity may treat queer students of color as afterthoughts, or lack the necessary training and commitment to best serve these populations.

Though these circumstances are common for QPOC students across all backgrounds, this book is specifically dedicated to Black LGBTQ+ students, with an acknowledgment that transgender experiences may differ dramatically from LGBQ+ experiences. Transgender folk reject the sex and gender categories they were placed in at birth, and therefore challenge heterosexist and patriarchal norms. The challenges they pose to established hierarchies of sex and gender mean that they share many of the same political struggles as LGBQ+ people. But queer politics, especially a civil rights–based model of queer progress, is not always inclusive of transgender people. Many transgender people publicly embrace the gender fluidity at the core of queerness. Others publicly choose a more stable pairing of gender identity and sexuality, and might not think of themselves as gender fluid. There are fewer support systems designed specifically for transgender people, so transgender folk may find it useful and affirming to join LGBQ+ organizations for fellowship. But spaces that accept and welcome LGBQ+ people may not be truly welcoming for trans folk. This includes LGBTQ+ student groups, which are not always safe havens for transgender siblings. Research shows, for example that trans-spectrum students have "more negative perceptions of campus climate, classroom climate, and curriculum inclusivity and higher use of campus resources."[26] The LGBQ+ community is linked to the transgender community through its cultural history, resistance to oppression, and fight for human rights. But the experiences and interests of transgender people and LGBQ+ people can be dramatically different.

Just as the "Q" in QPOC needs to be unpacked, the phrase "people of color" requires scrutiny. "People of color" is not a synonym for "Black," but the phrase "people of color" is often substituted for "Black" for several reasons. Merely speaking about race is often uncomfortable for white people and others invested in the myth of color blindness. To name Blackness is to invoke difference and make racial injustice audible and historically specific. Racial specificity calls attention to whiteness as well, and making whiteness explicit is the first step toward destroying the notion that white perspectives and experiences are neutral or normal. Naming specific racial categories forces white people to reckon with their privileges and power.

Another reason why "people of color" has become a fashionable phrase is that it implies similarity and unity among nonwhite people. This move may be well intentioned, and it may enable people of color to find commonalities across their experiences and support each other. However, exaggerating these similarities masks colorism and anti-Blackness within non-Black groups, diminishes the role of ethnicity in constructions of Blackness, and ignores the particular history of Blackness as a racial and political category in the United States. The noncitizenship, enslavement, murder, rape, segregation, exploitation, and incarceration of Black people are legally inscribed in ways that they have never been for other people of color. Educating enslaved Black people was prohibited by legislation in every southern state before the Civil War. For all these reasons, Black students and Black colleges are worthy of special attention.

HBCUS THEN AND NOW

In 1865, approximately forty Black people had graduated from college in the United States.[27] Most HBCUs were created in the immediate aftermath of the Civil War, when educating the children of previously enslaved people was nothing short of revolutionary. The white planter class in the postbellum South wanted to keep Black people impoverished and uneducated so that Black workers would be forced into sharecropping and other vulnerable jobs. But as Carol Anderson notes, racist tyranny in the South was not merely intended to control Black labor. "The whole culture of the white South was erected on the presumption of Black inability."[28] Black ignorance and poverty were the self-fulfilling prophecy of the white social order, justifying the physical brutality, political silencing, and economic deprivation of Black people. Substandard schooling for Black children was an essential mechanism of Black oppression. Political elites steered funding away from public and private Black colleges, and often used the accreditation system to place newly founded Black colleges at a disadvantage by denying accreditation or failing to rate the schools at all.[29] Still, between 1854 and 1895, ninety-two Black colleges were founded.

The radical politics of Black education and uplift were constrained by political pressure to produce a certain kind of free and educated Black person—one who would be integrated into southern society without threatening white-supremacist capitalism and patriarchy. HBCU students were not meant to question norms of gender, respectability, or morality. They were expected to demonstrate their fitness for integration and adaptation to Jim Crow. Cleanliness, discipline, adherence to Christian teaching, and sexual modesty were nonnegotiable conditions for respect. Queer desire and behavior were not acknowledged. The pressure to live up to these expectations came from faculty and administrators at the schools, but also from white religious societies, government officials, and philanthropic organizations, who were the financial lifeblood for HBCUs.

Much of this political pressure remains today, and it is exacerbated by the financial crisis in higher education. Colleges depend on student enrollment for their operating budgets, and Nathan Grawe estimates that by 2026, the college-going population could decrease by as much as 15 percent.[30] High school graduating classes will have a greater percentage of students of color and a wider range of academic abilities, and more American students will come from families that cannot pay the full cost of attendance. Colleges are struggling to meet their enrollment targets, and mergers and closures of schools in financial distress will become more common. The combined enrollment of all HBCUs increased from 234,000 in 1980 to 293,000 in 2015, but this growth lags far behind the enrollment across all colleges and universities, which nearly doubled over the same time period. HBCUs are also enrolling a smaller percentage of the Black college student population, as 9 percent of such students enrolled at HBCUs in 2015, down from 17 percent in 1980.[31]

HBCUs are at risk under these conditions, and their relationship with the Trump administration and the Republican Party during the first year of Trump's presidency increased the uncertainty. In February 2017, Trump invited leaders of several HBCUs to the White House for a meeting. The administrators who participated saw it as an opportunity to gain access they would not otherwise have, but skeptics saw it as a tactic to cover for Trump's hostility toward Black people. In May of 2017, the skepticism seemed to be validated, as Trump suggested that federal funding for HBCUs might be unconstitutional. Trump issued the statement after signing a bill with a provision authorizing federal financing for repairs to HBCU facilities, a program that had been in place since 1992. The Congressional Black Caucus blasted Trump for making such a dubious claim, and he later retracted his statement.

Despite the initial shakiness of the Trump administration's relationship with HBCUs, conditions stabilized. According to Johnny C. Taylor, the president of the Thurgood Marshall Scholarship Fund, federal funding for HBCUs remained consistent under Trump even amidst budget reductions for the Department of Education.[32] HBCU leaders continued to meet with both Trump and Republicans in Congress, and it appeared that their diplomatic efforts bore fruit. The Trump White House moved the HBCU Initiative from the Department of Education to the President's Office, forgave $330 million worth of debt incurred by HBCUs for Hurricane Katrina cleanup, and reinstated year-round federally funded Pell Grants, which allow economically disadvantaged students to continue their education through the summer and complete their degrees more quickly.[33] Federal investment and student aid account for 25 percent of HBCU funding.[34]

There is diversity with respect to the financial standing and student population of America's 101 HBCUs, but HBCU students often have fewer financial resources than students at PWIs. Because socioeconomic class status is such an important determinant of educational attainment, HBCU students also have lower standardized test scores upon admission and take longer to complete their bachelor's degrees than students at PWIs. Given the wealth gap between Black and white families, this is no surprise. In 2004, the median net worth of white households was $134,280, roughly ten times the $13,450 median for Black households. After the financial crash in 2008, median net worth for white households had fallen 24 percent to $97,860, but median net worth for Black households had fallen 83 percent to $2,170. In other words, the average Black household had two cents for every one dollar of wealth held by the average white household.[35] HBCUs are about six thousand dollars cheaper per year than PWIs,[36] but since the 1970s they have faced steep competition recruiting the most academically distinguished Black high school students. HBCUs also contend with a long history of contingent funding from philanthropic organizations and what can only be described as discrimination at the hands of state governments and banks.[37] As a result, a handful of HBCUs have bright financial futures, but far more are in danger of losing accreditation or shuttering their doors in the next two decades.

Still, HBCUs remain indispensable to Black education, and students thrive both during and after their time on campus. A study by Education Trust compared HBCUs and PWIs with similar percentages of students who receive Pell Grants and found that recipients at HBCUs had better graduation rates.[38] HBCUs account for just 3 percent of undergraduates nationwide, but 15 percent of all Black bachelor of arts (BA) graduates and 25 percent of Black graduates in science, technology, engineering, and mathematics (STEM) fields.[39] Research also suggests that HBCU graduates feel better prepared for life after college, and HBCU alumni report being more engaged, purpose driven, and fulfilled at work.[40]

Several HBCUs posted record-breaking numbers of applications and incoming students in 2017, and schools posted double-digit gains in enrollments from 2015 to 2017.[41] Dillard University is one such college to benefit from this trend, as it attracted 22 percent more incoming students during that time period than in the years prior. Dillard president Walter Kimbrough attributes the boom directly to HBCUs' history of serving Black students, especially in the light of current events. Referencing the antiracism protests on campus at the University of Missouri during the 2015–2016 academic year, Kimbrough explains,

> People are asking for more Black faculty, more Black staff, Black living spaces, Black-centered curriculum. Well, HBCUs have provided these things for almost 200 years. And so I think people are now asking a question to say, "What's important to me?" And if those things are important, they're looking to say, "Well, an HBCU offers that, and why don't I just go to the place that has those things?" The other part of the conversation with students and parents that I'm hearing is that they are concerned about their students being in those environments that they feel are hostile with macro- and micro-racial aggressions.[42]

Critics of Black colleges are not especially interested in the ebbs and flows of HBCU finances and politics, or the demonstrable benefits that accrue to Black students at HBCUs. Instead, they simply point to the student population and question whether such students are even worthy of admission to college in the first place. Racist stereotypes of Black intellect and Black culture that were attached to Black colleges in the nineteenth century continue to shape the debate about HBCUs today. White college students' political radicalism is often celebrated as a rite of passage, but Black college student radicalism is threatening to white benefactors. It is no surprise, then, that the emphasis on respectability prioritized by Black colleges in response to racism during their founding remains a key feature of life on HBCU campuses.[43] Maya, a student at Birch University, disdains the school's conservatism.

> MAYA: I was excited about coming here, and it's been a great experience, but I do feel like I got let down in the social side of Birch, because the people here are traditional. They're not really progressive. They'll talk about race, but they're real surface level about race. I mean, it's just 'cause we're at a HBCU so you kind of have to know something or a little something about race, and feel comfortable enough talking about it. Yeah, they're conservative. I would say that. Like you can't talk about anything too progressive, like sexuality, like gender identity, or people get really upset with you.
>
> MICHAEL: Do the students get upset, or the faculty? Who are you talking about?
>
> MAYA: All of them. The students, the faculty, and it's mainly the alums of the school who have just so much to say about all of these different things.

The conservative underpinnings of some HBCUs do not quell their students' radical potential, however. Many of the students most constrained by conservatism on campus take it upon themselves to advocate for social justice and change the culture. On campus, Black life is reimagined, and young Black people train each other to be agents of political change. This was true in previous eras as well. Martin Luther King Jr. attended Morehouse, and the deeply religious, impeccably dressed public image he projected met his college's expectations for respectable manhood. But King's politics were radical, as he put his body on the line in the face of state violence, espoused an ideology of supra-Christian radical love, and took unpopular and dangerous positions against racism, poverty, and war. Repression at HBCUs is not all-consuming. Community members are often supported as they speak truth to power, whether they are students or leading public intellectuals like Ta-Nehisi Coates and Nikole Hannah-Jones, who have found a home for their work at Howard.

BLACKNESS, QUEERNESS, AND POWER

Though I am Black, I wrote this book as an outsider with many privileges. I am a professor who interviewed college students on college campuses, where deference to professors is expected. I have tenure at my college and economic privilege in comparison to most college students and most Americans. I am a northerner, and I have spent almost my entire life in or near the New York, Philadelphia, and Boston metropolitan areas. I do not have a southern accent, and I did not use southern Black vernacular during the interviews with students, the majority of whom attended schools in the South. I am relatively light-skinned in comparison to most Black people. My skin tone is frequently read as a sign of class privilege and often insulates me from discrimination and insults based on colorism. And finally, though I did not disclose my sexuality and/or gender pronouns unless students inquired, I am straight and cisgender.

One of the advantages of entering an interview as an outsider is that the interviewee is usually happy to assume the role of expert in the conversation. He/she/they will take the time to explain things that they would not explain to someone who shares their experience. A disadvantage is that the person being interviewed may not trust the interviewer to take care of their stories or share intimate details about their lives. I did my best to earn trust at every stage of the interview process, beginning by reaching out to students through intermediaries they already knew who understood the purpose of my research. I promised to maintain students' confidentiality throughout the process, and I paid the students fifteen dollars each for participating as a small token of my appreciation for their time. Students knew the book was about Black LGBTQ+ experiences, and they wanted to talk about their lives, but I also let them guide the conversations as much as possible. I did not ask personal questions about their sex lives or their experiences coming out, though many students were eager to initiate conversations about those topics. I reminded them that they could stop or cancel the interview at any time without forfeiting payment. Students were overwhelmingly generous and enthusiastic, and they were excited at the prospect of being part of the book. They appreciated that someone cared enough to hear their stories. None of this, however, erases the power imbalance when a straight cisgender professor asks LGBTQ+ students about their identities and their lives. They might have told someone they trusted more fully something different than what they told me.

No matter how careful and well intentioned, this book is no substitute for the unmediated testimony of Black LGBTQ+ people. Ethnographic work is shaped by power, and many scholars believe ethnography is theft. When professors publish books and articles about vulnerable people, we often gain status. The people whose words fill these books, however, are not guaranteed to benefit from publication in any way. Both during and after working on this book, I have tried to support queer Black folk in my personal and professional life. But again, my relationships with, and love for, queer Black folk do not eradicate the problems caused by a straight cisgender man writing about LGBTQ+ people. Problems linger not only because straight cisgender people have power in patriarchy but also because professors like me are trained to ignore and suppress queerness when our research involves talking to people.

By "queerness" I do not mean same-sex attraction. I mean "queerness" as a nonbinary, uncertain, and/or fluid state of being. We often arrive at queer places in our conversations and our work because gender and sexuality surface when they are not supposed to: in a glance, or a stirring, or word or joke with too many meanings, or when we try to ignore discomfort for the sake of propriety. Sociologists are trained and encouraged to eliminate these moments from our work so we can see and hear things clearly, avoid confusion, and get to "the truth." We are trained this way because ignoring queerness reinforces the naturalness of the political and professional systems we live and work in, where the body and mind are disciplined in ways that affirm white cis-masculinity as the most accepted and powerful mode of being, writing, and teaching.

My invocation of the contradictory yet coherent "Black queertidian" and "queer mundane" affirms the fluidity and instability of day-to-day life. Placing "mundane" and "queer" next to each other on the page produces friction that opens space for understanding beyond the straight/queer binary. But I do not have what I would call a committedly queer methodological approach (more on this in chapter 2). I do not dwell in uncertainty, or speculate about absences or silences in the interviews. I do not read each student's performance, or describe their

self-presentation in great detail, or queer the boundary between interviewer and interviewee by writing about how I felt as I conducted the
research. There are places, especially when discussing communities of
students and their organizations, where the boundaries between straight
and queer may seem obvious and become habitual.[44] Such habituality
is often considered a failure or anathema in queer studies. So this book
might not be queer enough for some, but I wrote what made sense to
me, given the conversations I had. The result is a testament to the students and, I hope, a step towards prioritizing their lives and voices. All
shortcomings are my own.

Several qualities enabled me to do this work despite my outsider status. Though I introduced myself as a professor, it seemed that most students paid little attention to my title because of my appearance. Several
students had not read the recruitment letter especially closely and initially assumed I was an undergraduate or graduate student. A handful
of them explicitly told me they made this assumption because I dressed
casually and, at the time of the interviews, looked younger than a typical professor.

Another factor that may have mitigated my outsider status is my
comfort as an interviewer. I have conducted hundreds of research interviews, and the reason I do the work and enjoy the process is that I am
genuinely enthusiastic about learning from respondents and grateful for
their company. I believe the students sensed my comfort and enthusiasm, and recognized that the reason I wanted to interview them is that
they are the experts on their lives. I expressed my gratitude repeatedly,
in writing and in person, and made every effort to accommodate their
schedule and preferences with respect to interview locations. These may
seem like small details, but they are indispensable to building trust, recruiting interviewees, and conducting effective interviews.

On a final note about the recruitment process, I want to be clear
about who gets to speak for Black LGBTQ+ people. This book features
young Black queer people who (a) self-identified as LGBTQ+, (b) were
enrolled in college, and (c) wanted to be interviewed.[45] Plenty of students received the call for interviews and decided not to speak with me.
Perhaps they feared repercussion on their campuses, perhaps their experiences were too painful to discuss, or perhaps they simply preferred
not to talk. The students I spoke with were courageous and honest, and

this book has a range of descriptions of what it is like to be Black and LGBTQ+ in college, but it is not a truly representative sample. Plenty of Black folk who engage in queer behaviors do not identify as LGBTQ+.[46] In addition, the number of Black LGBTQ+ people who never make it to college is unknowable, and the costs of Black queer childhood can be overwhelming. It is hard enough to get to college if you are economically insecure, as Black Americans disproportionately are, and even more difficult if you are poor, Black, and queer, enrolled in a public education system designed around punishment and surveillance rather than child development. The mental and physical health costs of poverty and racism are exacerbated by the pain absorbed by young people whose families reject or punish them because of their gender identity and sexuality. The LGBTQ+ youth homelessness crisis is proof of these hardships, and it is a crisis that disproportionately impacts Black and brown children who move out because they are unwelcome in their parents' and guardians' homes. Those young people do not have the chance to sit with a professor and reflect on their experiences. Most of their stories are not in this book. So the students I spoke with do not speak for all of their peers, even if they share many of the same experiences and opinions. These qualifiers do not make the interviewees' stories any less valuable; they just remind us that we can only behold the tip of the iceberg, and we owe both the seen and the unseen our attention.

I did not write this book because Black LGBTQ+ folk are gifted with some sort of magical "second sight" thanks to their experiences. Black LGBTQ+ people are not the mystical solution to society's problems. From Bayard Rustin to Alicia Garza, Black LGBTQ+ people have been indispensable to Black liberation movements. But this book is not an implicit exhortation for them to assume the mantle of Black political leadership because they owe it to their siblings. I wrote the book for three simple reasons. First, the people I spoke with are too often ignored, silenced, and harmed. Raising their voices is a prerequisite for recognition, restitution, and justice, though I acknowledge that these voices are mediated by me. Second, the experiences and ideas the students shared demonstrate how race, class, and gender work together as vectors of power. And finally, this book sheds light on how all colleges and universities can be improved. With these reasons in mind, let the campus tours begin.

[1]

GETTING TO CAMPUS

Deron, a senior at Douglas University (a public HBCU), grew up in a mostly Black suburb of a large southern city. His parents separated when he was young because his father was imprisoned, and he was raised by his mother and grandmother. The family lived on a peaceful cul-de-sac that Deron called his first "safe space." Deron's public-school lottery placed him in a performing arts school from second until seventh grade, and while there, he developed a passion for dance and gymnastics. When he had to switch to a new school with a different curriculum for his eighth-grade year, he was terrified. Deron knew he was different from his classmates, and he did not know how they would react to his mannerisms. Some of those fears were confirmed when a few of his new schoolmates began bullying him, but he was never a victim of physical violence. After a few months, he said, "It didn't really affect me bad, because the friends I had at the time, they were just really supportive." When he told his friends that he was bisexual and, eventually, that he was gay, none of his close relationships changed. "It felt good to have that little group of friends that I could always go to and know that I wouldn't have to be afraid. And then I got the courage to try out for the high school, performing arts high school, and I made it my ninth-grade year, and I was there. And while I was there, I came out."

At home, things were different. Deron's mother had known he was gay since he was a small child, and she made Deron confess to her before high school began. Deron explained, "I guess she was just sad, 'cause she knew that she had a gay son, but she just didn't think that I would realize it at such a young age." Her response was to keep Deron away from other gay people and push Deron to disdain the LGBTQ+ "lifestyle" without condemning her son. Though he still enjoyed dance and gymnastics, Deron was in a malaise as senior year approached and he had no idea what he wanted to do after graduation. But his life changed when his mother began dating her new partner, Mark. At first, Deron said, "I was on the defense with any dude that I met that she was dating. Like I'm not going to be nice, but I'm not going to be mean either. But [Mark] started to show us how much he loved us, without having to say 'I love y'all,' and he just made me really appreciate having him around." One day, Mark asked Deron about his future. Here is what Deron told me about their conversation:

He was like, "Have you ever thought about [HBCUs]? And I was like, "No." I'm just like, "I'm probably just going to go to community college and stay here." He was like, "No." He was like, "I want you to shoot higher than that." Like, "Don't limit yourself." And then he talked about when he was here at Douglas, he met some really good people. Like, he's still friends with his Douglas friends now. And he told me he got a second family from Douglas, and that's what I want, personally. But I never thought about going to an HBCU before. . . . And at the time, I was really active in sports, so I was like, okay, I might as well major in physical therapy. That'll be nice. And then when I told Mark that, he was like, "I'll pay for you to go to school," and he told my mom she didn't have to worry about anything. And this was before I got really close with him. He was just like, "Yeah, I'm going to pay for his college, 'cause I see something in him that he doesn't see, so I want him to have the experience."

This is not the sort of story we usually hear about queer Black boys and the men in their lives, especially when elders in their family are not supportive of LGBTQ+ people. Mark and Deron's mother were friends before they began dating. Mark knew that Deron was gay, perhaps even before Deron was forced to admit it to his mom. And despite Deron's mother's attitude, Mark loved Deron and "saw something in him" that the boy could not see. This "something" was powerful enough for Mark to invest in Deron emotionally and financially. Part of Mark's investment was recommending his alma mater, a public HBCU, as a school that would provide Deron with a home and a second family.

Taylor, a senior at Linden University, took a different route to college than Deron. She spent her childhood in an economically depressed Black neighborhood of a different southern city, and she was not fond of her surroundings. "People aren't nice, and it's a lot of influences around you that can influence who you become when you grow up. . . . You see the drug dealers at the corner store selling drugs. It's not like it's hidden." The high school she attended shared many of the characteristics of her neighborhood, including high rates of poverty and violence, but she never told me she felt unsafe at school because of her sexuality or gender presentation. Rather, she described a general sense of anxiety about the neighborhood and gang disputes that spilled over into the school, and the reality that a fight might break out at any moment.

Despite the inhospitable school environment, Taylor was determined to go to college. Her father set clear expectations for both Taylor and her brother, even though he had not finished college himself and could barely afford to support his family financially. In fact, Taylor's dad had a very specific idea of the school she should attend: Juniper University, the public HBCU he briefly attended. The financial aid process, however, became a hurdle, and eventually she settled on a two-year stint at a local community college, which did not suit her. Taylor's perception was that many of her classmates wanted "a certificate to go straight to the workforce," or were simply unmotivated. "Like in my mind," she said, "it was just like a waste of time, 'cause I felt like everybody around me has no push, and it's just like I'm sitting here hanging around with all these people that have no push." She was determined to move on to a four-year university, but in order to get there she had to address the problems with her father.

The first time Taylor applied to college, her dad pushed her to go to Juniper, partially because he went there, but partially for other reasons. Right around the time she finished high school, Taylor told her father that she was attracted to women and that she was in a relationship with one. Juniper was only a few hours away from Taylor's neighborhood, but Taylor's father forced her to apply because it would separate her from her girlfriend. "He felt like she wasn't right for me," Taylor said, "but the way he came about it, it wasn't like, he came about it like as if, 'I care.' He came about it as if, 'I don't want you with her 'cause she's a woman, period.'"

As community college wore on, things were tenuous. Taylor still wanted to go to a four-year college but had soured on Juniper because the school was indelibly linked to her dad's disapproval of her sexuality. Her new target was Linden University, another public HBCU not too far from home. She put herself through community college without financial support from her family, but she needed her father's military benefits to secure the best financial aid package possible on her next round of applications. But Taylor was not comfortable living her life around her dad, and the two of them were barely speaking. Mysteriously and slowly, things started to change. Taylor could not quite put her finger on it, but she told me that her dad began joking about her being stuck in community college, almost goading her to get out and do something more. This was a cruel jest; had he been more supportive to begin with, Taylor likely would have enrolled at a four-year college immediately after high school. But Taylor only took minimal offense at her father's making fun of her, and she used his teasing her to mend the relationship. She explained,

> He did that [joking and teasing], and it was like, we ended up rekindling our relationship, and I told him, I said, "Honestly, dad, I want to go to Linden, and I want to get my degree. But I'm going to need your help." Because, like I say, I used his army benefits to get into school. So he helped me. Actually, he really helped me get into Linden. So once I got into school, our relationship basically is, I wouldn't say great, but it's good now. Like, we talk. We call each other. And he knows about my sexuality. He's okay with it. He's not in denial about it anymore. Like, he calls my significant other what they are, my girlfriend. That's exactly what he called them. So it was just a lot. That's what swayed my decision to come to Linden, 'cause it was so much being put on me being at the community college. So I was like, okay, I have to get out of here, and the only way I can do that is by rekindling my relationship with my dad so he'll pay for school.

Deron and Taylor had the seeds of their college choices planted by mentors or family members. Deron's mentor, Mark, and Taylor's father made the recommendation because they had attended the school in question and because they hoped that the university would serve a specific role in the teenagers' development. In Deron's case, Mark hoped that Douglas would give Deron a sense of belonging. In Taylor's case, her father believed that Linden was a better educational option than community college and that moving away from home would put an end to his daughter's romantic relationship. Neither student, each of whom had already affirmed their LGBTQ+ identity before graduating high school, expressed any reservations about attending an HBCU because the school would be inhospitable to queer people. Financial considerations, familiarity with the school, and the advice of the family member or mentor were the factors that made the colleges realistic options for the students.

These factors are commonplace among prospective college students, regardless of gender identity and/or sexual orientation. But there is no simple process that leads to a final decision about where to attend college. All these components—familial preference, student preference, finances, institutional prestige, and geography—are in motion simultaneously, sometimes in cooperation with each other and sometimes in tension. In these cases, however, Black queerness is the interstitial fluid flowing through the decision-making process, touching and shaping each component, sometimes explicitly and sometimes in silence.

There is little research on Black LGBTQ+ college students' school selection. Considering the stereotypes about Black homophobia and transphobia, as well as students' lived experiences within their home families, one might expect acceptance and visibility of LGTBQ+ people on campus to be a major factor in students' decisions about where to enroll. Surprisingly, few of the students I spoke with explicitly told me that campus climate for LGBTQ+ students drove their decision. Financial and familial considerations dominated the college-choice process, but perhaps the most important thing I learned is that we cannot treat each element of the college-choice process as discrete or self-contained. Students consistently discussed family, finances, geography, campus climate, prestige, and other factors with reference to each other.

RESPONDENTS AND THEIR COLLEGES

As mentioned in the introduction, students responded to a call for interviews with Black LGBTQ+ students, so the phrase "LGBTQ+" proved inclusive enough for several identities. However, one of the most striking things about our conversations and the demographic information I collected is the range of identities affirmed by students. I conducted all of the interviews in person, and each student, as well as any faculty or staff mentioned during the interview, was given a pseudonym. The questionnaire I asked them to complete after each interview asked students to report their sexual orientation *and/or* gender identity, and I told them that they did not have to answer any questions they preferred not to answer. The students described their sexual orientation and gender expression in the following ways:

- Eighteen students identify as "gay" and use "he/him" pronouns.
- Twelve students identify as "lesbian" and use "she/her."
- Twelve identify solely as "queer." These twelve students either did not reply to the question about pronouns, or they prefer "they," or they are comfortable with "his/her/they."
- Five students identify as "bisexual" and use "she/her."
- Three students identify as "pansexual/queer" and did not list pronouns.
- Three students identify as "nonbinary." One did not list pronouns, one prefers "they," and one listed "he/her/they."
- Two students identify as "bisexual" and use "he/his."
- Two students identify as "pansexual" and use "she/her."
- Two students identify as "queer trans." One of these students did not list pronouns and the other prefers "they."
- One student identifies as "panromantic asexual" and uses "she/her."
- One student identifies as "bisexual trans" and listed "he/her/they" as accepted pronouns.
- One student identifies as "bisexual nonbinary" and listed "none/they/he/her" as preferred pronouns.
- One student identifies as "bisexual queer" and listed "none/they/he/her" as preferred pronouns.

- One student identifies as "bisexual queer nonbinary" and listed "none/they/he/her" as preferred pronouns.

The prevalence of queer/nonbinary identity is significant, as twenty-three of the sixty-five people I spoke with invoked "queer" or "nonbinary" to describe themselves. A 2020 study suggests that only around 6 percent of LGBTQ+ people nationwide select "queer" as their primary identity category. Those who do usually fit at least one of three criteria: they are cisgender women or genderqueer/nonbinary, they are younger than most LGBTQ+ people, and they are highly educated relative to most LGBTQ+ people.[1] Clearly, the sample features young and highly educated people, but the prevalence of genderqueer/nonbinary as a primary identity among the students is notable.

Students describe both sexual orientation *and* gender identity, as "queer" and "nonbinary" were paired with other words like "pansexual" and "bisexual" (though not all who identified as pansexual or bisexual identify as genderqueer/nonbinary). Students were not required to give a specific type of answer on the questionnaire about their sexual orientation and/or gender identity. But the information they gave suggests contemplation of how these pieces fit together and willingness to use as many descriptors as necessary to fashion a label that fits.

I was only able to interview three students who identify as transgender for this book. In fact, none of the three students ever specifically used the full word "transgender" to describe themselves, as they preferred "trans" instead. The experiences of transgender people can be markedly different from those of LGBQ people even though trans folks are included in the LGBTQ+ abbreviation. Animus towards transgender folk is certainly prevalent among cisgender straight people, and LGBQ+ communities are not exempt from transphobia. I recruited students through their affiliation with LGBTQ+ student organizations on campus. But if those student organizations are not welcoming places for transgender people, my efforts would not have reached a large number (perhaps the majority) of transgender students at each school. I am not aiming for generalizability with a sample this size, but I wish I had been able to speak with more Black trans folks.

I want to underscore one final detail about the trans students I spoke with, pertaining to their choice of pronouns. Two of the three students identify as "queer trans," and the other identifies as "bisexual trans." None of the three students insist on a single, traditional sex/gender set of pronouns. Instead of selecting one of "he/his" or "she/her," two students listed "he/her/they," and one student declined to answer. I do not know why this is and I won't even hazard a guess out of respect for the interviewees. It is notable because many transgender folks exclusively embrace either "he/his" or "she/her" as their pronouns; the exclusivity is often a meaningful part of the transition.

In addition to gender expression and LGBTQ+ identity, I collected information about how and where the respondents were raised. About half of the people I spoke with (thirty-two) came from a household where at least one parent or guardian had earned at least a bachelor's degree from a four-year college or university. One respondent gave no reply to this question, which means that at least thirty-two of the sixty-five students are first-generation college students.

I also asked the students to estimate the yearly income of the parents or guardians who supported them growing up. Thirteen students came from households with an estimated annual income of less than thirty thousand dollars or described themselves as "poor." Twenty-five students came from households with estimated annual income between thirty thousand and one hundred thousand dollars, and eighteen students came from households with annual income of one hundred thousand dollars or greater. Nine students gave no answer on the questionnaire and did not discuss their socioeconomic class with clarity during the interviews.

These figures are imprecise and can be misleading. First, income is not wealth, and the wealth gap between Black people and white people in America is a far more appropriate measure of racial inequality. The median white family has roughly ten times the wealth of the median Black family, and the disparity will not be resolved by equalizing Black and white educational attainment or wages.[2] Income does not account for other quality-of-life indicators, such as access to health care, residential proximity to environmental hazards, and other meaningful dimensions of one's economic life. Second, the students come from many different places within the United States, and a household income of fifty thousand dollars in rural Mississippi affords an entirely different standard of living than it does in San Francisco. Third, economic security and class status can fluctuate over the course of a young person's life, and students may slide between socioeconomic classes several times before they enroll in college.

So the income information I collected does not neatly sort the respondents into distinct class categories. However, it does give an indication of the range of economic circumstances represented in the sample, and it speaks to the socioeconomic diversity of the students. The specific impact of finances emerged in far more useful and detailed ways during the interviews themselves.

Diversity of social class was complemented by geographic and residential diversity, as I spoke with students from every region of the United States and every sort of residential community. Twenty-nine students described their home town as "urban," twenty-nine described it as "suburban," and seven told me they came from "rural" communities. This is another area where the lines separating the categories can be grey, in part because the sprawling layout of many American cities makes it difficult to tell where the city ends and the suburbs begin. But again, during the interviews students spoke with great authority about the places they had known, and their descriptions of those spaces and communities provide tremendous insight into how space and geography influence perceptions of residential community.

Finally, I want to call attention to students' affirmation of immigrant identity. I did not directly ask the students if they or their parents were immigrants, nor did I categorize them by their family's generation in the United States, for example, first-, second-, or "1.5-" generation American. Still, eight respondents either explicitly identified with an ethnic group that distinguished them from African Americans and/or referred to their family as "immigrants" or an "immigrant family." Again, the specific number of respondents is far less important than learning about the ways immigrant and ethnic identity shapes students' experiences. This is a layered and explosive subject in the interviews.

Describing the colleges and universities I traveled to for this book is more difficult because of my commitment to confidentiality. Still, there are several important details about the colleges and universities worth noting. I visited a diverse group of HBCUs. Five of the nine schools I went to are public universities, and the other four are private institutions. The private colleges are, generally speaking, more selective than the public universities, but the selectivity gap within the groups of HBCUs was not nearly as prominent a topic among students as the perceived selectivity gap between HBCUs and PWIs.

Seven of the nine HBCUs were located in or close to a city with a large population and diverse economy beyond the commerce generated by the school in question. Five of the nine schools had undergraduate populations of fewer than five thousand students, though several of the universities I visited had significant graduate and professional school populations that pushed total student enrollment well over ten thousand. And finally, seven of the nine HBCUs featured student populations where more than 80 percent of enrolled students were Black when I visited. Black students accounted for more than 70 percent of the population at the other two schools. This may seem trivial, but many HBCUs are significantly more racially diverse than they were at the turn of the century. As I explained in the introduction, it was important for me to visit HBCUs where Black culture was unquestionably the dominant culture of the campus. Pseudonyms are assigned to all colleges and universities. Here is the list of HBCUs:

- Aspen University (rural/suburban, public)
- Birch University (urban, private)
- Cedar University (urban, public)
- Douglas University (urban, public)
- Evergreen University (urban, public)
- Fieldrose University (urban, private)
- Hickory University (urban, private)
- Juniper University (urban, public)
- Linden University (urban, public)

The PWIs I visited had a greater range of enrolled undergraduate students. Four schools had an undergraduate population of greater than thirty thousand students, and one school had an undergraduate population of fewer than ten thousand. Black students were a decided minority at each university, accounting for greater than 10 percent of the student population at only one of the PWIs. The group of PWIs also featured two schools with an undergraduate application acceptance rate below 30 percent, a trait indicative of their national prestige. The list features a mix of public and private institutions located in both urban and suburban areas. HBCUs are overwhelmingly concentrated south of the Mason-Dixon Line, and most of the PWIs are as well. Here is the list of PWIs:

- Adriatic University (urban, public)
- Barents University (urban, public)
- Caspian University (urban, public)
- Java University (urban, private)
- Tasman University (urban, private)
- Timor University (urban, public)
- Weddell University (suburban, public)

I could not compile a truly representative sample of colleges or Black LGBTQ+ students. I did not have the freedom to do so, given the way I selected the schools and recruited students, and achieving true representativeness is not an appropriate aim of a study based on sixty-five interviews. I am, however, delighted by the broad range of students and stories that found their way into this book. I began the process by searching the Internet, including social media, for publicly listed Black LGBTQ+ student organizations. Once I identified an organization, I contacted the faculty or staff person who appeared to be most knowledgeable about the organization based on publicly available information. Only after speaking with the appropriate faculty or staff person and going through all the safeguards in place to protect students from unwanted research inquiries did I make initial contact with the students from the organizations. The student leaders of the organizations were wonderful ambassadors for their communities, overwhelmingly gracious hosts, and indispensable to my recruitment efforts. One of the first questions I asked each student was, "How did you choose your college?"

FINANCES AND COLLEGE CHOICE

A 2016 study analyzed search data from over one million high school students to shed light on how students' college preferences shift from their first year of high school to the last. In the first year, students are captivated by prestige and name recognition, and Ivy League schools are overrepresented among students' top twenty choices. By senior year, however, students have a more pragmatic approach, informed by their high school performance and perceived chances of being admitted to highly competitive schools. Instead of prestige, students' preferences are shaped by geographic location (their top choices are relatively close to home) and cost of attendance.[3]

Another 2016 study found that almost 20 percent of students who are admitted to their top-choice college decide to go elsewhere due to cost of attendance. The next strongest reason for declining one's top choice is campus environment, which was cited by 9.4 percent of students, but additional financial considerations, such as financial aid, scholarship support, and value, were separated from the "cost of attendance" response. When all the financial responses are considered in concert, *roughly 40 percent of admitted students decline to attend their top choice for financial reasons.*[4] Again, this figure does not account for students who never even applied to the school they most wanted to attend because they knew it would be too expensive. The findings are consistent across students with different standardized test scores and racial backgrounds, but racial disparities in student loan debt highlight these considerations for Black students. Thirty-nine percent of Black people between twenty-five and fifty-five years old have student debt, compared to 30 percent of whites and 29 percent of Hispanics. Black people also have higher amounts of debt, roughly forty-three thousand dollars on average, than their white (thirty-one thousand dollars) and Hispanic (thirty thousand dollars) peers. A staggering 21 percent of Black college graduates default on their loans within twelve years of beginning college.[5]

Cost of attendance and financial aid are crucial to respondents' decisions about where to attend college, no matter what kind of school they attended. Jason, a twenty-one-year-old student at a private HBCU, made this clear when he told me, "I came down here for school mainly because they gave me enough money. So financial aid is a big deal for college students. Put that in your book!" He liked several other things about Evergreen College's profile, but he was not focused on the school because it was an HBCU or because of its prestige.

Jason was committed to attending college, but his relative openness to all options allowed Evergreen to make the decision easy by offering the most money. Gwen, a twenty-one-year-old at Caspian University, a public PWI, was not especially interested in college. She grew up in a small town in the Midwest where very few people had college degrees, and her parents were not among them. Although Gwen knew she wanted to leave her home town, she no longer wanted to be a student. "I didn't actually want to come to college at all," she told me. "But they kind of just gave me the most money, and like, it's a good school, so like, I'm not going to say no to Caspian. 'Cause then it's like, I don't know what else I would do." Gwen's description of her college choice melds financial considerations with other factors. When she told me, "I'm not going to say no to Caspian," Gwen did so in a tone that suggested it was obvious I would understand Caspian's appeal because of its reputation, not simply because of the money it offered.

A college's or university's ability to extend itself financially is sometimes interpreted as a sign not only of its reputation and prestige but of its willingness to invest in Black queer students. Candace attends Adriatic University, a large, public PWI with a national reputation for high academic standards. During the spring of her senior year of high school, Candace was considering several of the colleges that admitted her, and she learned about an event for Black prospective students at Adriatic just one week in advance. Though Adriatic offered considerable financial incentives if she enrolled, Candace did not have the money to visit the school for the prospective-student event, so she took things into her own hands. She called the admissions and financial aid office and explained that she was from a low-income household and could not afford to travel to the event. When the person she spoke with on the phone told her they did not have money to fund her travel, Candace began emailing individual staff members, and one of them, a Black woman, Dean Williams, emailed her back. Candace recounted,

[Dean Williams] was like, "Oh, where are you from? So your flight would be out of [major city]?" And I was like, "Yeah." And then she was like, "Okay, well would you like to miss school on Friday or Thursday?" And I was like, "Yeah, I don't mind." And she was like, "Okay, cool. My assistant will send you a ticket." And I was like, "Whoa!" Like, wait a minute, that happened like *that*! And just upon coming here, like meeting her, and the way she was just like, she was so ready to take care of me. She was like, "You belong here."

None of this would have happened if Adriatic had not had the money, but the financial health of the institution was not enough. It took the initiative of a prospective student and the commitment of a dedicated employee to make Candace's visit happen. Once Adriatic was able to get Candace on campus, Dean Williams's personal recruitment became the determining factor in Candace's choice to attend. Candace's life on campus has not been free of trouble caused by racism and sexism, but Williams's insistence that Candace belongs at Adriatic remains emotionally invaluable to Candace.

Note the Black queertidian character of Candace's story. She faced a decision influenced by the factors we know are common to all high school students: geography, institutional prestige, and finances. But Candace's choice was also shaped by her comfort on campus not only as a Black woman but as a Black queer woman. Her face-to-face interaction with a Black woman employee of the university made her feel both welcomed and valued. Had Candace's meeting with Dean Williams gone differently, she would likely have attended a different school.

Some students I spoke with expressed a clear personal preference for HBCUs early in their college-choice process, but had to abandon those hopes for purely financial reasons without regard for a school's reputation or their comfort on campus. Stories like Valerie's reflect the shifts in Black student attendance in higher education that began in the late twentieth century, when PWIs began competing with more fervor for high-achieving Black students. She explained,

> My mom, being like, an immigrant, she doesn't know about the college process. And so I was very pro-Black at the time, and I was like, "Ooh, I'm going to go to [an HBCU]." But then that was fake news, because they only gave me eight thousand dollars, and I was like, "Well, that's tragic." And then I applied to Barents [a public PWI] through the program, and this is like, honestly a miracle. 'Cause I was like, "Hmm, that one girl said she went to Barents through the program." . . . Thank the Lord, I got accepted, and for my class, we get, our tuition is paid. And so that's where I went, even though I didn't want to go to Barents. Because I was like, I've been in predominantly white spaces my whole entire life. I'm tired of this. But there's all these people who gave me money.

Unlike Deron, Valerie did not have a strong connection to an HBCU or an alum educating her about the college process. Like several students I spoke with, she was still drawn to HBCUs because of experiences with racism in high school, but those colleges were unable to offer the financial support she needed. Ultimately, Valerie was pushed toward Barents University not by a mentor but by her immediate social network, as she happened to know someone from a previous class in her high school who applied through an admission program designed for students like her. Hers was a choice by default.

Still, many of the conversations about finances and college choice were more layered than a cold calculation about affordability. Like Deron and Taylor at the beginning of this chapter, students often report that affordability is the dominant factor in their decision, but their interest in colleges and universities is sustained by people close to them. Jewel, another student at Barents, began by telling me, "I was not going to go to a school that I had to pay out of pocket for." But the reason she homed in on Barents rather than another affordable school was that

> I had, I guess, one particular mentor who went to Barents and became a math professor. And so I, even back in middle school, kind of knew that I wanted to eventually emulate her decisions, and wanted to kind of become her, in a way. But I knew that like, if I wasn't able to get the financial aid, like, it was over. I guess the next part was also that I knew I had to stay in [my state], 'cause I qualified for [the program], and that goes back to financ[es]. And it was close to home. So physically moving me and my stuff from [my city] wouldn't be difficult.

Jewel moves back and forth between the different reasons she chose her school. She begins with finances and then shifts to explain the math professor she knew and the initial exposure to Barents. Importantly, Jewel is struck not by the professor's description of what college is like but by what kind of person she might be when she graduates from college and builds her career. Jewel then switches to talking about the role of geography in her decision-making process, which is tied to her financial situation. Though finances often have the most force, all of these ideas are connected in the mechanics of college choice.

FAMILY AND COMFORT AT HBCUS

For years, researchers in the field of college choice held that the process unfolded in three stages, all of which are driven by parental involvement. In the predisposition stage, students in sixth through ninth grade are first exposed to college and motivated to explore what college holds primarily by their parents. Even if parents are not yet playing an active role in the application process, they are encouraging their children to see themselves as college students. The second stage is the search stage, where students begin to narrow down the schools they will apply to. This narrowing is influenced not only by practical considerations, such as cost and distance from home, but by input from their parents, who provide both explicit and subtle feedback about whether their children's preferences are realistic. The final stage is the choice stage, and at this point, parental involvement is more intensely focused on the financial implications of the college choice.[6]

Racist myths of Black familial pathology suggest that Black parents, especially Black fathers, are not involved in their children's lives to the extent that they should be, and therefore Black students are navigating this process largely on their own. Stereotypes of Black culture also suggest that studious Black children are swimming upstream against the fear of "acting white" in school, and the idea that academic success is somehow at odds with Black authenticity and a strong sense of Black racial identity. These myths have been repeatedly disproven. A 2013 study by the Centers for Disease Control found that despite the fact that a smaller percentage of Black fathers were married to the mothers of their children, Black fathers spent more time, on average, with their children than white fathers did.[7] Prudence Carter, Angel Harris, and others have shown that the fear of "acting white" thesis is false. Black parents place just as much emphasis on educational attainment as white families, and Black children's fear of being chastised for "acting white" is simply not a determinant of their behavior in school or their academic achievement.[8]

But emphasis on academic achievement is not the same as support for the college application and matriculation process, which often requires technical knowledge and financial resources. As we have seen, Black parents' inability to pay for college has clear effects on the college choices of their children. The colleges themselves often make up some of the disparity in economic capital.

What about social and cultural capital? How do students with parents who do not have the cultural knowledge or social connections to navigate the process close the college-choice gap? Amy Bergerson has forced a reconsideration of the three-part college-choice theory based on the experiences of economically privileged white students, as her work sheds light on the social and cultural dimensions of the process for Black students.[9] Bergerson affirms that parental involvement is indispensable to the prospect of attending college across racial and economic backgrounds. When Black parents do not have the requisite cultural knowledge, students turn to extended family and mentors to compensate. For Black students, familial or kin involvement, not just parental involvement, is key to exposing young people to college and helping them make their way to campus.[10] I found this to be especially true among students who chose HBCUs.

My aunt's actually an alumna from Evergreen, so she told me about it, and then they also gave me like pretty much a full ride, like paid for tuition and everything like that. So that kind of made like the decision a lot easier. And then I came down and visited. But this was like almost when I made my decision to come to Evergreen. So I came down and visited, and I liked it. Like I was saying before, with like, southern hospitality and things like that. Like, I came down to Evergreen and everyone's like, "Hi, how are you doing? Welcome to Evergreen," and everything like that. So yeah, so that kind of made my decision easier too. (Eric, Evergreen)

My grandfather went [to Cedar]. He was captain of the football team. My aunt went here. My stepmother went here. So generation after generation. Like we literally, for family reunions, we go to [the football game], and half the family sits on the Oak side and half sits on Cedar side. Like that's been my tradition since I came into this world. And my godmother went to Oak. All I know is HBCUs, so that's my only option in my life. And I have to find another type of education also. Unfortunately, I went to [a predominantly white] high school in Alabama for a little while, and that mistreatment, I can't do it again. I wasn't going to do it again. (Zoe, Cedar)

I'm not opposed to being uncomfortable. But just from my past experiences going to the school, middle school and high school, it was like I was surrounded by predominantly white people, and except for the small group that I may have had in like the African American club or my friends. And so I just wanted to be around a whole bunch of people that looked like me and wanted to accomplish the same goals I wanted to accomplish, [people who] were driven. And so I was sold on that part. And my sisters, two of my sisters went to HBCUs, so they were always advocating for HBCUs. (Sydney, Douglas)

College choice is a family affair. Grandparents, godparents, siblings, cousins, aunts, uncles, and stepparents all play roles in guiding these students toward a decision, either by introducing students to HBCUs or by strongly advocating for them. This advocacy was considered along with other factors, like campus climate and treatment from other students, as the decision is made. In Eric's case, Evergreen made the decision easier by offering him a full scholarship, but in the next breath he mentioned how welcome he felt during his campus visit. Evergreen is a private school and is better positioned to offer such a package than the average public HBCU, but the money spoke louder when amplified by Black southern hospitality.

Zoe gave me the sense that she never considered attending a PWI at any point in the process. HBCUs were the only options, and were baked into her family's traditions. Though she eventually settled on Cedar, she did not describe a hierarchy of HBCUs as she recounted her decision process, nor was she pressured to attend the specific HBCUs that other family members had attended. Importantly, Zoe explained that she became even more committed to the path her family laid out for after her experiences in middle and high school. She told me that she was racially profiled by police and school administrators, and socially isolated and harassed by classmates and teachers for her appearance, most notably her skin tone and hair. These are the types of experiences that Dillard University president Walter Kimbrough hypothesized were responsible for the recent surge in HBCU applications, as noted in the introduction.

Sydney described her sisters' influence, but like Zoe, she was motivated to find a setting different from her high school. She said that the HBCU environment is more comfortable for her not simply because the students at HBCUs look like her but because they have the same pride in accomplishment. Again, Black cultural pride in academic and professional achievement directly rebuts the stereotype of Black hostility to academic success.

Victor, a bisexual nonbinary student at Linden University, adds depth to this type of Black pride. He was first exposed to HBCUs through observing and admiring one of the most prominent men in his community. Though both of his parents eventually completed their college degrees, Victor grew up poor. The prominent mentor from his neighborhood appealed to Victor personally and encouraged him to go to an HBCU not simply because the education he got would be good for his financial prospects but because the teaching would counter the lies Victor had been told about Black people by the American education system. As Victor told me,

> Probably had the most prominent man in our neighborhood, was always clean cut, came to church, gave big offerings, just everything, but he lived in our community. So he really just inspired me to want to go off to a college, but more importantly, how important the Black experience was. 'Cause he always said, "Who could teach you better than your own?" And that always rang with me, because I was just like, you're right. Why wouldn't—I would much rather want to learn from a Black man about the Black experience, or a Black woman on the Black experience, or even something as far off as somebody brown, but someone of the diaspora teaching me and dismantling what I thought was correct education for a Black man in America.

Though HBCU students received positive messages about HBCUs from family members or mentors in their neighborhoods, very few students told me that these messages came from within their high school. When HBCUs were framed favorably in high school, they emerged as possible college choices because the interviewees knew older students who had gone on to HBCUs. Only one student among the forty HBCU students I spoke with described a high school guidance counselor or teacher as someone who encouraged them to apply to or attend HBCUs. Only one student mentioned an athletic coach as someone who played an active role in exposing them to HBCUs. It is difficult to interpret this

absence as neutrality. The implication is that teachers, guidance coun-
selors, and other high school staff either did not view HBCUs as worthy choices for their students, or were not invested enough to earnestly
engage their students in any discussion about choosing college. A few
students also described being steered away from HBCUs by their high
school classmates. Perhaps surprisingly, it was not white classmates who
cast doubt on the viability of HBCUs but Black students talking among
themselves about which colleges they should attend. Chris, a gay student who treasured his first year at a large, public HBCU, described how
these concerns rubbed off on him as he was deciding where to go.

> I had skeptical views about it 'cause I was like, I know that in the world
> we live in where it's predominantly white people. Well, not predominantly
> white people, but like, CEOs are white, or they're going to look at the bet-
> ter things. So me going to an HBCU, I thought I was going to be counted
> out. I thought that jobs were going to look past me because my thing says
> "Aspen." My resumé says I graduated from Aspen with this GPA. As op-
> posed to my friend graduating a PWI D1 [Division 1], and she's making
> those grades that I make at an HBCU, so they would look at her before
> they'd look at me.

In this excerpt, Chris does not express concern about the content or
quality of the education he will receive. The college's prestige is directly
tied to his employment prospects after college. He was initially worried
that an HBCU education would be viewed as inferior and disqualify-
ing by potential employers. Racism is a powerful undercurrent running
through these fears, as white opportunity hoarding and networking
certainly limit the employment and financial prospects of Black college
graduates. A recent study showed that white people without high school
degrees are about as likely to be employed as Black college graduates.[11]
But after spending a year at Aspen, Chris is less worried about his job
prospects because of the networking opportunities afforded to him
while on campus. He believes the connections students make through
extracurricular activities and the alumni network give HBCU graduates
advantages over their peers at PWIs. He explains, "I also let her know
that, again, as I told you, that PWIs, yes, it's good. Yes, like, the jobs are
there. But at HBCU, I feel like the same ways we get discredited, we get

credited for it. We get jobs because of the people that we know, because of the organizations that we're in, because of the things that we do on campus puts us in those places. Being active at an HBCU can get you to the places that a PWI can't do."

Annette also discussed her concerns about the labor market as a motivating factor in her selecting an HBCU. After stints in the navy and the army reserves, she returned to her home city and had a long conversation with her mother about improving her employment prospects. She decided to pursue a college degree but worried about what awaited her on campus. "[Mom] knew I was struggling looking for employment. So she mentioned, 'Why don't you go to school?' And for me, I was thinking about going to [a university] downtown, but then as I realized it and talked to her more, she was like, it would be better if I went to an HBCU. So I thought about it, and then I was thinking, I guess she's right, considering everything that's going on in the world, and how Blacks among the minorities are one of the most discriminated, especially LGBT Blacks."

Annette and her mother do not have a comfortable relationship because Annette's sexuality and gender expression are not fully accepted by her family. Despite these issues and her mother's limited resources, family input played a key role in Annette's school-choice process. Annette's mother was concerned, for reasons that are somewhat unclear, that her daughter would not thrive at a PWI. Annette interpreted this concern in the context of the current revival of unabashed white supremacy and discrimination against Black people and other racial minorities in the United States.

Annette's comment about discrimination suffered by queer Black people is the only instance during the interviews where perceptions and expectations about intersectional queer Black life on campus were explicitly mentioned as part of the college-choice process. Douglas Burleson surveyed 119 queer students in high school, college, and graduate school to identify the factors that influenced their college choice. He found that quality of education and the school's reputation were by far the most important factors for the students' selections. Student organizations (including, but not limited to, LGBTQ+ organizations), having a gay-friendly campus, diversity, and academic support were the next most important factors, followed by financial aid and housing. Students who described themselves as more "out" about their sexuality were more likely to report that prospective colleges' campus climate for LGBTQ+ people was a major consideration when they selected their college.[12]

Like Annette, many respondents did not feel comfortable affirming their sexuality or gender expression while living with their parents before college, and the traditional out/closeted paradigm was not developed with queer Black people in mind. The absence of explicit discussion of Black queerness and college choice was striking, especially when compared to respondents' comments about the racial climate on campus. Still, there were times during the interviews when the importance of queer comfort could be inferred from respondents' accounts. The diversity of Blackness queer Black students found on campus opens space for a queer reading of the college-choice process.

> It's like more relaxed when other Black people are around each other. Just, I feel like we can be more real, and, I don't know how to explain it. Just, yeah, feel like you fit in without having to try so hard, 'cause with such a vast variety of Black people, there's also like different kinds. So you just find somewhere to fit in right. (Shannon, Juniper)

> And then coming to Evergreen I took an enrichment tour in high school and stepping onto campus I felt I was at home. The campus atmosphere of being really family oriented, everyone being really friendly. Seeing how everyone expresses themselves the way they feel and the way they want to express themselves really brought me to campus to make me feel like I was at home. (Easton, Evergreen)

Both Shannon and Easton describe the sense of welcome and ease they felt as Black students on a predominantly Black campus. Their racial comfort is not based on uniformity of experience; it grows because they cherish Black diversity. They believe they have space to carve out individual identities, but also that there are communities within the Black student body to which they might belong. Importantly, these are students' recollections of the college-choice process, rather than their experiences as enrolled students. Still, a culture of Black achievement, Black diversity, and racial comfort, amplified by the advice and experiences of their kin, are the forces leading these students to HBCUs. Sexuality and gender expression were rarely explicitly discussed when students recalled their decision to attend their HBCU, but there is a queer reading of "diversity" as affirmed by the students, and Burleson's study indicates that LGBTQ+-specific concerns do enter into the college-choice process.

PRESTIGE AND COMFORT AT PWIS

Financial and geographic considerations were just as important for PWI students as they were for HBCU students. But among PWI students, there was very little mention of family or kin history, knowledge, or love when it came to college exposure or college choice. They also spoke less about how their identities, racial or otherwise, informed their thinking about whether the school they chose would be a good fit, or whether they expected to find students with similar beliefs and values on campus. Patricia, a senior at Fieldrose University, told me she used to watch the NBC sitcom *A Different World* with her grandmother, and the two would gossip about the characters. That television show introduced her to HBCUs and sparked her imagination about the mystique and fun of Black college life. Patricia's grandmother's support for her college fantasies gave her college aspirations a familial grounding. PWIs have plenty of traditions, pageantry, and mystique, and there is no shortage of films and television shows about life at those colleges. But none of the PWI students talked about their exposure to, or curiosity about, PWIs the way Patricia did; there was far less romanticism and familial enthusiasm in these students' accounts.

Discussions about prestige revealed additional differences between PWI and HBCU students' reflections on college choice. In the quotation in the section above, Chris expressed his concerns about the prestige of Aspen University. He was worried that white employers would not take his job candidacy seriously because Aspen is an HBCU. Those fears were assuaged by alumni who returned to campus and seemed to be financially comfortable and successful. Chris's concern about prestige is somewhat transactional, in that he cares about the school's reputation because he will trade on that reputation for a job after college.

Prestige was mentioned more frequently and in more different ways in my discussions with the PWI cohort than in my conversations with the HBCU students. On balance, the PWIs I visited had lower acceptance rates than the HBCUs, and two of the three most selective schools in this book are PWIs. So many PWI students applied to and enrolled in their colleges because they knew that admissions were competitive and they interpreted competition as an indicator of quality. Recall Gwen's statement that "I'm not going to say no to Caspian," when it offered her admission and financial support. That sense of obligation to seize the opportunity to improve one's life is echoed by several students, especially at Adriatic University, one of the most competitive schools I visited.

I just knew Adriatic was more like, what's the word for it, it has more prestige behind it. And then coming from such a small county, I kind of want to strive for that, something bigger. (Roland)

I didn't really want to go to college, but now that I had to go to college, I only picked a couple schools that I really wanted to go to. So they were kind of like, they were all mainly competitive schools, which was kind of unusual, because everyone around me, like this school was an impossibility for a lot of people. (Kerry)

Several HBCU students made similar statements about the importance of college as a tool for social mobility. One of the first students introduced in this chapter is Taylor, who switched from a community college to a four-year college specifically because she wanted to surround herself with motivated students with similar career goals. Annette returned from two stints in the military and spoke with her mother about obtaining a college degree in order to get a better job. Chris spoke about how an HBCU degree might affect his job prospects once he graduated. So HBCU students are making similarly strategic decisions about the colleges they attend, and they have a sense of their place in a social hierarchy. However, the emphasis on institution-specific prestige simply did not appear among HBCU students in the way that it did among PWI students.

Another point that presented itself more clearly in my discussions with PWI students was that there were specific offerings within the academic programs at PWIs that drew the students to their colleges. Earlier in the chapter we heard from Jewel, who went to Barents specifically to study math because she had a mathematician mentor who was a Barents alumnus. Harold, who founded the Black LGBTQ+ student group at Java University, selected his college specifically because of its computer science program and the discussions he had with computer science majors during his visit as a prospective student. Kerry went to Adriatic University because she knew it was a competitive school, and she knew she would be able to pursue her interests in film and theater. Other than medical school, which was an area of interest across both student groups, HBCU students had little to say about how their specific academic interests influenced their college choice.

These findings do not mean that HBCU students and prospective students do not think HBCUs are academically prestigious. Clearly, some HBCUs have greater name recognition than others and are nationally known as prestigious institutions. The list of schools I visited was not determined by college rankings or prestige, so what I heard from students was certainly shaped by the colleges in the sample. But the HBCUs I visited are not especially obscure institutions (at least among Black folks), and many of them attract students from outside their geographic region. Still, the conversation about prestige at HBCUs took a different shape than its counterpart at PWIs. This suggests that there is more to learn about how HBCUs cultivate a sense of prestige among students, alums, and prospective students, including whether those strategies and tactics differ from those employed at PWIs.

One area in which students' reflections were both similar and different is the importance of diversity on campus as a factor in college choice. The HBCU students quoted above were attracted not only to the racial safety and familiarity of Black colleges but to the Black diversity they saw during campus visits. PWI students did not have the same sense of racial familiarity, but said similar things about the value of diversity on their campuses.

> I talked to a lot of the students, they talked about how they felt like even though Java is a big school, they could still find some sort of community, and so there was a smaller group of people they could hang around and enjoy. And so I think that's definitely part of why. (Morris, Java)

> It's very cliché, but I felt like, when I was here, there were so many different types of people here that seemed to coexist on the same campus. . . . I think when I looked at the college, and I wanted somewhere where it

wasn't like, everybody had the same mindset, or the same political views, or the same ideas on religion. I just wanted a place where there existed everybody, so that when I was trying to discover who I was, I would be able to have sources of people that were different. (Olympia, Barents)

I think after I stepped foot on this campus and got the tour and saw the things that they were trying to do as far as like inclusion, that really kind of captured it for me, because the other schools talked about it, but they didn't really take you into the spaces that show that inclusion was a priority. So I was like, "Yeah, this is where I want to be." (Summer, Caspian)

This testimony moves beyond students' sense that diversity on campus allows for learning from difference and finding a social niche. At least two of the PWI students used their campus visits to figure out whether the lip service PWIs paid to diversity and inclusion was credible. The first example of this in the chapter was Candace's visit to Adriatic, where her meeting with Dean Williams assured her that she had found the right place and would be supported at her college. The second example is just above, where Summer came away from her campus visit especially impressed with Caspian University's commitment to diversity and inclusion. Again, the impressions made during campus visits do not always hold once students are actually enrolled, and other students at Caspian never felt the sort of comfort or commitment that Candace did. Nevertheless, the point is that PWIs seem more credible when something happens during a campus visit to convince the students that their commitment to diversity is legitimate.

Students consider diversity in several ways as they make their decisions about where to attend college. The HBCU students I spoke with sought diversity within the comfort of a mostly Black community. Though non-Black enrollment at HBCUs has increased over the past two decades, the schools I visited featured a significant Black majority. The HBCU interviewees did not report that their colleges boasted about racial diversity as an element designed to appeal to prospective students. It does not seem as if these HBCUs are selling diversity in the same way as do PWIs, where Black students want to be convinced that they can thrive on a campus with many different racial groups, and are looking for concrete signs of support for Black students in particular. None of the conversations I had suggested that Black students at PWIs had a weaker sense of their racial identity than their HBCU counterparts.

BLACK DIVERSITY

Where is the Black queertidian in the college-choice process? When I talked to queer Black students about how they selected their schools, they cited the same factors that all students consider: finances, geography, prestige, and family influence. These answers are completely ordinary. Finances had the most influence on the selection process, but students often talked about the different factors with reference to each other. An obvious example of the complementary nature of these considerations is the relationship between finances and geography. In-state public universities are often the most pragmatic options for prospective students from families without savings for the full price of a college education.

But Blackness, queerness, and queer Blackness color what might otherwise be mundane decisions for these students. Sometimes, Black LGBTQ+ collegians enjoy support from their families and kin, especially those who champion HBCUs. Their supporters impart the value of education and the value of embedding oneself within a community of Black students and professors. There is a dual meaning at play here between familial and racial kinship. Often, there is a mutually reinforcing relationship between the support respondents receive from HBCU advocates at home, and new friends and family they find on campus. This sort of on-campus kinship was not discussed by students who attend PWIs. I only interviewed twenty-five students from PWIs, so it is possible that some Black students at these schools have similar feelings of kinship extending from their home families to their new families on campus. But the interviews suggest that these values are more central to the college-choice process for HBCU students, and should be celebrated and built upon by HBCUs seeking to distinguish themselves.

Sometimes, however, the motivation behind familial guidance is harder to discern. Explicitly or implicitly, parents' and guardians' opinions may be shaped by prejudices and suspicions about whether a college will nurture or "correct" their child's queerness. In other cases, parents have little to say about the college-choice process, and the silence leaves room for multiple interpretations. Some parents and guardians may not have the time, knowledge, or financial resources to contribute to the decision. Others may be estranged and distant because they do not understand their children, or do not accept them for who they are.

Queerness also influences the importance of diversity at both HBCUs and PWIs. None of the interviewees explicitly told me they selected their school because it appeared to be welcoming for queer Black people or LGBTQ+ people more broadly. Perhaps this is the case because they ruled out the possibility of finding a school that celebrated LGBTQ+ people and their communities early in the college-decision process, so it was not an important consideration. Or perhaps they looked for signs of such welcoming on the Internet and during campus visits, but found none. In addition, many students were still questioning their sexuality and gender expression while making the college-choice process, so those students might not have sought out queer communities on campus at all.

Despite the lack of explicit prioritization of queer-friendly campus life, students told me they were attracted to schools with many different types of students. They prioritized this value because they thought it would be easier to fit in socially in places where diversity was evident. It is not much of a leap to infer that queer students and LGBTQ+ student communities were among those students searched for during campus visits. Not only this, but if "diversity" is a priority for Black queer students, and if what students mean when they say "diverse" is a campus where they can see and imagine themselves (Black queer people) living comfortable public lives, then the meaning of "diversity" is queered by students looking for it whether they make this queering explicit or not. If standard conceptions of visible multiculturalism on campus are translated into images of different groups of students, the traditional PWI campus inspires pictures of Black, Hispanic, Asian, Native American, *and* LGBTQ+ students as proof of diversity. White people are normalized and empowered, without need to make a "special contribution" to multicultural diversity to prove their worth. LGBTQ+ students, when they are part of the picture, are an addendum—a bonus category, surely secondary to the racial and ethnic categories, perhaps because queer identity is often more ambiguous than racial visibility for people of color. But these students are looking for *Black in-group diversity* and

Black queer diversity, both of which queer the checklist required for traditional multiculturalism in the PWI diversity model.

This chapter is a window into queer Black students' college-choice process, with special attention to the students' support systems and motivations for going to college in the first place. The next chapter more fully explains the idea of the Black queertidian, as students describe themselves in mundane ways as they provide a sense of the rhythm of campus life.

[2]

THE BLACK QUEERTIDIAN

Candace, the student at Adriatic University whose college recruitment was detailed last chapter, told me about the evening of her awakening.

> It was kind of like a chat and dinner type of thing at the LGBTQ+ center downstairs. I would say it was really eye-opening, because I realized for the first time that like, I guess being part of the LGBTQ+ community is not a thing people do. Like, it's not a thing people really *do*. It's just who they are. And I feel like a lot of times, especially in my culture, we view that as an action, and it's like you want to be defiant. Like, you want to be *extra* and things like that. But it's like, no, this is just who these people are.

When Candace refers to stereotypes of Black queerness in her culture, she describes the hostility towards LGBTQ+ people who are "extra." In all likelihood, the hostility is more frequently spurred by "extra" femininity, as embodied by transfeminine and femme-of-center gay men, but she does not specify which gender performances are deemed excessive. As noted in the introduction, the risks of violence for embodying femininity and femmeness are of a different kind than those associated with performing masculinity and mascness. However, the excessive, exacting, and prideful performance of any gender puts *all* queer people at risk of condemnation and violence. Candace deploys this inclusivity and invokes the LGBTQ+ community as a whole, insisting that the notion that all queers want to be "extra" and "defiant" is false.

Candace's comment, however, seems to run against the grain of essential work in Black queer studies. E. Patrick Johnson invokes "quare" instead of "queer" in homage to his southern Black grandmother, who "uses 'quare' to denote something or someone who is odd, irregular, or slightly off-kilter—definitions in keeping with traditional understandings and uses of 'queer.' On the other hand, she also deploys 'quare' to connote something *excessive* [emphasis added]—something that might philosophically translate into an excess of discursive and epistemological meanings grounded in African American cultural rituals and lived experiences."[1] This unruly flowering of meanings complements Eve Sedgwick's explanation that "queer can refer to . . . the open mesh of possibilities, gaps, overlaps, dissonances and resonances, lapses and excesses of meaning when the constituent elements of anyone's gender, of anyone's sexuality aren't made to signify monolithically."[2]

Queer theory and queer studies, then, are alternatives to stable empiricism and social theory. They disrupt traditional analyses, embracing fluidity and spillover in gender, sexuality, and other matters, and throwing categories into crisis. Ahmin Ghaziani and Matt Brim explain that queer research methods "question the origins and effects of concepts and categories rather than reify them in an allegedly generalizable variable-oriented paradigm, . . . reject the fetishizing of the observable. . . . [and] embrace multiplicity, misalignments, and silences."[3] They also note the importance of self-narration as a queer methodological alternative to misleading notions of researcher neutrality, objectivity, and invisibility.

So we have to reconcile Candance's insistence that belonging to the LGBTQ+ community is not about being "extra" with the accepted implication of queerness as an analytic concept fueled by excess. Fortunately, the reconciliation is straightforward. Candace simply says there is more than one way to be LGBTQ+. The diversity of queer life and personhood, *including mundane queer moods and experiences,* undoes the queer *stereotype* but reveals the truth and power of the queer analytic *approach.* The differences among LGBTQ+ people and between the seasons of their lives prove how limiting static categories and language can be, thereby validating queer studies and Black queer studies.

As I mentioned in the introduction, this book and the Black queertidian concept do not share many of the disruptive trademarks of queer theory or queer methods. Where, then, in the tradition of Black queer studies should *Black and Queer on Campus* and the Black queertidian be situated? I return to the excerpt from Johnson, who continues, "This reconceptualization foregrounds the ways in which lesbians, bisexuals, gays, and transgendered people of color come to sexual and racial knowledge."[4] *Black and Queer on Campus* describes the ways queer Black college students come to gender, sexual, and racial knowledge. I would not call the Black queer mundane a full-fledged *theory*, queer or otherwise, because of the monolithizing tendencies of theory.[5] If theory aims for generalizability and describes the relationships between different components of a social system, the Black queertidian is not a social theory of Black LGBTQ+ people or communities. Instead, I think of the Black queertidian as an interpretation. More specifically, it is my interpretation of the ideas and experiences related to me by self-identified Black LGBTQ+ college students. Here is what makes it valuable:

1 We are in a historical moment when Black queer fabulousness and radicalism are celebrated, commercialized, and accepted as never before in white American popular culture and media. We need to position the Black queertidian alongside the Black queer fabulous and fly in order put them in dialogue with each other for the sake of accuracy, at the very least. Black queer life is not *only* fabulous/fly, just as it is not only dangerous (in both the hopeful and the tragic sense).

2 Lauding Black queer spectacle at the expense of the mundane can elide the violence Black queer people face on a daily basis and may obscure the ways racism shapes queer experiences. A mandate to celebrate beauty in the fabulous, fly, and spectacular may also prevent us from finding beauty in the ordinary, quiet spaces of Black queer life.

3 The accounts in this book are seldom found in sociology, higher education studies, Black studies, or gender studies. Disregard for Black LGBTQ+ people remains commonplace.

The Black queertidian is not an invalidation of Black queer pride and fabulousness/flyness. My interpretation is not a substitute for, or summary of, Black queer people's lives. It is not a generalizable theory of Black queerness or a prescription for Black queer politics. It is a synthesis of the insight I gained from the students I spoke with, and an opportunity to approach analyses of Black queer life with a different lens. Before returning to students' testimony, I need to spend some time reinforcing the first two points above: the commercial rise and acceptance of Black queer fabulousness/flyness in American popular culture, and the value of preserving the Black queertidian as complement.

BILLY PORTER AND *POSE*

Billy Porter grew up queer in a divided home. His mother loved and nurtured his personality and flare for the dramatic, and his homophobic stepfather abused him from the time he was seven years old until he was twelve. At age fifteen, Porter moved out for good, completing his education at a prestigious arts high school in Pittsburgh while living in a motel. He paid his rent and other expenses by working at an amusement park, graduated high school, and moved on to the Carnegie Mellon School of Fine Arts. The way Porter tells it, he saved himself. None of the adults in his life had the power or courage to stop the abuse he endured or support his dreams, so he solved his own problems by remaining true to who he was and becoming independent. "I was able to extract myself from that toxic energy without fear, without guilt. . . . I wish more young people could get to the space of *I don't need your tolerance, I don't need your acceptance. What I demand is your respect for my humanity*."[6]

Porter began his Broadway career in a 1994 production of *Grease*, and was signed to a recording contract as a (presumably straight) R&B recording artist in 1997. In 2005, he wrote and performed his one-man show titled *Ghetto Superstar*, which was recognized at the GLAAD Media Awards. From there, his stardom remained unmistakably queer, and when he stepped into the spotlight as the drag queen Lola in the original 2013 production *Kinky Boots*, everyone knew acclaim would follow. He won the Tony Award for his performance, made several other appearances on television over the next five years, and began his reign as Pray Tell on FX's *Pose* in 2018. In 2019, Billy Porter became the first openly gay Black man to be nominated and win in any category in the Emmys. Having worked in show business for roughly thirty years, Porter reflects tellingly, "In the past, as an out, queer actor, they generally tend to cut our dicks off. We are not sexualized people," he says. "Even when they started telling stories of love, they were always white boys. I have spent my entire career never having been an object of anyone's affection in anything—until now."[7]

His status as an entertainment industry icon grew from his appearance at the Golden Globes Award Show in January 2019, when he wore a dazzling silver suit with a pink cape. He upped the ante at the February 2019 Oscars as he conducted pre-show interviews on the red carpet in a Black velvet tuxedo gown. "I knew it was going to be a thing," he said. "I didn't know it was going to be a *thiiinnng*."[8] At the Met Gala later that year, he sat atop a chaise as a winged, golden, Egyptian-inspired "Sun God," as six topless men carried him into the party.

Porter has suffered much criticism from conservatives and bigots, especially after he reprised the tuxedo gown for his 2020 appearance on *Sesame Street*. Predictably, his reaction has been, "If you don't like it, don't watch it."[9] But the moral panic swirling around Porter's Black queer fabulousness on the Right has been counterbalanced in mainstream media by fawning and applause for Porter's talent, unapologetic personality, and aspiration to be "a walking piece of art."[10] A *Vogue* magazine headline declared, "Billy Porter Just Made the Most Fabulous Entrance in Met Gala History."[11] *Time* echoed those sentiments almost exactly with its proclamation, "Billy Porter Had a Glorious Entrance to the 2019 Met Gala."[12] And almost a year later, CNN published a piece titled "Why Billy Porter's Red Carpet Style Transcends Fashion." The author, Mariani Cerini, trumpets Porter as "the fashion activist we never knew we needed until he arrived on the red carpet and smashed convention."[13]

It is important to explicitly describe the "conventions" Porter is "smashing." Porter has made his intentions quite clear: he sees himself as a Black queer disruptor of both race and gender norms, and an outspoken critic of the racist, homophobic, and sexist inequities that shape the entertainment industry. The quotation above from Porter about the desexualization of gay men was not just about gay men but about the paradigms of respectability and desirability that kept *Black* gay men from being love interests in film and television. The Egyptian sun-god performance at the Met Gala queers an indisputably African and Black icon of decadence and royalty, as the other guests hoping to shine at the ball are swallowed by the sun-god's shadow. The CNN article includes a quotation from Porter that illustrates his intentions, and he foregrounds Blackness. "From this (Oscars) moment, I want people to understand that you don't have to understand or even agree with other people's authenticity or truths, but we must all respect each other. People are going to be really uncomfortable with my Black ass in a ball gown—but it's not anybody's business but mine."

And yet, Porter's quotation is the only time the word "Black" appears in the CNN piece. In the aforementioned *Time* and *Vogue* articles about the Met Gala, the word "Black" is absent. Porter is not to blame for the erasure of Blackness in the reporting about his career and fashion choices. Embracing fabulousness as a Black queer aesthetic does not deracialize the person performing it. Black queer fabulousness is not anti-Black. It is not an attempt to make oneself more appealing to white liberal and moderate onlookers, or to rebrand Black queerness as, simply, queerness. However, as a case study, media coverage of Porter shows that one of the outcomes of his fabulous success is the drowning out of Blackness in applause for Porter's vision, courage, and queerness.

Oprah Winfrey's 2017 conversation with RuPaul is an even more dramatic example of this erasure and deracialization. The article summarizing their conversation is titled, "Oprah Talks to RuPaul about Life, Liberty, and the Pursuit of the Fabulous." Oprah begins with an explanation.

OPRAH: This month we're asking the question "What defines you?"
How would you answer that?
RUPAUL: At this moment? I'm everything and nothing at all. I'm Black,
I'm white, I'm male, female. To me, seeing all the facets of yourself is
the next level of our evolution—understanding who we really are.
OPRAH: I love that. So you don't put yourself in any kind of box.
RUPAUL: None of them felt like the right fit.
OPRAH: Because why do you have to define yourself?
RUPAUL: You don't have to![14]

When Porter's fabulousness is stripped of its Blackness by the media's treatment of his style and performance, it is a distortion of Porter's explicit intentions. In RuPaul's case, the performer deracializes theirself, affirming racial transcendence as a complement to gender fluidity. In both cases, mainstream celebration of the Black queer fabulous opens the door to whitewashing, reinforcement of acceptable bourgeois queerness, and disregard for the ways racism shapes LGBTQ+ lives.

One of the highly visible platforms that regularly avoids these pitfalls is *Pose*, a television show that features Black queer and transgender people in front of and behind the camera. *Pose* is unapologetically fabulous as characters and visual representations of Black queer ballroom culture in 1980s and 1990s New York are striking and spectacular. Mj Rodriguez, the Black Hispanic transgender woman who plays Blanca, reports that acting on *Pose* "feels like a form of activism," and says the show "gives me hope that we can change people's hearts and minds."[15] Storylines celebrate ballroom culture without ignoring the struggles and trials of its characters, including the struggle against racism. *Pose* also depicts Black queer sex in ways that Porter describes, without positioning respectable white queers at the center of its stories or portraying such intimacy primarily as eroticism driven by danger. Characters are sexual beings who are not defined by their sex lives. Viewers see mundane moments of beauty, dignity, and pain that are undeniably queer but not always glamorous.

Porter is front and center in many of these scenes. In *Pose*'s second season, Pray Tell (Porter) becomes a caretaker and confidant for a younger character on the show, Ricky (Dyllon Burnside), a young Black man who is diagnosed with HIV but not noticeably ill. Pray Tell had served in such a role before, as he comforted his lover, Costas, through his losing battle with AIDS in the first season. This time, however, Pray Tell is also burdened by his own HIV-positive diagnosis. The two transition from caretakers to lovers as Ricky initiates sex after watching a movie on Pray Tell's couch. The scene is stunning, considering the history of gay sex on television, especially sex between gay Black men on television. The poignancy of the scene and Porter's role in it were amplified in May of 2021, when Porter revealed to the world that he had been HIV positive for fourteen years. There is no precedent for the simulation of the physical acts of sex, the focus on the two men's passionate and vulnerable facial expressions, and the postcoital moment when they lie still, holding each other in the nude. The scene is especially significant because it illustrates that the physical and emotional needs of HIV-positive gay men do not magically disappear after their diagnoses. The need to be touched and loved, to live sensuously, to seek and give pleasure, remains in Pray Tell and Ricky. Witnessing these characters fulfill each other quietly and lie naked in the afterglow is both ordinary and striking.

Ricky moves into Pray Tell's apartment and becomes even more of a caretaker. In another scene, Pray Tell lies drunk and angry on his couch, worried that he has forsaken his closest friend, Blanca, and sentenced himself to suffer through HIV/AIDS without any emotional support. Despite Pray Tell's drunken and somewhat rude ramblings, Ricky gently comforts his lover, ushering him off the couch and toward the bed, where Ricky kneels down to take off Pray Tell's shoes before tucking him in. In the morning, Pray Tell wakes up hungover, and Ricky has made him breakfast that includes eggs, fresh coffee, and headache medication. Pray Tell slumps into the chair across from Ricky, groggy and half-dressed in a pajama top and socks, embarrassed by his behavior the previous night and surprised by Ricky's dedication. "You stayed," Pray Tell says softly, as he reaches out across the table to take Ricky's hand, in another mundane affirmation of Black queer compassion. One of the elements that makes both the sex scene and the breakfast scene especially striking is Pray Tell's comportment as ballroom MC, when he embodies queer Black fabulousness in all its confidence and flair. But at home with Ricky, we see a far less flashy and self-assured Pray Tell, wrestling with his own fears and guilt, reliant on the counsel and care of a younger gay Black man. Ricky is more than a hot young sex object for Pray Tell; he is someone Pray Tell leans on. The intimacy they share is both queer and recognizable to everyone whose loving partner has tucked them in after a hard night and eased them into the following day.

Pose is full of such moments of queer care and community building, and it also provides insight into the ways white patriarchal society regards queer Black and brown folk. The romance between Stan (played by Evan Peters), a white businessman married to a white woman, and Angel (Indya Moore), a Black Latinx transgender sex worker, is fertile ground for exploring the acceptance and implications of Black queer fabulousness in broader (white) American culture. The two meet in the first episode of the first season, when Stan goes cruising for a prostitute. Despites Angel's profession, her relationship with Stan is far more than transactional. They go to a hotel room where Stan asks Angel to undress for him, but instead of having sex, he just wants to talk. Violence committed against Black trans women is a national epidemic, but the relationship is not framed by the ever-present threat of physical harm when it turns sexual. The characters are emotionally entangled with each other, and this entanglement extends to Stan's wife Patty (Kate Mara), who confronts Angel about her relationship with Stan one night.

The two women sit at a table near the window in a nondescript diner. Patty sits stiff as a board in her chair as the dialogue unfolds.

> PATTY: He paid you for sex the first time you met. That's why he sought you out?
> ANGEL: We didn't have sex the first time. He mostly wanted to talk. It wasn't dirty or nothing.
> PATTY: Did he talk about me?
> ANGEL: No, not really. But I already knew, if that's what you're asking. He took off his ring to try to hide it, but I always know. And I never feel guilty either. I figure, who am I to judge what goes on between people? Why they need what they need.

Immediately, the viewer understands that Stan and Angel's relationship is more than just physical. From their first encounter, Angel perceives that Stan is married, but whatever he is struggling with cannot be completely reduced to a problem with his wife. She does not feel guilty for giving Stan what he needs, either emotionally or sexually. Patty directs the conversation back to sex.

> PATTY: Did he use protection?
> ANGEL: Every time. We're not together. I was the one who broke it off. I felt like he wanted to keep me. Like a doll.

These are not the typical power relations between a cisgender heterosexual white woman and a Black trans woman, or between a Black trans sex worker and a cisgender white man. Angel is the one with the power to end it, and she explains to Patty that her reason for doing so was not sexual or physical but emotional. Angel could not stand the feeling that Stan wanted to keep and control her, and her need for independence trumped any financial, sexual, or emotional reward for continuing to see Stan. Patty then asks Angel about ballroom culture, and what it means when Angel calls the Hall her home. She is confused because Angel appears to be a woman, and she asks, "How could a woman be a drag queen?" Angel is amused and replies, "I'm a transsexual." Patty is stunned, and the music shifts to an eerie timber to emphasize her unease. She responds shakily.

PATTY: I don't believe you.
ANGEL: Why thank you. It's a compliment, you know?
PATTY: No. Stan would never do that. You're a woman.
ANGEL: One hundred percent.
PATTY: Prove it.
ANGEL: [Incredulously] What, you want to see my dick?
PATTY: [Insistently] Yes.

Angel refuses to show her genitals. Her womanhood is unshakable. Patty's disbelief about her husband and his desires is not grounds for Angel to give Patty the proof she requires. The conversation ends, and Angel remains the same as she was before it began: confident in herself and comfortable with her relationship with Stan.

The conversation between Angel and Patty occurs during the sixth episode of season 1, bur it invokes a similar scene from episode 2, set in the same restaurant. Angel and Stan sit against the backdrop of the diner's grimy window as Stan confesses his admiration and desire for her. He explains,

I'm no one. I want what I'm supposed to want. I wear what I'm supposed to wear, and I work where I'm supposed to work. I stand for nothing. I've never fought in a war, and I probably won't ever have to because the next one is going to kill us all. I can buy things I can't afford, which means they're never really mine. I don't live. I don't believe. I accumulate. I'm a brand. A middle-class white guy. But you're who you are, even though the price you pay for it is being disinvited from the rest of the world. I'm the one playing dress up. Is it wrong to want to be with one of the few people in the world who isn't? To have one person in my life who I know is real?

After Stan tells Angel why he wants her, Angel warns that she will not sacrifice her dignity and remain relegated to "scraps under the table" in her relationship with Stan. He offers to buy Angel an apartment in exchange for her giving up sex work. In a subsequent interview, Indya Moore revealed that this scene is the one she played out during her audition for Angel. "I related to that—being in the shadows, expected to pick from low-hanging fruit, coming from a space of not having anything. Angel stepping into her power—'This is what I need from you'—that was really powerful and beautiful."[16] Clearly, this is an empowering scene for Angel and for Moore, and it depicts an affirmation of dignity and genuine desirability that is uncommonly attached to fabulous Black LGBTQ+ people, and Black trans women in particular, on television. Again, Stan's desire burns not simply because of Angel's appearance or sex appeal but because of her courage and authenticity. Stan's monologue directly challenges the notion that transgender people deceive themselves or the society they live in. To the contrary, transgender people live their truth, and everyone else obeys the lies they are told.

And yet, close examination of Stan's monologue reveals the trouble with his comparing Angel's authentic Black queer fabulousness to unremarkable white manhood. Stan sees himself as powerless. "I'm no one. . . . I stand for nothing," he says, but cisgender straight (and straight-passing) white men are the most privileged race/gender demographic in the United States. His abdication cannot erase the legal history of a country based on the presumption that straight white men are the only people entitled to the full protection of the law and the sovereignty of their bodies. Stan's belief that he stands for nothing is an invocation of white invisibility and false neutrality. He complains that he buys things he cannot afford and will never really own. But the grace he, as a white man, is afforded as a consumer, as an applicant for credit, and as a carrier of debt (he buys Angel the apartment) is an immense and unjustly derived privilege. The creation and protection of white property and the extension of white credit were the basis of the American slave economy, which is the foundation of American capitalism. He complains that he does not "live" or "believe" in a country where white colonizers violently established and sustained Christianity as national religion. He laments "I accumulate," as if white excess accumulation were a personal burden, instead of the immoral and inevitable result of the exploitation of Black, brown, red, and yellow people for white profit.

Finally, Stan asks, "I'm the one playing dress up. Is it wrong to want to be with one of the few people in the world who isn't? To have one person in my life who I know is real?" Angel reacts favorably to Stan's pleas. The music in the scene changes, and she appears to be genuinely surprised, flattered, and moved by his words. Angel stands up for herself, but does not challenge Stan's self-pity. She remains poised and self-aware and does not profess her love for Stan or soothe his self-loathing. But this exchange is a sleight of hand whereby the powerful somehow becomes powerless. Ordinary white manhood looks to the Black queer fabulous for inspiration and salvation, but the Black queer fabulous is not, and will never be, means for white patriarchal redemption. If Stan wants to escape the luxurious prison he lives in, he must dismantle it himself, not ask to be rescued by someone "disinvited," murderously, as the statistics demonstrate, from white-supremacist patriarchy. The writers and producers of *Pose* do not craft a story that validates this redemption fantasy. But the orientation of the two characters toward each other, the earnestness of Stan's monologue, and the way it is received conspire to reposition white patriarchal suffering and Black queer fabulousness in places they should not be.

LENA WAITHE IS BOLD AND BORING

Like Billy Porter, Lena Waithe is a Black queer trailblazer who ascended to pop-cultural royalty with an Emmy Award. In 2017, she became the first Black woman nominee and winner in the Outstanding Writing for a Comedy Series category. As both a writer and an actor, her fingerprints were all over the Netflix show *Master of None*, but the episode that secured the award was titled "Thanksgiving," and Waithe based it on her experience coming out to her family during the holiday. In a *Time* interview about her triumph, Waithe was quick to point out the women whose shoulders she stood on, including fellow Black queer actor and writer Wanda Sykes, who had previously won an Emmy for Outstanding Writing for a Variety or Music Program. But she did not report having experienced great injustice within the industry because she is Black and queer. She explained, "I've felt my gender and identity mostly in success—not in trying to come up—where certain white men were thinking they knew more than me or feeling resentful that I was more successful. But for the most part, people didn't care that I was Black or female or gay."[17]

Waithe's relatively benign assessment of the way her identity affects her career is not reflected in her approach to activism. She is a consistent and courageous spokesperson for Black people, queer people, and Black queers. Like Porter, she used her platform at the Emmys to make a statement. Speaking directly to her "LGBTQ+IA family" during her acceptance speech, she affirmed, "I see each and every one of you. The things that make us different—those are our superpowers. Every day you walk out the door and put on your imaginary cape and go out there and conquer the world, because the world would not be as beautiful as it is if we weren't in it."[18]

Months later, she donned the superhero's cape at the 2018 Met Gala. The theme of the party was "Heavenly Bodies: Fashion and the Catholic Imagination." Waithe wore a white shirt under a black tuxedo draped by a massive Pride flag as a cape/cloak stitched into the shoulders and lapels. In an obvious rebuke of the Catholic Church's institutionalized history of discrimination and bigotry directed towards LGBTQ+ people, Waithe explained, "You talk about church and Catholicism, it's about—you were made in God's image. . . . The theme to me is be yourself."[19] The flamboyance of the cape enhances Waithe's dapper queer aesthetic, demonstrating the ways Black queer fabulousness can be expanded to folks who are masc-of-center.

One year later, Waithe returned to the Met Gala with another statement. The theme of the 2019 party was "Camp: Notes on Fashion," and Porter's aforementioned embodiment of the glistening Egyptian sun-god captured much attention. But Waithe came through with a statement of her own, wearing a light-blue satin zoot suit with the words "Black Drag Queens Inventend Camp" stitched in black on the back.[20] The suit's pinstripes were vertically arranged song lyrics drawn from queer classics like "We Are Family" by Sister Sledge. The gold buttons on the jacket were metallic faces of the real pioneers of camp, including RuPaul. Waithe's companion for the evening was designer Kerby-

Jean Raymond, who wore a matching white suit with a quotation from recently deceased rapper Nipsey Hustle on the back. Raymond's jacket urged onlookers to "fix your credit, pool money, buy back the block." These celebrations of Black and queer autonomy and ownership caught all the light, thanks in no small part to Waithe's array of golden accents: her hair (buzz cut and dyed), stud earrings, necklaces, and the rings on her fingers. In these public moments Waithe intends to stand out, and she directs onlookers' attention to the people and political issues that matter most to her.

At other times, however, Waithe assumes a more understated persona. Nowhere is Waithe's character more beautifully rendered than in *Vanity Fair*'s March 2018 cover story authored by National Book Award winner Jacqueline Woodson (who is also a Black lesbian). The digital publication of the story includes several photographs by Annie Lebovitz and a brief video conversation with Waithe as she shops and dines on an ordinary day in Los Angeles. The video begins with Waithe sitting down at one of her favorite eateries, nonchalantly announcing, "I'm a creature of habit, which means I'm also boring. I always go to the same spot and order the same shit."[21] This Black queertidian admission was reinforced by additional comments about the way her style is received by the broader public. Jacqueline Woodson reported, "As much as anyone appreciates a compliment about their 'look,' she says she doesn't *need* it. 'Being Black and gay, having dreadlocks, having a certain kind of swag, and dressing the way I do,' she explains, she is sometimes told by certain well-meaning admirers or fashion wannabes, '*That's dope, you're cool.*' 'I don't feel validated by that. . . . I don't want to be White. I don't want to be straight. I don't want to blend in. . . . I try to wear queer designers who happen to be brown and makin' shit.'"[22]

The *Vanity Fair* piece was published before the 2018 Met Gala, where Waithe wore her Pride flag cape. She knows she is a budding fashion icon but does not need the attention. She downplays her originality with the language she uses to praise Black queer designers. Waithe's presence among the Hollywood elite is an exception, but her self-image needs no personal glorification or embellishment. She is captivating and confident, and also mundane and "boring."

Waithe's Black queertidian life is captured by photographs of Waithe and her fiancée, Alana Mayo.[23] Three images in particular set the mundane and moving mood of Woodson's profile. The first two, one of Waithe in her car and one of Waithe fixing her hair in the mirror, sit side by side about halfway down the webpage of the article. The car photograph is shot from the passenger seat, as Waithe sits with her left hand on the wheel, apparently speaking to the others in her vehicle, with her right hand slightly raised to emphasize whatever conversational point she is making. The caption simply reads, "Waithe sits in L.A. traffic," painting the most commonplace Los Angeles experience one could imagine, and the expression on Waithe's face is focused but cool and neutral. Immediately to the right of that picture is a photo of Waithe standing in her apartment bathroom adjusting her hair. Lebovitz's camera is behind Waithe and over her shoulder, such that we can see Waithe's face in the mirror as she stands in a heather grey t-shirt. The lighting in the picture is warm and tan. The bathroom appears fairly small and the walls are bare. None of the fixtures are fully visible, but the hints we get suggest they are modest. A roll of toilet paper is attached to the wall in the lower left-hand corner of the image, and the caption reads, "Waithe fixes her coif."

These images were curated for the article but that does not mean they depict Waithe falsely. Many of them appear to be candid, capturing moments and rituals performed countless times each day by ordinary people. The unapologetically queer character of Waithe's ordinary existence is brought to life not only by her personal style—Woodson calls attention to the masc/femme sides of Waithe's hair, dreadlocked on top and shaved close on the sides—but by the presence of her partner, Alana. The final photograph of the two women in the piece appears to be posed, as Waithe and Mayo hold each other on the couch. But the more strikingly mundane image is a shot of the couple in their kitchen. Mayo sits at a white marble counter, perhaps two feet away from Waithe, who stands cooking eggs at the stove. Waithe wears red Chicago Bulls sweatpants and a white t-shirt referencing the Black Lives Matter movement, wielding a spatula inches from the eggs. Her back is to Mayo, whose mouth is open in midconversation with her left hand slightly extended toward her lover. An engagement ring with a large, clear stone rests prominently on Mayo's left ring finger, and two plates with two strips of bacon each sit in front of her. The refrigerator in the background is wide open and carelessly stocked full of drinks, condiments, and other such things, its doors decorated with magnets and crooked photographs. This is a lazy, bacon-and-eggs morning for the engaged couple, seemingly unconcerned with the camera, going about their business. But the engagement ring shines light on the queerness and beauty of their comfort showing the whole world their commonplace domestic life.

The profile closes with a telling quotation from Waithe about her self-image and purpose. Woodson, quoting Waithe, writes, "I didn't realize I was born to stand out as much as I do. But I'm grateful. Because the other Black or brown queer kids are like, 'Oh, we the shit.'" Lena flashes a huge smile, then shakes her head with wonder.

This is an encapsulation of Waithe's sense of her own ordinary and extraordinary power as a Black queer woman. She is still coming to grips with her power and has not let success grow into self-aggrandizement. Her activism takes at least three forms. First, as described above, Waithe is a mirror for queer Black and brown kids who draw pride and confidence from her accomplishments. Second, she takes ownership of the Black queer stories she tells as writer and actor. And finally, she is a steward for Black queer folk in the industry, as she tells Woodson, "Activism is me paying for a writer to go to a television-writing class," and "[executives should] take my call when I call you about this Black queer writer over here who's got a dope pilot." The understatement of these endeavors does not discount the spectacular queer Black radical activism that paved the way for Waithe and many others. She keeps that tradition alive as well, with keen attention paid to her queer kin in her fashion choices and award acceptance speeches. In so doing, Waithe embodies the coexistence of the Black queer fly and the Black queer mundane.

BLACK QUEERTIDIAN LIFE

Students follow Black LGBTQ+ celebrities closely. Black queer popular culture ties their social groups together and gives them something to debate with their friends. But they do not just follow the plot lines and characters from *Pose*; they follow specific performers and creators. The entertainers' lives and experiences inform students' ambitions. A handful of students told me they wanted to be famous, and they specifically wanted to be famous for working in the entertainment industry, which was perceived as part of the LGBTQ+ lifestyle and welcoming to queer people. As Brandon, a student at Aspen University, told me, "And there's more opportunities if you're gay. You can be a fashion designer. You can be, you know? Michael Kors is gay. Who else is gay? Everybody's gay. Not everybody, but everybody in the industry is gay. Frank Ocean. Queen Latifah."

Students' positive impression of the entertainment industry combines with the way they are perceived by others. In affirming the fabulous and fly side of their personalities, the students who perceive themselves as more colorful and outgoing invoke entertainment as part of what makes them who they are.

> I want to be a famous model. I really wish they had, like, this reality TV show that I could go onto so I could get noticed and then do stuff later on. I don't know. And sometimes, like I'll be talking about my goals and I'll be so uncomfortable saying them, but it's like, you have to say them. You have to believe in them. You know what I mean? And you have to say them to small-minded individuals sometimes so you can keep going, like, okay, I'm not going to let that phase me, whatever. But yeah. And people tell me that all the time. I've been told that since I was like little. Like oh, you need your own TV show. You need your own this. You're funny, you're funny, you're cool, you're handsome.

Ervin, a nonbinary student at Juniper, gives a similar description of how people's impression of them informs career goals. "Everybody says I should be a comedian, and I don't think I should be a comedian. I'm more leaning towards being an actor. So, like, everywhere I go, there's somebody bound to laugh. Usually I'm talking to my friends, so I know what I'm saying to them, but I will catch a giggle or a snicker laugh here and there, and when I turn around, I'm just like, 'I'm sorry, you know, 'cause you're not used to this. This is your warning.'"

In contrast, Jace, a student at Tasman, described his outgoingness purely in terms of his passion for poetry, music, and self-expression, rather than others' opinions of him. But he still has the drive to be famous, as he explained, "My main goal, ideally, I would be famous, be a musician and get paid to do that, and just perform all the time. That would be so much fun. I would love that." These students use different labels to describe their sexuality and gender identity, and they express themselves differently in dress and conversation. But they share a sense of pride and a sense of themselves as outgoing and captivating. There were also a few instances where students described themselves as unique and outgoing without the pursuit of attention or fame as a complement. Matt told me, "I'm a little weird. So I'm into holistic stuff, so I'm very into, like, crystals, incense, or lamps, stuff like that. I'm just very big on just getting our medicines from, like, the earth and not really synthetic. I'm just an open book. Like honestly, ask me anything and I'll tell you. Like, there's no reason for privacy. Just be yourself, 100 percent."

These students are among those who most strongly affirm Black queer fabulousness as key to their identities. But it was far more common for students to describe themselves in more subdued terms. Sometimes they described personalities that were a mixture of introverted and extroverted. They could be bold on occasion, or with the right company, but also thought of themselves as relaxed and understated.

I'm a really chill person. It's like I'm chill, but at the same time it's like not. So I like to hang out with my friends, go to movies, go to the hookah bar, just do different fun things. I like being around friends and family all the time. (Bradley)

Kind of laid back. I'm more of a hanging out with close friends type of person, really small group of friends type of person, but I'm also a really, in my opinion and other people's opinions, outgoing and really goofy, and also very like into my studies. (Lana)

My daily life has just become very routine and mechanical, so I, like I'll wake up. I'll go to class. I'll eat. I'll go back to another class. Go to sleep, and then wake up, I'll eat dinner, and then I'll go to sleep again. And it just starts, every day is the same. And I'm usually feeling just kind of a sense of like mundanity. . . . I think of myself probably more as an introvert. I like being home. And that kind of conflicts with my desire to be always in the city and always around kind of chaos. (Kerry)

It's kind of hard to describe, but the type of person I am, I guess I'm more like quiet, like introverted. But once I do meet somebody and really get to know them, I'm more outgoing and start talking a lot more. But before then, I'll just be the person to the side or something. (Roland)

If Bradley, Lana, Kerry, and Roland were somewhere on the middle of the spectrum, there were even more students who described themselves as ordinary and introverted, far from the stereotype of Black queer spectacle. When I asked the open-ended questions like, "How would you describe yourself?" or "What kinds of things are you into?" these students said,

I'm a fourth-year computer science student here at Java. Generally in my free time, I just kind of like to read. I'm learning how to sew and cook. Stuff like that. Pretty chill. (Morris)

One my favorite things to do is read. Especially when I was younger, because I was a big introvert, and my family were extroverts. So I spent a lot of time alone and reading, kind of just like, one of my favorite things to do is like, get lost in another world. (Olympia)

I just really care about people, and I'm just trying to make people feel good about themselves all the time. And in my free time, I'm a cheerleader here, so when the season was hectic, I didn't have any free time, but now since the season's over, I really just chill with my friends, and I smoke. (Deron)

I feel like I'm a pretty chill, laid-back, reserved person. I mean, well recently, I've become a part of like my creative writing group here at Evergreen, so I've been trying to get more into poetry, rather than just like an outlet, as a form of communication, I guess. Yeah, I don't know. I like movies. . . . Oh, I love museums. I love art museums and stuff like that. (Eric)

These students are "chill" and "laid back." Some of the hobbies they describe are expected pastimes for college students, like smoking and reading. Others are somewhat surprising, like sewing and going to museums. Either way, the interests and activities students talk about do not have much to do with spectacular queerness. This does not mean that students always actively downplay their LGBTQ+ identities as they go through their days, or that the kinds of worlds they imagine and escape to in movies and books they consume are not queer. The students are no less queer for their reserved personalities and mundane lifestyles.

E. Patrick Johnson writes about southern Black gay men who "draw upon the performance of 'Southernness'—for example, politeness, coded speech, religiosity—to instantiate themselves as 'legitimate' members of Southern and Black culture, while, at the same time, deploying these very codes to establish and build friendship networks and find life and/ or sexual partners."[24] He explains that this embrace of dignified, comforting southernness is a reaction to repressive sex and gender dynamics in the South; there is legitimate fear of transgression. But performing respectable, recognizable southernness is also a means of transforming southern affects into tools for queer world building. So it is possible that students' invocation of a "chill" and "laid-back" lifestyle is doing similar work. It is highly doubtful they read me as southern, but if they read me as a cisgender and straight authority figure within the world of higher education, they may feel pressure to live out the stereotype of the reserved, nerdy, and therefore "good" college student. As the interviews went on, however, students were not interested in performing this sort of respectability. They wanted to tell me the truth about who they were and how they really lived because so few people seemed to care. And when I specifically gave them the opportunity to tell me what they did with their time, the way they described most of their days reinforced the impression of the mundane. Just as Johnson argues that Black men's southern queerness may enable the construction of social networks and partnerships, there is no doubt that students' queertidian days opened up social possibilities that they had not experienced before college.

These descriptions are notable not only because few people care to ask Black LGBTQ+ students these questions but also because of stereotypes of college life. In her book about college hookup culture, Lisa Wade describes the pressure college students feel to live exciting lives once they arrive on campus. Much of the excitement is supposed to be found in hookups, which produces pressure to have stories to tell and to adopt a casual attitude toward sex. Like several others, Wade finds that the pressure to hook up belies the truth that college students are not having nearly as much sex as most people think. For Black LGBTQ+

students, dating and sex are different calculations (more on this later), so Wade's work does not map directly onto the people I spoke with. But the general sense that college is supposed to be fun, exciting, and hedonistic still shapes outsiders' assumptions about what students actually do all day. For both straight and queer students, college is not nearly as thrilling as it is portrayed to be in film and television. I asked students not only how they would describe themselves but what their average day was like. The answers from three different students give us a sense of the ordinary ways students spend their time. Cara begins by painting a picture of life in her social group.

> CARA: Go to class, rush to the next class, just keep it going like that. Meet my friends. I may meet them like how I did today. We usually sit outside here like where you saw us, sit on the brick wall right there, when it's hot that's what we do. Listen to music. We just socialize with each other, go to class, and then meet back up again.
> MICHAEL: Do you like that? Do you wish that you were doing other things, or is that pretty much what you want to be doing?
> CARA: I guess that's pretty much it. I'm boring. I don't really like doing too much. I'm boring. Some sleeping in [laughs].

I hasten to add that Cara underplays her activity level and contributions on and off campus. She is a leader at Douglas University, where she repeatedly advocates for marginalized students, including vegans and her queer classmates. She also works for a reproductive health organization in the city Douglas is located in and serves as a mentor for Black high school students at a public school near campus. But on most spring days like the one when I talked to her, she made time to congregate with friends and just unwind. Cara presents more on the femme side of queer and talked about her experiences as someone who frequently passes for straight, but at least two of the friends I saw her with that day were more masc-presenting. They seemed totally comfortable claiming space on their HBCU campus. Though Cara told me about the ways LGBTQ+ students are disadvantaged and sometimes mistreated at Douglas, she did not feel policed or harassed by faculty, staff, students, or campus security employees. She and her crew exhibited an easy ownership and comfort with their daily routine.

One of the key components of that routine is studying, and students had a great deal to say about their work and their experiences while class was in session. But studying together after class is also an important part of forming social bonds between Black queer students. When I asked Valerie, a queer pansexual student at Barents University, how she spent her time, she said, "I'm just there, sitting on the couch [in the LGBTQ+ space], doing my homework. And whenever my friends are there, we're just there talking. Me and my twin live literally a five-minute walk from each other. This is my apartment [gestures with hands], this is hers. And so sometimes I go over to her place. She comes over to my place. If we have enough time after like a school day, we just stay there till like 12:00 a.m. doing homework together."

Barents is a large, public PWI, and the importance of having dedicated space for LGBTQ+ students should not be overlooked. The Black queer students I spoke with had mixed things to say about their relationship with LGBTQ+ student organizations led by white students, a topic I address later in the book. But there was almost universal agreement about the usefulness of the physical spaces dedicated to LGBTQ+ students, even when those spaces were mostly used by non-Black students. Valerie points to one such use—the LGBTQ+ center is a study space for her and her "twin." The friend Valerie refers to here is another queer Black woman, who, like Valerie, grew up in a family of immigrants. This mutual recognition and invocation of kinship between two students is an example of the sort of "found" rather than "birth" families young LGBTQ+ people build. Valerie's emphasis on the physical closeness of their apartments reflects the social and emotional closeness the "twins" share. She did not tell me about sexual attraction or relations between the two. I cannot rule out that those feelings were key to the friendship, or the possibility that Valerie sent that message and I missed the cue during our interview. Regardless, I walked away deeply affected by the language of "twinship" and mirroring, and the comfort in seeing oneself in a study partner who smooths the academic journey through college.

Sometimes, however, students described their daily routine without any of the warmth and connection that Valerie conveyed. Luke, a senior at Weddell University, has a few close friends, but had very little to say about how those friendships shaped his time on campus. I asked him about how he spent his time,

LUKE: I guess I'm more of an introvert than anything, but it depends on like the situation or like the space I'm in. Usually for fun, just sitting around like talking with friends, or mainly watching TV, movies, or YouTube or reading, listen to music. I like to walk a lot.

MICHAEL: Yeah. So pretty much just a kind of a regular day routine, class, work, and then at the end of the day is when you do most of your socializing and stuff like that, hang out?

LUKE: Yeah.

MICHAEL: Do you ever do anything for fun? Like, do you go to parties? Do you go to shows? Do you go to bars? The social side of your life, is it pretty much just on campus hanging out?

LUKE: Pretty much. I'll go to like the store, maybe Target, Wal-Mart. I go to the movies every now and then. But I'm not really like a party person or a club person. Bars, I've never been to a bar before, but I want to. So I guess that's like, a goal. I don't know.

Luke was an engaging interviewee, but my experience talking with him fit his self-description. He had a sharp sense of humor, but never really got excited or animated during our conversation. He did not have good things to say about his experiences at his PWI, either in or out of class. Social opportunities were limited by homophobia, general racism, and the racism of the mostly white LGBTQ+ community on campus. He was not frustrated because he wished for more stereotypical college excitement; despite my somewhat leading question about parties, he was frustrated because of the looks he got from classmates and the disrespect he perceived from his professors. I am using his testimony as an example because it raises the question of whether the mundane lives of so many of the people I spoke with might have been richer and more colorful if not for their experiences with institutional and interpersonal bigotry. Though the students did not explain their day-to-day lives in these terms, it must be the case for some of them. But still, there were plenty of folks like Luke who expressed no real aspirations for a spectacular social life. The impression I got was that he really wants to lead the quiet life he does; he just wants to be able to do it with more kindness and support from his college community.

This chapter began by describing the Black queertidian, explaining how uncritical celebration of the Black queer fabulous and fly can disguise oppression and misrepresent Black queer life. A more thorough examination of Black queer popular culture and celebrity reveals how the mundane complements the Black queer fabulous and fly. My interviews with students lend legitimacy to the ordinary moments that exist beyond the world of radical spectacle. Students describe themselves in ordinary and "boring" ways. When I asked them to talk about how they actually spent their time, they were comfortable telling me about all the quiet and unremarkable things they did at college. Of course, there might have been some reluctance to talk to me about things they deemed too personal or thought I would disapprove of, such as sex, drug use, or maybe even political radicalism. But they did, in fact, introduce many of those topics at other points during our interviews, and I tackle those subjects later in the book. None of those dimensions of their lives invalidate the ways they describe themselves above or diminish the value of foregrounding ordinary Black queerness.

The Black queer mundane is not just about being boring. It is about recognizing how the ordinary times and spaces of Black queer life become spaces of connection, beauty, and self-affirmation. We can hear hints of this truth in the way Valerie describes her friendship with her twin, and the spectrum of Black queer joy and pride is wide enough for both the spectacular and the unremarkable. Black LGBTQ+ student organizations are key sites for exploring all these possibilities.

[3]

ADJUSTING TO COLLEGE

Ava grew up in a small town in the Mid-Atlantic region of the United States. She was raised by extremely religious parents, both of whom were major figures in her local church. Gender and sexuality were so strictly policed that she and her sisters were not allowed to wear pants or shorts outside the house; only dresses or skirts were permitted. Nobody in her household drank alcohol, smoked, swore, or attended parties outside the church. It was a massive culture shock when Ava moved down south to attend Birch University, an HBCU in a major southern city. It took her some time to get used to her independence and socialize with peers who had completely different life experiences prior to college, but she loved being on campus.

One reason Ava enjoyed her first few years of college is that she did not completely abandon the lessons and values she learned during childhood in an orthodox Christian home. She prioritized honesty, selflessness, charity, hard work, humanity, and humility, and she found outlets for all of those values at Birch through joining student organizations and introducing herself to activism. When Trayvon Martin was killed, she felt the pain of her classmates and a calling to take action. She grew into her role as a community organizer, and the people she met through that work became her closest friends. Those comrades, both on and off campus, were the first people who introduced her to the idea of queerness and the spaces that LGBTQ+ people carve out for themselves.

Ava was a senior when I met her, and she was still in the process of figuring out her gender identity. She uses "she/her" pronouns and identifies as a woman, but does not know what the word "woman" means to her just yet. She told me that she just wants to "wear and be whoever I feel like" and that sometimes the LGBTQ+ communities she finds herself in can be restrictive in the same way her parents' community was. But she continues to explore LGBTQ+ spaces and takes comfort in her relationships with queer Black organizers and allies on campus, unlike her relationship with her family. She told me,

> I'm right now working on rebuilding my relationship with my parents, because for the first few years, I kind of went MIA. Not even just for my parents, but I didn't reach out to my brothers and sisters and aunts and uncles, and I just fell off the radar. And nobody knew, or really knows anything about my life. And I've been really trying to make an effort to change that, because I know that—I feel like part of it also is my own projections, because I had those examples of what happened when my other siblings and cousins would try and live their lives and what happened. I didn't want that to happen to me. I grew up with a close relationship with my dad. And my mom loves all of her children. . . . But I know that I also was just afraid of what would happen if I tried to talk to them about it, and so I ran. And I ran for three years.

Fear, guilt, and uncertainty suffuse Ava's account of the preceding three years. She did not tell me that any of her siblings or cousins are LGBTQ+, but any expression of independence by children in her family seemed to be met with punishment. It stands to reason that Ava's rejection of sex and gender norms would be among the most egregious violations of her family's culture, and it is no wonder that she went into hiding. She has not completely severed communication with her parents, and her description of her relationship with her mom and dad is touching. She loves them, appreciates them, and admires them deeply, in some respects. But these feelings of attachment and appreciation lead to a heavy sense of guilt, as Ava wonders whether the fear she feels is justified. She is unsure whether they would act the same way towards her as they do when her siblings step out of line. She feels liberated by college, and has grown into adulthood as a queer organizer, but she feels pressure to settle on a more stable identity and reverse the erosion of her family ties.

Ava's story contains so many of the facets of this experience across the group. This chapter is about the transition from home to college for Black queer students. It reinforces what we already know about the importance of leaving home for Black queer people, and sheds new light on the core functions of Black LGBTQ+ student organizations at colleges and universities.

LEAVING HOME, ARRIVING ON CAMPUS

Students' experiences at home encompass more than just their experiences in elementary, middle, and high school. We have to understand their schooling experiences in the context of their lives with their families and in their neighborhoods. Of course, talking about "the Black family" is fraught with all sorts of stereotypes and misinformation. The presumption of Black familial pathology is a racist myth designed to justify segregation, policing, mass incarceration, and the continued destruction of the social safety net in the United States. Numerous authors and researchers have debunked this myth, demonstrating that "absent" Black fathers are not absent at all,[1] "welfare queen" Black mothers do not exist,[2] and the very notion of "the Black family" is a distortion that cannot account for the role of kin networks in Black survival and joy.[3] We also know that Black children's "misbehavior" in school is not a product of their upbringing but a racialized tactic of punishment and control, as numerous studies reveal bias in school discipline and surveillance for Black children.[4]

One area of the research that is not quite as robust, however, is the exploration of how experiences within Black families influence the lives and identities of young Black LGBTQ+ people. There are several different angles to approach this issue from, but Antonio Pastrana studied it by trying to figure out how family support structures influence Black LGBTQ+ people's willingness to publicly affirm their queer identity. First, a caveat: being "out" is not a stable status, or an event that happens once, when one leaves the closet, and then never again. Further, the closet metaphor and notion of a single, definitive "coming out" was never theorized with Black people, transgender people, or Black transgender people in mind.[5] It is also true that in Black and Hispanic families, tacit understandings of sexuality often preclude formal announcements of one's sexual orientation and gender identity.[6] So the notion that outness is courageous and liberating is often developed through white and wealthy understandings of queerness.

With that caveat in mind, Pastrana's study is important because it confirms a reasonable intuition about how family life impacts Black LGBTQ+ people. He finds that the more supportive one's family is—the more open to nontraditional gender expressions and willing to affirm connections to LGBTQ+ communities—the more likely it is that Black LGBTQ+ people are "out" to their families.[7] Few of the students I spoke with described their birth families as supportive environments. Trent, a twenty-one-year-old student at Barents University, explained, "Growing up also, my mom was always like, 'Being gay is for white people.' Like, 'Black people aren't gay. It doesn't happen.' So like just, people always saying, like you know, 'gayness is for white people,' stuff like that, it's kind of just shaping one's mind to believe that, you know? And that's why we see white people have movies about queerness and all that kind of stuff. And also, like, queer people of color are the ones that like don't get to survive as long as white people, white queer people."

A study by Christopher Petsko and Galen Bodenhausen speaks directly to perceptions of gay as white. Their research shows that "when Black and Hispanic men are described as gay (vs. not), they become stereotypically 'Whitened' in addition to seeming less stereotypic of their own racial groups. This 'Whitening' effect is explained by Black and Hispanic men's seeming more affluent when described as gay (vs. when not), an effect that holds even when controlling for changes in these men's stereotypic femininity."[8] In addition to these findings, which span across racial and ethnic groups, this sort of hateful mythology of gayness as a self-hating, culturally "white" hobby is bound with anxiety about masculinity and Black resistance to racism. In an attempt to affirm Black pride in the face of white cultural encroachment and erasure, the notion of queerness as a weak and white way of life exerts a powerful hold within Black communities. Of course, we know that queer Black people lived and thrived in Africa long before European colonists brought antigay Christian mythology to the African communities they invaded and exploited. But the powerful impulse to reject racism and colonialism through affirmation of heteronormative Black and Christian "purity" plays out in countries throughout the transatlantic world. Queer Black people perceive greater disapproval from their families than white LGBTQ+ people, and numerous studies have shown that Black people are more likely than white people to express anti-LGBTQ+ attitudes. As Mignon Moore notes, "Much of the racial differences in expression of attitudes are attributed to the older age, lower levels of education, and greater religiosity of Blacks in research samples. However, Blacks of the same religion and with similar levels of education as Whites were still more likely to express negative attitudes towards homosexuality."[9]

Importantly, Trent interprets his mother's attachment to the myth that being gay is for white people through the lens of both popular culture and the cold statistical reality of Black life in America. These pop-cultural reference points that seem to validate Trent's mother's worldview affirm the importance of Black queer pop-cultural breakthroughs described in chapter 2, as figures like Billy Porter and Lena Waithe demonstrate the power of representation as fuel for resilience and self-making for young Black LGBTQ+ people. Narratives of Black queer life in American popular culture are especially important in the context of a culture where Black queer people are, historically, first to die, because they are pariahs and deserve AIDS, or because they are framed as "deviant" sex workers or predators unworthy of safety or protection. So when we see these people and their stories on screen, it is vital that they not only appear, but live and thrive, so that students like Trent have alternative material for self-fashioning. The physical danger of living as a Black queer person, especially if femme, is underscored by Patricia's account of life in her home town, which was especially hostile to LGBTQ+ people. She told me,

If you had "sugar in your tank," like they say, you got beat. You know? You were the one who got picked on. And I feel like growing up and them always seeing that, and then, you know, they're in a generation in the eighties too where the AIDS epidemic broke out, and they also have that mentality like "Oh, if you're gay, you're going to have AIDS, or you're going to get diseases." It's just, I feel like honestly, it's just ignorance being from their location in the culture that engulfed them. And I feel like that's something that's really one of the reasons a lot of Black people in the South have not really been able to be as accepting of the LGBTQ+ community.

Patricia is from a rural Black community in the South, where she says that violence towards gay men was normalized in both rhetorical and physical attacks. Of course, bigotry towards LGBTQ+ people is a national phenomenon, with few safe havens for Black queer people on either side of the Mason-Dixon Line. I hasten to highlight the work of Carly Thomsen, E. Patrick Johnson, and others who argue that ignorance about rural communities facilitates the erasure, or at least the illegibility, of rural LGBTQ+ people and Black rural LGBTQ+ people in particular. Over and over again, Johnson's research illustrates the mundane and sweet potency of queer Black southern life.[10] So I am not presenting Patricia's testimony about her experience as a queer Black girl growing up in the rural South as a universal truth about what life is like for Black people in similar communities. But Patricia, who also attends an HBCU in a southern city, is especially upset by the regional dimensions of Black homophobia, imparting a sense that the "backward" southern understanding of AIDS is stuck in a time before the biological and social science of the disease was laid bare.

As Cathy Cohen's book *The Boundaries of Blackness* shows, the devastating impact of HIV/AIDS in Black communities was the result of several factors: malicious governmental neglect, institutional racism, widespread belief that homosexuality itself is a disease, and the unwillingness of Black institutions, like the Black church, to recognize and address the problem. But Patricia feels that the place where she grew up exerts a kind of "ignorant" and ahistorical hold on the folks in her town, who remain hostile to their LGBTQ+ neighbors because that is the way it has always been. Tamika, a student at Caspian University, also referred to the violence of life at home when I asked her about where she grew up. She said, "I tell people all the time, like, it's rare for me not to go to bed to the sound of gunshots at night when I'm at home. So with that being said, it's not like it's the worst place on the planet, but there's a lot of baggage in Ironville that I really want to get away from. My Christian family, the heteronormative ideals of my family, and so forth. But I do miss them, so I do have to go back every once in a while."

Ironville (a pseudonym) is a midsized midwestern city that never recovered from the impact of late-twentieth-century deindustrialization of the American economy. It would be hard for Tamika to find comfort at home because her family lives in an impoverished neighborhood, and that poverty gives birth to illicit economies with unpredictable local violence. This is the broader environment within which her family's "heteronormative ideals" are situated, and so home, both inside and outside the house, is far from welcoming. Still, the final sentence of her testimony points to a broader theme worth highlighting: few of the students I spoke with had cut themselves off completely from the families they left behind when they moved away to college. Ava, the first person introduced in this chapter, is a bit of an exception. There are many reasons for maintaining these ties, and love and financial intertwinement are chief among them. But the point is that there are few clean breaks from life at home when students arrive at college. Students may have moved out, but they have not completely moved on.

After I asked the students what their home town was like, I asked them what school was like in the place where they grew up. Some of them recounted almost their entire educational history, beginning with elementary school, moving through middle school, and then finally the high school they attended immediately prior to college. Most of our conversation, however, focused on their experiences in high school, and taken as whole, I felt as if I had toured every single type of high school in existence in the United States by the time all the interviews were complete. So it is difficult to paint their stories with a broad brush, and one of the main contributions of this chapter and this book is to illustrate the diversity of Black LGBTQ+ stories. But this diversity cannot drown out the reality that, on balance, high school is treacherous for most Black queer students.

It is treacherous not only because they feel they are disliked by their teachers and peers but because they are unsafe. A 2020 study by the Gay Lesbian and Straight Education Network (GLSEN) revealed that "over half of Black LGBTQ+ students (51.6%) felt unsafe at school because of their sexual orientation, 40.2% because of their gender expression, and 30.6% because of their race or ethnicity." Over fifteen hundred

Black LGBTQ+ students were surveyed for the study, and they reported widespread verbal degradation and physical harassment. Students knew they were targeted because of their sexuality/gender expression, race, or both. The 40 percent of students who reported experiencing both racial and gender-based bigotry felt the most devastating effects; they had the lowest levels of school belonging and highest levels of depression. As a group, these students were also more likely to skip school because they feared for their safety.[11] And this is why it is important to be mindful of which Black LGBTQ+ students enroll in college and then end up in the sample of people to be interviewed. Those who have the worst time in high school might not make it to graduation, let alone college. If folks with such painful histories were able to matriculate, they might not want to talk about their lives with someone like me. So it bears repeating that this is not a representative sample of all Black LGBTQ+ college students. But those who spoke with me made massive contributions, broadening our understanding of all the different ways an educational setting influences their ideas about themselves. Jason describes a painful experience after transferring from a predominantly white public high school to a mostly Black Christian school for the rest of his education. "It was, like, majority Black. And that experience was, I feel like, more familiar to me. But if I want to talk about, like, when it comes to the LGBT thing, I feel like those schools like destroyed me in thinking of like my own identity and stuff, because you know, Black people are homophobic as hell, or whatever. And I feel like if I was still at the school I was at ninth grade, I probably would have been more accepted."

At first glance, a simple narrative emerges here. Jason was not especially comfortable as one of few Black people at the white public school, but he did not perceive intense homophobia at that institution. The Black school was the problem for Jason, and perhaps this is unsurprising when we consider the religious dimension of its educational program. So the Black school provides a haven from racism, while the white school provides safety from homophobia. But other students I spoke with told stories that clearly challenged the mythology of the enlightened white school as the best learning environment for all queer students, including Black LGBTQ+ students. Cat, a nineteen-year-old bisexual student at Caspian University, went to a public high school with very few white students in a large midwestern city. She described it as "very historically

Black," and she "really enjoyed that experience in terms of just the history and just the people that you see coming out of the school. So it was really a fun experience."

The dominant characteristic of the school was its Blackness. It gave Cat a sense of place in a legacy of successful Black students, which fueled her academically and provided a fun atmosphere for learning and socializing. Her high school was, in fact, the school with the largest percentage of Black students of any school she attended, having enrolled at more racially mixed schools before then. Jonelle, a twenty-one-year-old student at Timor University, had a different experience navigating the transition, as she changed from a mostly Black setting in middle school to a mostly white one in high school. As she began ninth grade, her parents moved so that she could attend an almost entirely white and well-resourced public school in a midwestern suburb.

> It was the best school in [that part of the state], and that's why my parents decided for me to go there. . . . But it was very difficult, 'cause I went to a predominantly Black middle school. My best friends were there, and like the way I grew up in terms of like race, I was told to—you know, with a Black person in white spaces, you know how to act in white spaces, but you aren't necessarily comfortable in white spaces. . . . And there were times where, like, you know, some of my classmates rode up to school with Confederate flags on their trucks. My brothers were threatened at an after-school football thing because they were really good players and they were the only Black players on the team. And they were saying that they couldn't take white players' spaces, or whatever. And they were threatened with weapons and things like that. So it's like, that was very difficult, and just living with that type of fear.

Jonelle is an exceptional student who excelled in high school and continues to do so in college. She never had any challenges keeping up with her schoolwork in high school, but it was extremely difficult socially. As a bookish, middle-class Black girl amid a sea of wealthy white classmates, she had very few friends. Her brothers had more fun, made more friends, and enjoyed more social status in high school because they were star athletes, but high status is not safety for Black people. The school was deeply racist in both covert and overt ways, as Jonelle was essentially isolated from her peers and subject to threats of violence. Jonelle is bisexual, and she never mentioned any struggles with that dimension of her identity as we discussed her high school experience. So it is possible to hear her story separate the intertwined strands of racialized and gendered experience and arrive at the impression that racism was a problem at her school, but homophobia was not.

Such an interpretation would fit the narrative of the well-resourced white school as a safer space for queer folks of all backgrounds than a Black (and poor, by stereotypical association) school. But just the fact that Jonelle did not mention fear of being attacked for her queerness does not mean she did not live with it. There are so many explanations for Jonelle's account. She might have been at a different place with her sexuality, or might not have thought of herself as bisexual at all until late in high school. Or perhaps she knew she was bisexual, but the threat of racial violence was so constant and severe that it left little space for the fear and anxiety provoked by homophobia. Or maybe she knew she was bisexual and was fairly comfortable with it, because her social life was so unremarkable and unpleasant that she never really felt she was losing anything or being denied the relationships she wanted to build. Or perhaps the people in her social circle were just as bigoted towards queer people as they were racist, but they did not perceive Jonelle as queer because she is straight passing. All this is to say, the absence of a narrative about homophobia and self-doubt in white high schools does not mean that white schools are comfortable spaces to be Black and queer. Alice's story brings depth to this insight. She told me,

> So eighth grade, I was secretly talking to this one girl. I heard that she liked girls and guys. So I started talking to this one girl, and that lasted until tenth grade, so went into my high school. And I kind of kept it very low key, still, because I came from a Christian household, Christian family, and I knew it wasn't acceptable, and especially coming from a Christian school. So I kind of kept that low key. And tenth grade, our relationship ended, but I decided maybe I should try what everybody else was doing, try to date guys. Didn't work, at all. So high school was a struggle, was a struggle the rest of my high school. Like I said, everybody at my school was the same. Everybody did the same type of things, so I kind of tried to conform to how everybody else was.

Like Jonelle, Alice attended a wealthy, predominantly white high school. Unlike Jonelle, Alice went to a private Christian school, but it is located in a West Coast suburb with a more liberal political reputation. The specter of racist terror that Jonelle described in her midwestern suburb was not part of Alice's school experience. While Alice never felt physically unsafe, she echoes some of the issues with racial and gender conformity gleaned from Jonelle's experience. Alice was not harassed by her white peers for being Black, but as with many high schools, there was a social cost to standing out, especially with respect to sex and gender expression. Fortunately, Alice was able to get through the difficult times, and by the time senior year arrived, she was less afraid to reveal her queerness.

> Yeah, high school was very rough until my senior year, I went to my first Pride festival in [large West Coast city], and my [aunt] took me, secretly, 'cause she knew. She took me and my best friend, I had my best friend come along with me. And she took us to Pride without my mom knowing. She said that we were just going to hang out for the weekend. I loved it. It was a great experience, and I went to [another city] too, like the next week. 'Cause it was, like, Pride Month, so I didn't want it to stop. So it wasn't until really senior year where I kind of became more open about it.

Comments from Alice and several other students show that there is a reinforcing relationship between the religious environment in the school and the religious environment at home. For these students, there really is no safe haven inside or outside of the house from a religious ideology that disdains LGBTQ+ people. Theirs is a regimented form of Christianity that influences all parts of their socialization and learning, and it is often intensified by explicit racism or implicit racial conformity and denial of Blackness. Importantly, the intervention that allowed Alice to lead a happier life was precisely in line with Pastrana's research on the importance of family supports for queer Black folks. Alice's aunt took her away from home and school, and into a Pride celebration in a major city. These parades have come under fire recently, especially when they are staged in wealthy urban areas, for performing a form of queerness that is corporately sponsored and overwhelmingly white. But both Pride events were liberating for Alice, so much so that they gave her the confidence to be more open about her identity when she went back to school.

Several of the students did not need to break free from the school environment to feel comfortable affirming their queerness. Fewer than a dozen students told me they had strongly positive experiences, as there were far more cases where they seemed lukewarm at best about their schooling before college. But what struck me about the students who did like high school were the different types of high schools they came from. Matt, for instance, lived in the same part of the country as Alice, and went to a very similar wealthy, white private school. He was out in high school, and also described himself as "a very open book," someone who had no qualms about showing people who he was. When I asked him if he enjoyed high school, he said, "Yeah. I was like, I'm like more of, like not to toot the horn, but I'm just like a very, everyone knows me, in a sense. So I guess kind of just, I don't know. I'm just friendly and it's not very—I didn't feel like bullied or anything, I guess, 'cause some people are, and just my mannerisms and I guess how I speak and carry myself, I could be a target for that, but I really wasn't. I was friends with heterosexual guys and everything."

Matt did not talk very much about the specific elements of school that he enjoyed; he just reported having a comfortable social experience. Later during our conversation, he told me that he was frustrated with the dating scene in college, which was a common theme among the students. Many of these frustrations began in high school, so his time there was not perfect, but he described himself as popular and successful both inside and outside of the classroom. He built confidence that he carried through the application process and into his time on campus.

In contrast to Matt, Albert provided a few more details about why he was socially successful and comfortable in school. He went to a completely different sort of high school than Matt: a selective and majority-Black public school in a large midwestern city. Still, he communicated a similar sense of ease and social success. When he compared his high school experience to his time in college at Tasman University, a selective and predominantly white private school, he smiled at his recollection that "high school was like a 'hood. I didn't have responsibilities. I didn't have to get a job, it was great. Now I gotta, like, work and do all this other shit." He was comfortable in his ordinary experience. He appreciated the absence of pressure and anxiety, the lack of responsibilities and spotlighting that he derived from going to high school in a "'hood," a community that never made him question his belonging. In this setting, he had plenty of friends, but unlike Matt and a few other students who told me they were friends with plenty of straight people, Albert's social circle was queer.

> But like, looking back on it, I realized I didn't have any straight male friends or straight friends who were cisgender, like, heterosexual men. Like, if I did make any friends that were men, they would be like gay, or they would later come out as gay, or later come out as bisexual, and I'm like, "Oh my god, I'm like so shocked" [feigning surprise]. It was kind of like, as I grew up, I kind of realized that the people around me were, gravitated toward me for a specific reason. Like they just, I don't know. Like, lots of people just came out to me.

When I asked Albert what explained this phenomenon, or why he thought so many queer folks gravitated towards him, he told me, "I think it's 'cause I'm really gay. Or people tell me that I'm really gay. So I just made people feel so comfortable." This is not comfort achieved through conformity or respectability. Albert's majority-Black public high school was in the 'hood and it felt like one, but it was a 'hood where someone with an unabashedly queer style could feel at home. It is possible that Albert became such an important resource for students because he was one of the only people at his school whom other LGBTQ+ students felt safe talking to. Several interviewees described outright hostility and/or cowardice from adults in their high school who were supposed to support them both academically and socially. In those cases, students like Albert who are more unapologetically queer can serve as both inspiration and a source of confidence. His publicly setting the bar at "really gay" may provide space for questioning students to take less dramatic steps into queerness. So Albert's enjoying high school and feeling comfortable there may not mean that the institution as a whole was a welcoming and supportive place for all queer Black students. Still, Albert's experience is an important example considering how infrequently we hear stories of fabulously queer Black students thriving socially in high school.

Chris adds another layer to these experiences because he exhibited a more understated personality during our interview than both Matt and Albert, and also because he talked about what it was like to come out during high school. He attended a wealthy private school in a southwestern suburb, and he had built up significant social capital before he came out. "I mean, at school, my senior year of high school, I mean, people liked me. Not tooting my own horn, but people liked me. They understood that I was me, even if I didn't tell them I was gay. So when I let them know that I was gay, it was just like, 'Okay. We've been around him like this, so why not?'"

Importantly, Chris did not describe a dramatic shift in his self-presentation that accompanied his coming out. He did not describe himself as "really gay" the way Albert did. So when he says that his peers thought to themselves, "We've been around him like this, so why not," the "like this" may refer to a sense of comfort that Chris's more reserved gayness or adherence to gender norms did not pose much of a threat to their usual social order. He also said, "They understood that I was me, even if I didn't tell them I was gay," presenting the possibility that many of his friends suspected or knew he was gay before Chris officially came out. This may have softened the social impact of his publicly affirming a queer identity.

Chris's example is part of a collection that highlights diversity among Black LGBTQ+ students and the high school settings they learn in. Comfort is not the norm, but their stories disrupt the notion that all high schools, or any specific types of school, are unquestionably terrible for queer Black students. Still, there is no question that most of the people I spoke with were more than ready to leave home and start their college lives. In her book about queer Black women and the families they build, Mignon Moore observes that physical separation from parental figures is a key step for Black lesbians of all types. Moving away from home allows the women described in her book to grow into their identities and more openly share their lives with the folks who raised them.[12] Many students express a similar sense of newfound freedom once they arrived on campus. Parker, a trans student at Weddell University, grew up in a rural southern town that bears some similarities to the southern Christian environment Patricia describes earlier in the chapter. "I grew up in a little country town," Parker said. "It was outside of [a southern city]. And it was very white and country. I was very used to micro, used to, like, any kind of like blatant microaggression. I was super into theater. And I had a very, very bland childhood. I was closeted, like most people are. My family is like, conservative Black Christians. And then when I came to college and [Black Lives Matter] happened, it was like, 'Oh, okay.' It was my chance to break away from all that."

The place of Black Lives Matter as a force in students' identity building should not be overstated, but in Parker's case, it played a key role because the courage of queer Black activists inspired them to break away from their previous life. Camila, on the other hand, did not seem to need any added inspiration. She was ready to announce her presence as soon as she moved into her dormitory.

> I knew that I was in [a southern city], and I was here by myself. I didn't have my family tying me down. So I remember, like, the first thing I was talking to my roommate about was, "I'm Camila. I'm from [a southwestern state]. I'm gay, so if you ever see girls in the room, just know that, you know, I'm gay." 'Cause I was really, I just wanted everybody to know, like, that's who I am. I didn't have to pretend to be anybody else anymore. And I felt like it was like open arms when I got to Birch. I mean, everybody was kind of like, "Oh, well, there's a whole bunch of different people here."

For Camila, it was not just that she had moved away from home. She moved from a more conservative place and community to a large and more queer-friendly city on the other side of the United States. There was a huge geographic and cultural distance between her family and her new environs. Birch is an HBCU, but she described her classmates' initial reaction to her as somewhat unremarkable—just a feature of the diversity of Blackness on campus. Later in the interview, Camila also reflected on her feminine style as a trait that might lead others to perceive her as straight in some social situations. She also talked about the ways that not all queer people on campus at Birch experience the same sense of welcome from their straight peers or their LGBTQ+ classmates. So while she felt comfortable almost immediately, many of her peers did not share that feeling upon arrival at college. Recall that at the beginning of the chapter, Ava explained how uncomfortable it was for her to grow into her new identity on campus. She "ran from" her family, cutting off virtually all communication, and is still in the process of figuring herself out. Another HBCU student, Victor, felt added pressure to stay within the lines of traditional gender identity when he first arrived on campus, because his matriculation to college was an opportunity he feared he would ruin if he fully embraced his queerness. "You know, I'm just a Black man just trying to make it," he told me,

> balancing out masculine, feminine energy. And in your freshman year of college, you're just still trying to. I was working three jobs my freshman year, so I didn't have time to be, you know, all hooked in and things like that. And then I was still battling from my Christian upbringing. So there was a lot of things that was battling within me internally. . . . It was scary for anybody that's young, because you're really just trying to figure out, you know, this is my dream school. I've given up so much to come here. I ain't trying to ruffle no feathers.

When I introduced Victor earlier in the book, I highlighted his admission that he was inspired to attend an HBCU by one of his mentors in his hometown. This mentor was a prominent figure in the church, a well-to-do professional Black man who exemplified success for Victor and many of his peers growing up. These different strands of respectability intertwined to form a specific narrative of responsibility and attainment, one that left little time and space for Victor to resolve the competing ideas he wrestled with. Additionally, Victor dealt with immense financial pressure. Though he was on scholarship, he had to work three jobs in order to cover his living expenses while on campus. Any sort of self-indulgence or coloring outside the lines might be fatal to Victor's college career, and he deeply feared not only the possibility of discontinuing his education but the sense of shame and regret that would cover him if he had to go back home. Ultimately, Victor adjusted during his first year and thrived thereafter, becoming a beloved and outspoken advocate for other Black queer students on campus. But the geographic distance he put between himself and his family did not lead to his kinfolk embracing his sexuality. Bradley, another HBCU student, also described struggling with the adjustment to college when he first arrived. But the geographic distance from home helped him tell his parents about his identity, and now he feels more comfortable.

When I was in high school, I was much more quiet about it, 'cause I didn't necessarily know how anybody would feel about it. I didn't even know how to necessarily process the bigger picture of what was going on. I just, at that time it was just, "Oh, I think I'm gay, but I don't know." But once I came to college, my first semester, it was kind of, like, stressful for me, because I really wanted to tell my parents, but I didn't know how to tell them. So once second semester came, I just text[ed] my parents . . . I never felt the need to try to be anybody else or try to date a girl, because I knew deep down they just wasn't for me. So it was like, I was open then, but now I'm just much more open and comfortable.

Bradley never pretended to be straight by dating girls in high school, but he was unsure and secretive about his sexuality. That anxiety did not immediately disappear when he arrived at college, in part because he somehow felt pressure to talk to his parents about his identity in a way that he never had. While he did not act on this feeling initially, he took the leap in his second semester, and landed in a better place. This story raises the question of whether there was something specific about the time spent on campus that gave Bradley the courage to send the text message and move himself to the next phase of his identity. He did not give a precise account of the elements of his time on campus that gave him the courage, but other students pointed to specific moments or activities they participated in that helped them achieve similar breakthroughs. Deron explained that although his mother knew he was gay,

While I was like, a teenager, she kind of kept me sheltered from the gay community. So it kind of made me develop a negative mindset towards LGBT lifestyle. I mean, even though I am gay, as far as participating in the community, she just shunned me away from it for a long time, and I had really negative thoughts about it up until this semester. I think it was late February, my first time going to [a gay club], and it *changed my life*. I just really enjoyed myself. It wasn't what I thought it was, and I've been putting myself out there in the same [social circles] just trying to be more comfortable with myself, working on building me up to the highest point so nobody can break me down.

Again, this could not have happened if Deron had stayed home. It was not the formal curriculum he was exposed to in the classroom but the informal social scene of the gay students on campus that introduced him to the broader social scene of gay life in his new city. Deron talked about his gay identity not just in terms of knowing who he is as an individual but in terms of his connection to a broader queer community, in his case, a queer community that includes gay Black men like him. His mother's efforts to cultivate resentment and suspicion, not only of gay people but of gay spaces, ultimately failed. Deron builds himself up in the company of other gay Black men, a process made easier by his social grounding at an HBCU. The number of queer Black students on campus may be much smaller on predominantly white campuses. Many students found this experience to be isolating, but Jonelle, a Black queer woman at a large, predominantly white public university, still managed to find "pockets" where she could build community, unlike her experience in a mostly white high school.

> So in high school, whatever race you were, you just sort of had to find your place in white spaces. So you had to like, integrate yourself in that way, or you're just going to be out, because it's all a white space. So if you don't want to be in that white space, then you're just out of the whole space. Whereas here, there are things separated into pockets. There is a Black community. There is a Latino community. There is an LGBT community. So not being in the white space doesn't mean you don't have a space. You're going to have less resources and it's going to be different, but you have a space to where you can go and be comfortable.

This description allows for multiple interpretations. On one hand, it is a simple story of exclusion and forced segregation. The white space is the majority space, and it is also the space with the most resources. But on the other hand, those who would rather not build their lives in predominantly white social spaces have options beyond individual marginalization. There are communities that are at least somewhat supported by the college, and Jonelle says that people like her find comfort in them. This Black queer place making on campus does not happen by accident, or purely because of the goodwill of the college or university. Recall Ava's account at the beginning of the chapter, where she trumpeted the role of Black queer student activists in helping her grow into her identity. Both on and off campus, Black queer people build community through organizations. Some of these groups are not officially affiliated with the school. In talking about their journey, Parker explained how the boldness and honesty of Black queer organizers in the nearest city spurred their self-recognition and growth. "I got involved with organizations on campus and in [the nearest city]. I met all these amazing Black queer organizers. I think after that, that's when I realized I was queer, being around Black queer people who were so open and who were like very honest about who they were, what they were about. What they're about, they used the words, I'm like, 'Oh, this is me too.'"

But most of the students came to these moments of self-recognition without leaving campus. Even in places where the politics of respectability and religion are integral to campus culture, visible student organizations are indispensable resources for the students. Jasmine immediately sought them out at Birch. "I had been closeted in that way until I graduated [high school]. The first thing I wanted to do when I heard there was a registered student organization fair, I was like, 'Okay, where are the gays?' So I found [the organization], and I went to their first meeting, and we all introduced ourselves. And I noticed that the president, the E-board, they were all talking about it being a safe space. And I said, 'Well how safe?' And then I kind of tested the waters a little bit, and that's where I officially came out as gender queer."

For Jasmine and so many others, coming into Black queer student organizations is part of getting acclimated to college itself. But on the whole, the student organizations are not solely focused on initial acclimation for first-year students. After speaking with the students, I saw clearly that Black LGBTQ+ student organizations have three key functions: increasing visibility and safety for Black queer students; supporting the health of Black queer students; and educating the entire campus about LGBTQ+ identity and experiences.

BLACK QUEER STUDENT ORGANIZATIONS

Kristen Renn sets the stage for the contemporary study of LGBTQ+ college students by pointing to the explosion of gay and lesbian student organizations in the 1970s. If the Stonewall Uprising was the match that lit the fire and resulted in the first gay student organization in the country at Columbia University, the shift in thinking at the American Psychological Association (APA) added fuel. Until 1973, the APA defined homosexuality as either a disease or a disorder. Five years after that designation was removed and roughly ten years after Stonewall, there were two hundred LGBT student organizations on college campuses across the United States. The proliferation of student organizations at colleges and universities forced administrators and student affairs staff to take LGBTQ+ students seriously as a constituency in need of support. In order to find out what sort of support was needed, university leadership began studying LGBT student life using campus-climate surveys. The underlying logic of this approach, and the mandate revealed by the findings of these studies, was that these students were, simply, normal.[13] They needed the same things that all students needed: attention from their professors and a supportive social and cocurricular environment to enrich their college lives and help them succeed inside and outside of class.

The "finding" of LGBT student normalcy was codependent on LGBT student visibility. The more visible LGBT students made themselves through organizational work, the more of them there were to study and learn from. The normalcy and visibility of LGBT students became a driving force in changing campus culture for all LGBT people, as nondiscrimination policies were expanded and the student-climate study became a tool used to capture the experiences of students, faculty, and staff. Renn reflects on the state of the research in the 1980s and notes that while many of the findings seem obvious and "quaint" today, we should not underestimate just how revolutionary it was to affirm LGBT visibility and normalcy on campus in the late twentieth century. And while such studies may seem quaint today as a result of this legacy of scholarly success, we should not underestimate the degree to which they are still needed at many colleges and universities across the United States. "Normalcy" as an aspiration has been dismissed, both by queer theory and by the diversity, experiences, and sensibilities of queer students, and Renn seems almost bored by contemporary LGBTQ+ research that rediscovers the importance of visibility. Carly Thomsen argues that visibility is not merely boring but harmful to LGBTQ+ liberation, as visibility and

awareness politics replace the collective action needed for radical institutional change.[14] But the findings are stubborn. The students I spoke
to are not obsessed with white ideals of normalcy or recognition and
acknowledgment from white people. They are still ignored to a degree
that limits their lives. They told me, emphatically, that we have not yet
achieved a state of affairs where Black queer visibility on campus can
be taken for granted. This is a problem because students cannot move
through space the way they want to, and the invisibility they describe
makes it more difficult to find like-minded folk to befriend and build
community with. The creation of a *visible and safe community* is the first
key function of Black LGBTQ+ student organizations:

> I believe that on campus, before I saw the group on the page, I didn't
> know that there was a larger representation of LGBTQ+. So I was like,
> you know, searching, and like you'd see, you'd hear about a few here and
> there, but it wasn't really like prominent like I had thought. So I wanted
> to get more like involved, and really try to connect with a lot of different
> people. So I think it just created a sense of community, at least for me,
> togetherness. (Sydney)

> I was just like, here is this space I can go to that I know are like me. So I
> just kind of went with open arms, and we just had different various dis-
> cussions. And it was kind of a form of community. A lot of them are still
> my friends now. So it was a cool little community to have when I first got
> here. (Camila)

Black LGBTQ+ student organizations are groups that students can
join so that they do not feel alone. There is strength in numbers for the
students, and the size and diversity of the Black queer campus community are not always immediately evident to students when they arrive
on campus. The organizations serve both open and closed functions,
closing their ranks in the name of the specificity and solidarity of Black
queerness, and occasionally opening themselves up to the rest of the
campus as representative of Black LGBTQ+ people. Joining such a group
and finding other people with similar experiences and outlooks actually changes students' identities and makes them more comfortable with

who they are. Jace, a student at Tasmin University, a selective, private PWI, discussed his first experience going to a meeting.

> JACE: I actually went for the first time like two weeks ago. So I'm going again this week. But like, my first time going, it felt like I had known these people forever. They're so like homey, and like, nonchalant, and like, I don't know.
>
> MICHAEL: That seems like a positive experience. You're going to go back, so I'm assuming there was something good about it.
>
> JACE: Yeah. I enjoyed it. I think what was stopping me was myself from sort of partaking in these groups specified for people, because I would tell myself, "Oh, I'm only half Black," or "I'm only half white," and it's like, I don't want to intrude, or like maybe these aren't my people or I can't relate. And I just kind of, like my own mentality really ruined a lot of opportunities in the past. But I'm kind of over that. Yeah. I [don't] really consider myself to be a different person as much anymore, I guess.

Jace grew up in a Black neighborhood in a large northern city, and had a miserable experience in high school. He was a fine student who excelled in writing and history, but he never felt comfortable at school. Many of his teachers had what he called a "white savior" complex, and his classmates, most of whom were Black, had little interest in socializing with him. He is, by his own description, straight passing, but never felt invested or interested in the type of masculinity performed by his peers. He experienced his discomfort not only as a rejection of patriarchy and heterosexism but also as a painful distance from "authentic" Blackness, amplified by the fact that one of his parents is white. But this one meeting was so powerful in both its Blackness and its queerness that it made space for Jace to claim all the dimensions of his identity in ways he had not before. Put differently, Jace's experience in the student organization strengthened not only his gender identity, which is still unsettled, but his racial identity. Affirmation of Black queerness is an affirmation of Blackness and a newfound ability to relate to others. The language Jace uses to describe this transition is worth underscoring. This homecoming ("homey") to people he felt he had always known, was enabled by the "nonchalant" atmosphere of the organization members and the meeting they conducted.

The fact that Jace felt a sense of belonging and comfort in the company of the organization does not mean that everyone in the organization acts the same way. One of the questions I asked the students was how they would describe the people in the group. Beyond the fact that the organization was composed of Black LGBTQ+ students, I wanted to get a sense of whether there were certain personality types or key traits that characterized the people in the organization. On every campus, students told me that the group was not dominated by one type of person or personality. Gwen, a pansexual student at Caspian University, explained, "I think it's really all different types. Like you have some people who are like, they're committed to the group, but they're not going to be the first person with their hand up wanting to say something in the conversation. Like, some people are really laid back about it. Some people are super up-front, and they like to talk about the group and advocate for the group. So it's a little bit of everything."

This affirmation of diversity highlights the coexistence of bold and understated styles and personalities in Black queer spaces. Community does not require a certain type of Black queerness; it thrives because all types of Black queerness, from the fabulous to the understated, are accepted and supported. The diversity of personalities and self-discovery that takes place in the student organization requires trust and a sense of safety in order for group members to reveal themselves and connect with others. The notion of "safe space" has been skewered by critics who feel that college students are too often coddled intellectually and socially, and allowed to retreat into communities where their views will not be challenged. Setting aside for a moment the disingenuous nature of many of these lamentations about "intellectual safety"—they are often thinly veiled attacks on marginalized people and progressive politics—the students I spoke with told me that the safety they created was not primarily about the safety to express ideas. The student organizations provide, very simply and sadly, a form of physical safety: a buffer against the harm that might be done to Black queer people by other members of their campus communities. Another student at Tasmin, Naima, made this clear when I asked her what the main purpose of the student organization is. She said, "I think it's a safe space where, like, there really are very few safe spaces on campus. They always say, 'Oh, safe space, safe space.' It's not safe. Like, even our crisis intervention teams are not safe. People here have abused their power. People here have hurt students, and there are only a few places where you're safe on campus."

And Abraham, who goes to Juniper University, a public HBCU with a different student profile from Tasmin's, articulated both the power of community and the imperative of safety for Black queer students.

> It was my first time making bonds with people to where it was like, "Okay, now I want to stay." Even afterwards that was my real first group of friends. We started hanging out to where we spent all our time together. We went to dinner, lunch, breakfast. I even spent a night at their house sometime because we formed that type of bond. Our organization became like a family. If we felt like someone in this family was being attacked by someone on this campus we jumped in and said, "Yo, that's not going to happen on our watch."

Abraham did not tell me that he or any of his siblings in the Black queer community had been physically attacked by people on campus. But he did say there were times when he and his friends felt unsafe, in part because the campus was open enough that visitors could enter and exit freely and it could be difficult to tell who was a student. As both Naima and Abraham make clear, however, there is a lack of trust in the authority figures on campus and a sense that one of the crucial services student organizations provide is physical and emotional safety. These students do not always rely on university employees or support systems to keep them whole; they rely on each other. This brings me to the second key function of Black LGBTQ+ student organizations, which is implied above, but needs to be explicitly stated: *they support the health of their constituents.*

Naima's distrust of the mental health services at Tasmin is not unique. Without my asking directly about it, students on nearly every campus, whether PWI or HBCU, told me they could not consistently trust the mental health services at their colleges or universities. Tracey, a student at Evergreen, explained, "Our counseling center, a lot of people just don't feel comfortable going to it because they know that the head of our department, Doctor Smith, she's a deep-down Christian. Imagine how that makes you feel if you're gay or transgender if you're going to her office to open up to be gay or a lesbian? I feel very uncomfortable. . . . I'm over here telling you things that undermine your religion. I do believe that mental health is a big problem in the LGBTQ+ community."

Students are acutely aware of the mental health challenges facing their community. Shannon, a nonbinary student at Juniper, told me, "I know most of us [in the organization] have some kind of mental disability or illness because of the way we grew up, I guess." And Bradley explained, "Especially being gay, like that's so much. So many things that happen as a child or as, just as we come into ourselves that we don't talk about that could possibly trigger a mental illness, and we don't even know because we just aren't educated on the correct things."

But the problem is not simply a lack of knowledge or a code of silence. Structural inequality drives the mental health crisis among young Black LGBTQ+ people. A 2020 study conducted by the Trevor Project sampled over twenty-five hundred Black LGBTQ+ people between the ages of thirteen and twenty-four. The researchers found that 44 percent of Black LGBTQ+ youth had considered suicide in the previous year, "including 59% of Black transgender and nonbinary youth and half of all Black LGBTQ+ youth ages 13–17 years old." The study also found that "60% of Black LGBTQ+ youth who wanted mental health care were not able to get it, with more than half citing affordability as the reason they weren't able to get it." As suggested earlier in the chapter, high levels of family support significantly mitigated the risks of mental illness for the respondents in the study, and by contrast, police victimization due to gender identity increased the risks.[15] So it is not the case that Black people simply do not know about mental health resources, or that Black culture is hostile to mental health care. Certainly, Black people harbor distrust of the American medical establishment, and with good reason, given the ongoing history of discriminatory racist treatment of Black patients by American doctors of all specialties. But the Trevor Project report shows that Black LGBTQ+ health disparities are driven not by distrust and cultural beliefs but by lack of access to health care and over-exposure to punishment that makes Black queers even more vulnerable. Gwen, a student at Caspian University, told me, "I think just being a psychology major in general, like hearing all the disorders that are out there. Like it really makes you wonder, like 'Oh, I could have that,' or

'Oh, I'm showing signs of that.' And having friends here who deal with the same things that I do, and I thought nobody understood until I got here and met people who dealt with it. 'Cause my family is like, I don't know. They're not anti–mental health, but if you say, like, 'Oh, I'm depressed,' they're like, 'Oh, you're not depressed.' So it's a whole new experience here."

Nick, a student at Timor University, had a similar story about his family's refusal or reticence to address their mental health issues. "I know a lot of times, my mom says, '[Nick], do you think you're the only one that's depressed?' She said that to me before several times, and I said, hmm. That's interesting, 'cause you're basically telling me that you're able to live with depression, and like not be treated for it. So, you know, I think that's the main thing, is that the African American community is so focused on being strong that we don't feel the need to speak up about things such as mental illness."

The question is, What do Black LGBTQ+ student organizations do with this information? Clearly, their members know that mental health is a serious concern for everyone in their community. They do not have the financial support to eliminate the barriers to professional medical treatment for members who wish to seek it. But they do help each other in multiple ways, including the very basic step of providing space for someone to talk about who they are and how they feel. Leaders of these organizations, like Zoe, however, have a valuable perspective on the depth and scope of the challenge, and on all the things a Black LGBTQ+ student organization can do. She explains her work and her approach at Cedar University, a large, public HBCU, in detail.

Being in college, and at an HBCU? "What's mental health? We don't do that. You better pray about that, baby." And we start putting on more and more programs, and the more students talk, the better we get. I pick the topic for that week. Like one week, it was, "I'm coming out," and it was like the first time somebody knew you were gay, tell your story. And when they started to tell their stories and they started looking at each other and realizing, "You almost got the same story I got, I can ride with you." I started making best friends in the group to the point that they started disappearing. I was like, "Hey, where are y'all?" They're like, "Oh, we're hanging together." I'm like, "Hey hey, don't stop coming! Hang with me though!" [Laughing] But, like, it was a bond, 'cause it's like, "I'm not weird. I'm not different. Everybody goes through this, and I have somebody to talk to." So we do a lot of that. Like we do a [painting event]. That's what all these portraits you see here [gestures at the wall], all of that came from events. All of these are done by students. We did words of kindness, where we do little notecards, and you write a quote on there about something positive that's going to move somebody that might be having a bad day. And then you go out, we just pass them out. And I really think that's the most positive thing that [we are] doing, is we're building mental stability.

Zoe begins by talking about the stigma attached to talking about mental health within Black communities and on her campus. Then she discusses the various programs she put in place as the leader of the student organization. Some of them are difficult conversations about specific topics, like coming out, and some of them are less structured events that are designed to give people the tools they need to express themselves. All of these activities are undertaken with the goal of building mental stability, and that is one of the most forceful elements of this excerpt. The student organization builds the capacity and agency of its members. They not only feel better as individuals when they participate; they behold their own power as agents of change and people who can impact others. The collective power and bravery to reach others only adds certainty and strength to their sense of community and safety around each other. Sonia, who is only intermittently connected to the Black queer student organization at Aspen, another HBCU, explains its value in ways that echo Zoe's comments. "They can come talk to you, as long as they know everything's confidential. Sometimes there's, they need someone to talk to. And with suicide and stuff like that, 'cause people still do that at school, in college. And it could be just as simple as their love life. They're confused. They don't know what's going on, like they can't find anybody. They feel lonely. [The student organization] help a lot of people in that sense to feel more welcomed into the school."

Both Sonia and Zoe describe organization members bonding with each other. In several excerpts above, students I spoke with talked about the lasting friendships they developed as members of their organizations. Zoe describes this beautifully, as she tells me that the friendships between members grew so strong that it actually became a challenge for the student organizations to keep them coming back. This was not uncommon, as some students were only occasionally active in their organizations because they felt they did not really need them the same way they had when they began their college careers. But these lapses are not failures. They speak to the lasting and sometimes hidden value of these organizations as groups that seed the ground of Black queer social life and connectivity. Not all of the connections are unendingly sustained by the organization, but they are often initiated in the organizational space.

Another way that organizations contribute to their constituents' health is that they carve out space for queer and questioning students to talk about dating and sex. There is much more to say about Black LGBTQ+ students' experiences with dating, a subject that is more fully engaged later in this book. But as part of this conversation about the main functions of student organizations, Zoe also described the different types of sharing sessions that the group provided for its members, including a conversation in which any student who felt comfortable could tell awkward stories about their dating life and hookups. The casualness of these conversations is a counterbalance to the shame and uncertainty many students feel about these topics, as well as the serious sexual health concerns Black queer students face. Hailey, another student at Cedar, told me that sexual education was one of the group's priorities. "For example, an event that we're having soon is going to be [name of party], so like we're trying to have like presentations on—I think something with dildos, something with strap-ons, like something with that, and we always have condoms just available. So sexual health is like key here."

The organization's status as a sexual-health resource center signals the third crucial function that Black LGBTQ+ student organizations play: they *educate the entire campus about LGBTQ+ identities and issues.* It is difficult to overstate what a prevalent theme this was in the interviews. The students' accounts made it clear that people in all corners of the campus at both PWIs and HBCUs need to be better educated about the terminology applied and experiences attributed to LGBTQ+ people. At both types of colleges, students talked about their own blind spots in their understanding of what it means to be LGBTQ+, and how many different ways there are to move through the world as queer people. On both types of campuses, students described problems with classmates, some of whom have no tolerance for queer people, and others of whom seem more open to affirming queer people and building community, but might have been afraid to say the wrong thing. At every place I visited, students talked about divisions within LGBTQ+ communities and among LGBTQ+ people about the labels they use, and disagreements about which queer folk really belong in which organization. But here, I want to focus on comments from students at HBCUs that specifically show the value of the student organizations' emphasis on education for their members and the broader campus community.

Ervin is not one of the two students who self-identified as trans when we met for our interview. He has not changed the name his birth parents gave him, but his parents used different pronouns for him than those he now uses. He describes himself as gay and androgynous and told me that he is sometimes misgendered and that people look at him in a confused way before they get to know him. He is not a regular member of the LGBTQ+ student organization at Juniper University, but he credits that group with giving him the freedom to rethink identity, both for himself and for the siblings he met during the meetings. He told me, "At first starting off, I just knew you were either gay, straight, or bi. And when I came to the group, I realized there were people who were asexual, non-binary, androgynous, transitioning. So polyamorous, polygamy people. Like there's a lot of things that I did not know when I first started."

Madison, a student at Birch, said something similar about the influence of the organization on her understanding of herself and the people around her. "So like their last meeting, they were discussing different gender and sexuality groups, so understanding that everyone doesn't identify as the standard gay or bisexual that you would think. And then also, we go over pronouns, which is another important thing that I learned just from being there, 'cause prior to that, I hadn't realized the importance of knowing different pronouns."

The student organizations are committed to education for their members first. As Madison, Ervin, and so many others attest, finding the language to talk about oneself and naming the diversity of Black LGBTQ+ life is an awakening. None of these explorations are included during first-year students' formal orientation to the campus, but this space for conversation and identity development is crucial to the students' college transition. In that sense, Black LGBTQ+ student groups fill a massive void that might otherwise be filled by programming and staff in the student affairs division of the college. In addition to providing this education for students, student organizations take it upon themselves to educate faculty, staff, and administrators. Zoe is one of several students who emphasize this point.

> The hardest people to work on at this point is the grown-ups. Not calling the students children, but it's the ones who are teaching them that are—the faculty is the issue. We have so many that are here to help us, but the few that don't want us are the problematic ones. And it's because of the fact they don't have knowledge of a lot of stuff. And that's why we do safe zone training. And you learn about the different pronouns, and how sexuality works, and you know, just identifying and understanding people. 'Cause it really has nothing to do with who you go home and sleep with. We all different somehow.

It is noteworthy that Zoe desexualizes the LGBTQ+ group and the sort of education it provides, especially because sexual education is part of the organization's mission. Deploying this sort of explanation in conversations with college faculty and administration signals that she does not think some "grown-ups" are ready to understand the full range of needs and experiences within the Black queer student population. She brings this conversation to them in the language of diversity—"we all different somehow"—which seems less threatening than the language of power, safety, and justice. But she chooses these tactics because some of the faculty on campus are either uninterested in or truly ignorant about Black LGBTQ+ issues.

Easton, a leader of the Black LGBTQ+ student organization at Evergreen University, explains when and why he realized that educating the broader community had to be central to his group's mission. "Last semester we were kind of trying to get people together and things like that. But there was a little, not even pushback from the administration. . . . We realized that in order to have events, we realized that people needed to be educated on the lifestyle before the events that we're having so they are able to understand what we're doing and the basis behind the event." Again, enhancing the visibility of Black queer students is central to the organization's mission. But when Easton planned events aimed at calling attention to Black queer life on campus, he sensed confusion and reticence from the administration as well as other students. They might have supported and collaborated with his organization, but they did not know what the organization stood for or what it meant for someone to claim a particular Black queer identity. In contrast to Zoe, when Easton and his organization shifted gears and began to focus more on educating their college community, they did so without leaning too heavily on the language of diversity, and without fear of the consequences of talking about power, safety, and justice in Black queer life. The organization was "educating them on the history of the LGBT community. But not even that. Educating them on the viewpoints of how the heteronormative community are oppressing the LGBT community. I wouldn't say in a comparison of prejudice and racism, but it's almost like that, how the heteronormative community is kind of oppressing the LGBT community in the sense of just being able to freely express themselves."

At HBCUs and on all campuses, both kinds of education are needed. Student organizations play key roles for their members, giving them the space and vocabulary to better understand themselves and speak their identities out loud. They also turn their energy and focus outward, giving that same language to everyone on campus who is willing to receive it, and pairing these more basic explanations of Black LGBTQ+ identity and experience with analyses of history, power, and oppression. They are essential to students' transition from home to college, providing a social structure for new students to enter. But not all students enter with the same degree of comfort with identity, and not all students derive the same social pleasures from the organizational setting. There must be other sources of Black queer social connection, and more to the story of Black queer bonding than friendship as a function of organizational life. The next chapter addresses these issues in more detail, beginning with ideas about LGBTQ+ identity development and "coming out of the closet," and moving to students' accounts of liberating friendships and chosen families.

[4]

COMING INTO THE LIFE

Brandon spent his pre-college years in the suburbs of a large southern city. He went to a racially diverse high school where he enjoyed his time with friends and did his work in class, but never felt inspired by school or closely connected to his community. During his senior year, his mother told him that he could decide whether he wanted to attend college, but if he chose not to, it would be difficult for him to find a job later in life. She encouraged Brandon to apply to Aspen University, the large, public HBCU she graduated from, and he did. When he was accepted, she moved with him, settling down in a community about thirty minutes away from campus so they could remain close.

Their closeness, however, was not entirely comfortable. Brandon always knew he was gay, and his mom had difficulty coming to terms with it. The truth remained unspoken until he forced her to confront it while they were on a vacation cruise together during his senior year of high school. One night, Brandon announced that he was going to a social gathering for LGBTQ+ guests on the ship. She sheepishly asked him, "Why would you go to that? You're not gay." And Brandon replied,

"I know you know. You have to know. Like, I've lived with you for eighteen years. You know. But you push it out your mind. You know." And she's like, "I had suspicions, but I didn't know." I was like, "You're acting like you don't. Like, just say you did so you can stop having a hard time believing it." You know? And then the whole time we were there, it was weird. But she made it weird. She was just like, "I don't know who you are." I'm like, "Yes you do. I'm the same person." And then sometimes she'd be like, "Oh, okay." Like sometimes, one day on the cruise she'd be, "You know, okay, I'm glad you came out." And other days she'd be like, "Get away."

In the months following the cruise, Brandon's mom gradually stopped vocalizing her disbelief and rejection. She moved toward an uneasy acceptance of Brandon's identity, an acceptance that never reached the point of full embrace, but allowed for a mostly supportive and loving relationship. When it came time for Brandon to leave home for college, she helped him make the transition to campus. Part of that process was choosing a roommate, and the one thing Brandon stipulated on his roommate preference form was that he wanted his roommate to be from the same part of the country, and, if possible, from the same metropolitan area that he lived in. Aspen was able to accommodate his request, and the two students connected on social media just before freshman year. When Brandon looked up his new roommate, Will, on Twitter for the first time, he could tell that Will was gay and told his mother so. When Brandon showed Will's profile to his mom, she agreed that Will was gay, but was not upset by it. Instead, she asked if Brandon wanted to go meet him. They picked a time to visit their dorm room together and start setting things up. At first, Brandon didn't know what to make of Will, even though they had so much in common.

It was like, off, at first. I don't know. 'Cause you know, you don't mess with everyone. I didn't know him. I was just [feeling like] "I don't know you." And so later on, like months go by, and I could tell we're getting closer and closer and closer. Like, I can't stay away from Will. Will is like, my best friend. Like, I live with him. That's just cool. I'm glad I met him though. I'm glad everything fell how it fell. I don't want to say I can't live without Will and [other friend], but if they weren't here, I feel like it would be different. I would be more . . . someone else. You know what I mean? Someone else rather than me. 'Cause I like to find a group that is comfortable with me being me, and if I am with a group that's not comfortable, I have to tone it down a little bit. Not really tone it down, but kind of like, not be the real me. You know what I mean? I could be the real me around them.

Brandon's mother plays a major role in both of the excerpts from our conversation. When Brandon told his mom about going to the LGBTQ+ event, he was not telling her anything she did not know, but he did describe the moment to me as "coming out." Her reaction was predictable; the experience of shame and rejection within one's birth family was devastatingly common among the students I spoke with. But there are other layers to Brandon's revelation that are equally important, as they shed light on the inadequacy of "coming out" as a construct for understanding how Black queer people negotiate their identities. He was not imparting new knowledge to his mother. Brandon's disclosure was less of an event for him than it was for her, and he did not mark it as a breakthrough in his own sense of who he is. He was already solid in his gay identity, and she was the one changing, being dragged toward acquiescence by her son. Their conversation on the cruise was not final, so it was not as if he came out to her once and then never had to do so again. She took steps forward and backward as she moved toward not only acceptance of her son as an individual but acceptance of the community that he belonged to. She demonstrated this acceptance later on by facilitating Brandon's initial introduction to Will and providing the modest foundation for what became a deep friendship between two young, Black, gay men. And on that foundation, Brandon built himself up and strengthened his own image with lasting, dependable friendships that validated his sense of personal authenticity and queerness.

Brandon's story features the two key themes of this chapter: the meaning of "coming out" for Black LGBTQ+ college students, and the possibilities of queer friendship and joy on campus. I begin by reviewing the debate over "coming out of the closet" as a long-troubled construct within queer studies. Criticism of this idea abounds on both theoretical and empirical grounds, and Black queer scholarship and experiences demonstrate that the notion of a single "coming out" event is woefully inadequate as a means to understand Black queer affirmation and community building. Students' commentary on this issue, however, does not amount to a forceful dismissal of coming out. They still find the idea somewhat useful as they describe what happens when they affirm themselves with their birth family and in other spaces. But when they discuss the effects of these moments and events that follow, it becomes even more clear that we should abandon the simplistic narrative of "closet" as concealment or prison and "out" as freedom or happiness.

None of the students described coming out as the moment they felt completely liberated or joyful, but they did share other memories of joy and contentedness with me. In recounting memories that brought them happiness, the students offered a mix of specific times when they felt alive and validated as individuals and in the company of their friends. They spoke carefully about the ordinary pleasure of friendship and its extension beyond one day, or night, or their time at college. Their stories demonstrate the power of the collegiate mundane as a setting for Black queer delight and empowerment.

COMING OUT

Before examining criticisms of coming out as the essence of, or prerequisite for, queer liberation, we have to acknowledge the appeal of the idea. It is compelling because coming out is regarded as an individual psychological process that leads not only to self-acceptance and affirmation but to political solidarity and power. As John D'Emilio explains, the story of LGBTQ+ liberation in the twentieth century is in no small part the story of changing the meaning of "homosexual" from a private act or behavior into a public political identity.[1] Queer people's collective recognition that they are subject to the same institutional and cultural forms of oppression leads to radical political solidarity. D'Emilio argues that the Stonewall Uprising in 1969 crystallized this realization for LGBTQ+ people across the country. The victims of police violence were targeted and attacked *because they were queer*, and they resisted and fought back because they demanded rights and dignity *as queer people*. The uprising led to a wellspring of queer activism, including Pride celebrations, galvanization of LGBTQ+ organizations that existed prior to 1969, and the birth of new groups that asserted themselves in the late twentieth century. Stonewall motivated LGBTQ+ people to come out not just for personal affirmation but as an example for others.

Coming out is a political phenomenon, but it is frequently discussed with reference to an individual psychological process of identity development.[2] In 1979, just six years after the American Psychiatric Association stopped listing homosexuality as a disease, psychologist Vivienne Cass developed a still widely referenced six-stage model for LGBTQ+ identity development. In stage 1, the person in question has a sense that they may be different from others and feels confused about it. Stage 2 is when the person recognizes that the feelings they have indicate that they are queer, and in stage 3, the "tolerance" stage, they tell other people about those feelings and begin to seek out the company of others like them. During stage 4, they more fully "accept" their identity, and in stage 5, they begin to take pride in it, becoming nonapologetic, possibly angry, and activist as they strengthen their ties to LGBTQ+ communities and distance themselves from predominantly straight social groups. The final stage is called "synthesis," characterized by acceptance, decreased anger, and reconciliation of their social identity both within LGBTQ+ communities and in other spaces. It is important to note that Cass understands that not all LGBTQ+ people move through every stage, and that settling at one stage is not condemned as pathological or incomplete growth. Still, the sequence of the stages suggests a certain type of progress, which has implications for happiness. If a person cannot truly accept their identity before reaching stage 4, and they stop concealing their identity (or come out) in stage 5, it would be difficult to make a case for self-acceptance and happiness without reaching the late stages of the model.

Cass's model was criticized and built upon throughout the late twentieth century, perhaps most notably by Ruth Fassinger. Cass's prioritization of individual identity with little connection to social context, questionable sampling method, commitment to a linear model of development, and failure to account for race, age, and class differences led Fassinger to develop a competing model with two parts and four stages rather than six. The first part pertains to *individual* identity development. While Cass's model is largely based on gay men's experiences, Fassinger's is based on lesbians'. Stage 1 is awareness of queer sexual desire. Stage 2 is exploration, which may include strengthening and exploring feelings of desire, but not necessarily exploring relationships with partners or engaging in sexual behaviors. Stage 3 is "deepening/commitment," wherein the woman accepts herself and resolves to pursue fulfilment as a sexual being. Stage 4 is the final stage, where the person more fully accepts herself as a lesbian and affirms her desire for women as part of her individual identity.

The second part of Fassinger's model pertains to *social* identity. In the first stage, the woman realizes that LGBTQ+ communities, rather than just individual people, exist, and they are not alone. The second stage is exploration, when the person seeks knowledge about these communities. Stage 3 is "deepening/commitment" again, which indicates a sense of solidarity with others who share their identity and face similar oppression. And the "synthesis" stage of the social identity half of Fassinger's model is a sense of comfort with membership in the identity group.[3]

Neither Cass's nor Fassinger's model is strictly described as a blueprint for "coming out." Both researchers allow for the possibility that coming out as a public declaration is not a requirement at any specific phase. It is unlikely, however, that someone would be "out" in the way we now understand the term without having reached the final or penultimate stage of either model. And importantly, the general argument of both models is reliant on the sort of linear progression that Fassinger points out as a weakness of the Cass model. There is uncertainty, exploration, realization, and then an unquestionably public move outward, into the world, with pride, and with the aim of joining a community widely recognized as LGBTQ+.

As Antonio Duran notes, the scholarship about queer collegians of color directly challenges these still-celebrated models of LGBTQ+ identity development, and the concept of coming out, in particular. Research shows that "queer collegians of color are less likely to disclose their sexuality publicly, adopt normative labels, or describe themselves as part of the queer community." For queer collegians of color, and Black college students in particular, the publicly accepted labels applied to LGBTQ+ people are not understood widely enough in the context of their lives to be consistently useful, and coming out is a process that is more selective and less public than it is for their white peers.[4] The gradual and ongoing nature of this process continues after college for the Black lesbians in Mignon Moore's book, *Invisible Families*. Moore eschews "coming out" and argues that the women in her book are instead "coming into the life." They learn how to be publicly queer, not in an imaginary raceless setting, but in queer Black social settings, which are the social worlds her respondents frequently inhabit. Coming into the life is "learning how to label and reveal oneself to others, and how to navigate the series of adjustments necessary to move through Black gay and lesbian subcultures."[5] This process is not linear; it is contingent and fluid. More specifically, it is a fluid navigation of *Blackness* as part and parcel of one's queerness, rather than a preparation for a final "synthesis" of deracialized social or personal LGBTQ+ identity.

Nearly two decades ago, Beverly Guy-Sheftall and Johnetta Cole discussed the phenomenon of conditional acceptance of same-sex relationships in straight, cisgender Black communities. They argued that even in homophobic Black spaces, such relationships were often tolerated so long as the partners in question did not garner too much public attention or boldly claim one of the labels of queerness.[6] More recently, Katie Acosta's book on sexually nonconforming Latinas (I pause here to note that "Latina" and "Black" are not mutually exclusive categories) provides a more detailed look at this phenomenon. Acosta shows that these women are not simply living between two discrete choices, acceptance or nonacceptance. They do not live as either "out" or "closeted," and many do not have clear coming-out moments with their families of origin. Instead, the women may bring their partners to family functions and other gatherings so long as they manage a delicate understanding that the romantic nature of those relationships is not discussed or emphasized.[7] In an article separate from her book, Moore observes an almost identical phenomenon, as she notes that Black respondents "had learned that it was not polite to refer to a partner as a 'lover' or to use terminology that approached anything sexual in nature when describing someone who was not a husband or wife."[8] Marlon Ross further explains this social negotiation and the choices queer Black folks make as they manage relationships with their kin. If the queer attraction and identity is obvious, Ross says, publicly announcing it, or "coming out," cannot easily be categorized as progress in the way that stereotypical understandings of coming out suggest. In fact, he says, "it can be judged a superfluous or perhaps even a distracting act, one subsidiary to the more important identifications of family, community, and race within which one's sexual attractions are already interwoven and understood."[9]

To all this evidence that commonly accepted ideas about LGBTQ+ identity progression and coming out are flawed, we must add the truth of transgender experiences. As an empirical matter, the lives and testimonies of Black transgender people have not been honored and accounted for in academic research. There is no established account of transgender identity development or "coming out" that is afforded the same authority as the work of either Cass or Fassinger. If there were, many of the same problems would likely present themselves, especially with respect to racial differences in the life experiences of transgender people. The unique and often terrifying condition of Black transgender life necessitates a complete rethinking of linear progress, coming out, and synthesis. For many transgender people, transitioning is intended, in part, to eliminate the need to announce oneself, or to further clarify one's gender in most settings. With respect to the identity-development models, what would it even mean to be in "synthesis" with a society or community where violence against Black transgender people is so often ignored? To put a fine, and perhaps too modest, point on the above: there is insufficient evidence that the most commonly held understanding of "coming out" applies broadly to Black LGBTQ+ people.

Even without the empirical weakness of the closet concept as a tool for understanding Black LGBTQ+ experiences, the idea of coming out can be dismantled on almost purely conceptual grounds. One of the most cited and formidable criticisms of the closet as a construct is Eve Sedgwick's *Epistemology of the Closet*. Sedgwick asserts that homophobic discourses are irredeemably contradictory, and their contradictory nature, or multiplicity, means that any argument in favor of dignity, rights, and empowerment for gay people will be undercut by the legal and cultural apparatus of patriarchy and sexism. At various times in American legal history, LGBTQ+ people have been denied civil rights protections because their status as a minority is not conferred by any single immutable characteristic, like race or sex. At other times, however, the act of sodomy has legally defined gay people as a minority group—a minority group whose defining characteristic is that its members break the law by committing sodomy and therefore forfeit protections. Whether minority-group status is legally denied or legally bestowed, the outcome is the same: denial of rights.

Sedgwick rejects the promise of the closet as a gateway to liberation for LGBTQ+ people. Queer people are under immense pressure to come out, because anything short of publicly declaring one's identity and sexual preference is interpreted as deception. Their refusal to come out is cast as a malicious deception, because it conceals deviance and the capacity for predation, the spread of diseases like HIV/AIDS, the sabotaging of traditional families and "family values," and other social ills. So if someone is hiding their sexuality, they must be hiding it for devious reasons, and the heterosexist pressure to come out is applied in the name of the *social good* in addition to the queer subject's personal growth. The harm of this logic lies in the fact that once someone is out of the closet, they are often criticized and stigmatized for not having come out soon enough. In addition, they are often penalized in myriad ways, including physical assault, familial rejection, religious condemnation, and educational, medical, workplace, and criminal-punishment discrimination. LGBTQ+ people are attacked and cast as betrayers on both sides of the closet door. Their safety and freedom are not, therefore, dependent on personal choice or development, as the closet narrative would have us believe. Safety and freedom are dependent on concrete changes to the legal and cultural institutions that make LGBTQ+ people suspect and queerness a crime, no matter how politely or secretly it is practiced.

Sedgwick's work has been criticized and improved by scholars like C. Riley Snorton, who have taken her to task for essentially ignoring race and the condition of Blackness in particular. Blackness as a starting point allows Snorton to observe, "Comparative interpretations of the closet rely on a set of logics that place darkness and enlightenment and concealment and freedom in opposition to one another. These logics are put in crisis in the case of Blackness, where darkness does not reflect a place from which to escape but a condition of existence. In other words, there can be no elsewhere when darkness is everywhere."[10] Snorton posits that representations of Black sexuality are a "glass closet" of hypervisibility, spectacle, and speculation. Hiding safely in the closet, therefore, is not an option for Black queer people, who are constantly surveilled and speculated about. Escape and happiness are not achieved through leaving the closet; again, one cannot abandon Blackness as a condition of existence. They must be achieved through shattering the closet and upending the knowledge/power project that the closet is built to facilitate, which is the surveillance, disciplining, punishing, and exploitation of Black people.

STUDENTS' EXPERIENCES COMING OUT

I did not ask students if they had come out or what it was like to come out. I did not think it ethically appropriate to request that they tell me about times when they disclosed their sexuality to others. But not surprisingly, students volunteered these moments of disclosure frequently during our conversations, as they talked about different periods, relationships, and experiences of their lives. I did not assume that they accepted "coming out" as an apt phrase for an experience they had or the process of disclosure. However, they did use the phrase frequently during the interviews, so the concept has value to them, even as their stories illustrate some of the problems described above. The first thing to say about the details of these disclosures is that coming out was usually a painful and upsetting experience for the people I spoke with. Almost none of the students found immediate comfort or acceptance from their birth parents or closest adult authority figures. I will not present a large collection of interview excerpts to illustrate the frequency with which students described the pain of coming out, because it is unnecessary. I will, however, focus on stories from two students that illustrate the range of factors and reactions at play when someone chooses or is forced to come out of the closet. Here is the first story, from Elizabeth, a student at Linden University.

Well, when I came out to my mother, I was in the seventh grade, because I was kind of forced out of the closet because of a relationship I had at school. And my cousin worked there, and she found out about the relationship that I had with a girl. And so she was telling, it went around to teachers, and the teachers were looking at me like, "Well, what would your mom say?" And I immediately thought, "Well, before it gets to my mom from someone else, I have to tell her myself." So I sat my mom down that night, and I was crying for like at least forty-five minutes to an hour straight, trying to tell her but I still couldn't. So then I took a deep breath and I was like, "Mom, I like girls." She was like, "Oh I know. I kind of figured." And she was like, "I'll always love you, but remember what the Bible says." And that right there, it was like, well, yeah, of course I know what the Bible says, 'cause we go to church every Sunday. I know what's preached over and over again about homosexuality in the Bible. But me as your daughter coming to tell you this about myself, that was not the answer I was expecting to hear. And still to this day, she would rather me not tell anybody that I was gay.

Note the compulsory nature of the disclosure, which invalidates the notion that coming out is a choice dependent on Elizabeth's personal qualities or position on a scale of development. It is a choice structured by her lived reality in a homophobic world, where she is vulnerable to punishment at multiple sites. The bonds of family betray her, as her cousin spreads the word without her permission. Once Elizabeth's teachers learn of her relationship, they threaten her, which forces Elizabeth to tell her mother so that her mom does not hear it from someone else first. The act of telling her mother was painful, and her mother was not surprised. Just as Marlon Ross suggests, Elizabeth told her mom something she already knew. The violation and cause of parental condemnation in this case is not the fact of Elizabeth's sexuality but its proclamation, exactly as described in the scholarship and other accounts. Elizabeth's mother then issues a statement of qualified love, suggesting the inevitability of religious condemnation, and Elizabeth's interpretation of her family's attachment to the church solidifies the feeling that she cannot escape God's penalty. The affirmation of qualified love was not a public affirmation, and her mother still prefers that Elizabeth keep her sexuality a secret. In summary, the institutionalized oppression of family, school, and religion conspires to attack Elizabeth, and her coming out in seventh grade did not result in any of the benefits that the theory of coming out or identity development would suggest.

The second story I want to highlight belongs to Mitchell, a twenty-year-old sophomore at Hickory University. Mitchell told his family about his sexuality when he was thirteen years old, during his eighth-grade year. In April of that year, he told them he was bisexual, "to give them a little hope," but in June he stopped pretending and told them he was gay. His parents immediately suggested that he was too young to know, but he told them he was absolutely certain he was only attracted to boys. After the initial shock of disclosure, his parents moved swiftly to suspicion and denial. Mitchell cried himself to sleep several nights during the first few weeks after their conversation. "Every single day around five o'clock," he told me, "they would call me into their room, and I would sit on the edge of the bed, and they would ask me why I am how I am." Mitchell would sit on the bed without offering any more of an answer than he had already given, pretending to watch television and sneaking glances back at his parents, who seemed to be staring at him. He would occasionally wake up in the morning to his mother putting olive oil on his forehead and praying over him as he lay in bed. On weekends, she would leave a bookmarked Bible in the room and tell him to read verses while she went out to run her errands. "And then we finally came to this big like milestone, to me," he said.

> And this was when I was like, a teenager. I felt like this was a milestone, and it still kind of is to me. I was maybe in my freshman or sophomore year in high school, and I remember we were driving home. I was on the passenger side. My mom was driving. And I remember coming home from school. I had my uniform on, and she said, "You know, you really are pushed forward with this, you know, this wanting to be gay thing." And I looked at her, and I was like, "I thought you told me that your child's happiness was the only thing that matters to you. Well this makes me happy." And she was just silent.

Mitchell's father never really engaged in a conversation about Mitchell's sexuality, and his mother seemed to increasingly adopt his dad's code of silence as her son approached college age. When I spoke with Mitchell, he was ready to start the conversation with his parents again, not because he believed they would be receptive but because their silence was holding back the rest of his life. "I'm like at the point now to where, I want y'all to start meeting my boyfriend and getting to know him," he explained. "I want you all to know him. Like, me and this dude been together for a year. I want y'all to get to know him. I've gotten to know his mom and everything, and I want him to start coming to the house to get to know you and my dad. You know, just so he feels comfortable as well, and just so I have an ease as well. Like I always tell him,

I'm like, 'I know your momma. You know, I'm ready for you to get to know my momma.'"

For Mitchell, coming out to his parents was not a one-time event; it is a repetitive and ongoing process. He tried to mitigate the damage by beginning with bisexuality as a less threatening on-ramp to the truth. When he told them he was only attracted to boys, it cost him years of awkwardness at home, as his parents alternated between silently staring at him, questioning how he could truly know, and trying to pray the gay away. As in Elizabeth's case, we see the interwoven threads of silence and religious condemnation in his parents' inability to recognize and affirm their son. Mitchell asked his mother if his happiness mattered to her, and she did not reply. He moved to college and built a contented life as a gay Black man at an HBCU, complete with a leadership position in his campus's student organization and a fulfilling romantic relationship. Despite his parents' repeated rejection, he feels the urge to "come out" yet again, and have a real "sit-down conversation" so that he can strengthen his relationship with his boyfriend and make his partner feel more comfortable. Through all of this, Mitchell still feels very close with his mother, and that is one of the reasons he persists in forcing her to face the truth. The best version of Mitchell's life holds space for his parents, but they are unwilling to claim it.

Given that so many students experience disappointment and pain when they disclose their sexuality to people close to them, it is no surprise that they hold negative views about the value of coming out. Students' comments suggested that they did feel significant pressure to come out to their birth families, friends, and others. In some cases, like Elizabeth's, the sources of pressure were clear, as students were forced to navigate threats and disapproval of people who knew the truth and spread information in ways that could damage relationships. In other cases, however, the pressure to come out seems to be a more nebulous social pressure, and many students spoke about it in raceless terms. None of the people I spoke with described the outcome of disclosure as an instant sense of freedom or finality. Nobody who discussed societal pressure to come out felt it was justified or at all useful, nor did they tell me that they came out because they wanted to make a political statement. Instead, they experienced this pressure as something they carried as a personal burden, and they objected to it on the grounds that it was a double standard and violation of their privacy. In response to a question about homophobia, Jason, a student at Evergreen, told me,

> Homophobia is some bullshit. Some bullshit. Like, why the fuck does it matter what the hell I'm doing? Like, I actually like just came out, like December, to my family and my friends, 'cause it was like a whole situation. We ain't gotta get into that. But I just finally came out, and thankfully I've been received kind of well. Like my family, they haven't disowned me. My mom was kind of in denial. My dad kind of, I feel like he's in denial but he says he doesn't care. And my friends were like, "Yeah, we knew." But I'm lucky enough to not have to deal with the vitriol and the hatred that homophobia has in society, even though things have changed in recent years.

Along the spectrum of responses to students disclosing their sexuality, Jason's account is one of the least painful. The fact that his experience still entails denial and feigned tranquility from his parents is an indication of just how low the bar is when LGBTQ+ people are searching for acceptable outcomes. Jason interprets other people's need to know as a product of homophobia. As Sedgwick and Snorton and others suggest, queer people are a source of great anxiety, and must, therefore, be scrutinized and decoded in a heteropatriarchal society. Jason's response to such prying eyes is to reclaim his privacy, which he does in the course of the interview. Even though I asked him about homophobia rather than coming out, when he brushes up against the details of his coming-out experience, he reroutes the conversation with, "We ain't gotta get into that," preferring to keep some things to himself. Jason cannot return to whatever secrets he kept prior to disclosure, and as a respondent to a call for interviews with LGBTQ+ students, he likely has little desire to do so. But the fact that he lives his life openly does not mean that he celebrates coming out or believes that his experiences of disclosure should be broadcast to others.

Jason's comments echo several points discussed above, including the notion that he was telling the people close to him something they already knew. Faith, a student at Aspen, had a similar experience, and she also defended herself by talking about her sexuality selectively. "I didn't tell everybody. It wasn't everybody's business. You know? But I know I told my friends. They was cool. They was like, 'Oh, I've been on it. I knew what's up.' And I actually had, like my play brother, he's gay too, but he just recently came out. Like, he would lie to us about it. We knew it. It was crazy."

Faith did not tell me whether she talked about her sexuality with her guardians, others in her birth family, or adult authority figures. Again, her description of coming out to her friends should be counted as a fairly positive one, given the range of stories I heard from the students. She also reflects on coming out from a different subject position, as someone who knew the truth about her "play brother" before he officially came out.[11] When she said that "it was crazy" that "he would lie to us," she did so without any vitriol or confusion. She spoke the phrase with an air of amusement, as if it was silly of him not to tell her the truth because she knew him so well. This is likely the same feeling her friends felt, and she did not suggest there was anything wrong with keeping the tacit understanding a secret, whether she or her play brother was the subject.

A final invocation of privacy in response to coming out amounts to a more forceful criticism of the idea of coming out itself. Like Jason, Zoe's comments below hint at the homophobia at the root of coming out, as she rejects the pressure LGBTQ+ people face as a standard that straight people do not. "I don't believe in coming out," she said. "Straight people don't come out. They don't wake up one morning and say, 'Mom, I'm straight.' No. So why would I wake up one morning, 'Mom, I'm gay'? No, I am who I am. Like, it shouldn't matter who I sleep with."

At other times during the interview, Zoe was a fierce and unapologetic advocate for the public standing of queer people. She was leader of the Black queer student organization on her campus, was highly visible in her position, and spoke with her peers about the value of open conversations about sex. So it is not as if she believes in disciplined desexualization as a personal or political strategy for queer people. She does, however, reserve the right to invoke privacy about her sex life whenever she wants to, and she seems to hope for a day when whom she sleeps with will not matter to others. Taken together, the comments from these three students demonstrate that there is a nebulous social pressure to come out. They practice many responses to this pressure, dependent on the circumstances they find themselves in. During interviews with me, someone they do not know all that well, it became clear that they still value privacy after coming out. The affirmation of their identity does not mean that everyone has a right to the details of their disclosure stories.

Students do not specify in which spaces they felt the pressure most intensely, though the fact that they were coming out into the established culture and expectations of their family means that they had to negotiate Black cultural spaces. One lens through which the Blackness of these spaces is revealed is students' collective concern about their families' religion and the frequency with which religion is evoked by authority figures to condemn or attempt to "fix" the students. Later in the book, I describe students' analysis of the connections between religion and homophobia, which they have thought a great deal about and believe to be undeniable. But if religion indexes Blackness only gently in these exchanges about the anxiety of stepping into Black social space, there was one comment in particular that explicitly named Blackness as the social fact that completely changes the cost-benefit analysis of coming out. I previously introduced Candace, the student who chose Adriatic University, a selective, historically white college, because of the efforts of a Black administrator at the college. During her time on campus, she has had several off-putting interactions with queer white students, which pushed her to socialize almost exclusively with queer people of color. As Candace explains, one of the things that frustrates her about her conversations with white LGBTQ+ students is that they do not understand why coming out is different for her. She explains,

They try to relate on like, "We're going through the same things." And it's like: no. Intersectionality exists, and there are problems here that I'm dealing with that you don't have to deal with. So don't make it seem like, you know, "Just tell your parents." I'm like, "Wait a minute. Relax! Have you ever lived in a Black home? No. Have you gone through like, Nigerian culture? No. It's more than that." And I feel like, especially being friends with people of color within that community has given me more understanding of why people are not so open in coming out. And it's more than just, "Oh, just be who you are." Because your family is really the most important part of you, so imagine if they don't even accept you. Like, it hurts more than people like to make it seem.

Black LGBTQ+ students reported a number of problems and disappointments with their white peers, including tokenism and explicit bigotry, that are detailed in the next chapter. This particular disappointment, however, stems from what seems to be a well-intentioned attempt to relate to Candace and assure her that she is struggling with the same issues white students do before coming out to their parents. But Candace knows this is not true. She argues that the experience of living in a Black home, and a Black and immigrant home in particular, is something white queer students know little about. In Candace's case, the problem is not just the risk that her home and family will suddenly become inhospitable but that her family is a part of her. So coming out is, for Candace, in part a betrayal of *herself*, not just a betrayal of others. She copes with the alienation from white queers and the continued personal struggle she faces by indulging in the company of other queer people of color. The value of student organizations is described in the previous chapter, but one detail that should be added to student organizations' contributions as spaces for community and visibility is that they directly address their members' (and potential members') struggles with coming out. In chapter 3, Jasmine explained that she had been out to her mother, but closeted to the rest of her high school. She actively sought out the LGBTQ+ student organization as soon as she arrived at her private HBCU campus, came out at the first meeting she attended, and felt comfortable thereafter. Not surprisingly, organizations do not simply rely on the initiative of individual members; they create opportunities with programming. Here is Mitchell's description of one of these events.

> Last year, Coming Out Day was beautiful. There was a board that they went and wrote on, and it was about "When did I come out?" And basically telling a brief story, just to encourage other people on how you can come out, or things you should do, and just knowing that you're not alone. And also knowing, 'cause a lot of people like this one, that you don't have it as bad as other people may have. And I had to realize that as well. When I gained my gay friends or whatnot, I had to realize that, okay, you may have went through some shit, but you didn't go through a lot compared to this person that is now in your friend group who dealt with the complete neglect of their parents and things of that nature.

This event accomplishes so many things for Mitchell and others who participate. It provides resources, confidence, and tactics for queer students who are thinking about coming into the life. The organization also builds friendships, and Mitchell continues to learn from his friends and draw on their support as he wrestles with the difficulties in his own life. Their experiences give him perspective that he could not have had without embedding himself in a network of queer Black people. Though his ongoing problems with his parents are dispiriting and devastating in so many ways, he is able to make sense of them and build resilience in the company of his friends. In this case, the spark for these connections and the knowledge they bring is a scheduled event planned by the organization. But at other times, this sort of learning about coming out happens in informal and improvised organizational spaces. Zoe describes one of those informal connections and learning moments, as she recounts the time she helped a friend of hers deal with discomfort after coming out to her family. The backdrop for this story is that Zoe's mom knew Zoe was gay, but the two of them had never explicitly discussed it.

The first time I ever said the words to my mother is for one of my [friends in the organization]. We were here, probably it was like a couple of weeks ago, and my friend was like, "I feel like my mom is going to be weird. We have a better relationship now after I told her, but it's still weird." I was like, "You feel uncomfortable?" She was like, "Yeah, everywhere." I was like, "Well, hold on." So I called my mom on speaker. And I'm like, "Mom." She's like, "Yeah?" I'm like, "I got something to tell you." So I was like, "Mom, I'm gay." She was like, "Girl, whatever." And then she just kept talking. And I looked at my friend. "I said, 'See?'" So she goes, "Ha, okay." I'm like, "This is how they act. There's nothing you can do about it." It's like, we have two choices here. Either they can really love it and be extra weird about it and be trying to link with every gay woman they meet, or you get the one that's going to put you in the closet and read the Bible to you for hours. So I said, "I think we'll take the one that's going to be weird." I said, "Don't think anything of it. Y'all relationship's going to get stronger." It's just, it's awkward. They don't know how to—they don't have the same training we have. They didn't come to school, they were not taught, "Okay, this is how you deal with this." I was like, "It's supposed to be awkward. It's okay. You'll get over it."

This is a powerful illustration of students drawing strength from each other. Zoe plays the role of mentor here, but we can also see how she is emboldened by her friend. In order for Zoe to give the support she wants to give, she takes it upon herself to do something she has never done before. Of course, at this point, Zoe does not consider telling her mother she is gay to be much of a risk. They seem to have a good relationship and understanding of who Zoe is, so the phone call is not a massive breakthrough in their relationship, but the language is new. Zoe's mother's reaction is almost comical, as is Zoe's ability to use the episode as a teaching lesson. Far from a crescendo, the phone call is laughable in its mundaneness, as Zoe's mother carries on as if Zoe had said something completely unremarkable, and Zoe carries on with her friend. Zoe's "coming out" on the phone was not significant in its own right, but she made it meaningful when she reframed the disclosure as an issue for straight people rather than Zoe and her LGBTQ+ peers: "This is how they act," Zoe says. Straight people are paralyzed and ignorant, without the tools and training to deal with queer life. Many straight people are bigoted, but many others are almost blameless (according to Zoe) because they are not taught how to behave. To blame them for a weird reaction, Zoe suggests, is to lack perspective as a queer person. The alternative reaction, a Bible-thumping condemnation, is far worse, so "I think we'll take the one that's going to be weird," instead of the one who is going to be vicious. Zoe's is a gracious reading of homophobia, ignorance, and silence, which she surely knows are problems. But Zoe offers her perspective to give her friend confidence. In the worst-case scenario, her friend will adapt to the awkwardness and live beyond it. In the best, perhaps the friend's mother will change. Either way, it is not her friend's problem.

Coming out is not a one-time event that unfailingly changes one's life such that the time before disclosure becomes irrelevant. It is not a clear threshold from private imprisonment to public freedom, or from self-denial to self-acceptance. It is not a natural stepping stone to queer politics. It is not always the same act for queer Black people as it is for queer white people or folks with other racial and ethnic backgrounds. It does not hold the same cultural value in the Black communities that the students belong to, which include Black communities on white campuses, Black communities on Black campuses, and Black families. Still, Black

queer students know coming out is significant. The meaning of that significance is often dependent on the social world one resides in. It helps
to be at least partially attached to a student organization that can serve
as a resource. Rather than encouraging Black LGBTQ+ folks to "come
out," which puts the pressure on a queer or questioning person to make
a move or proclamation, student organizations often focus on "inviting
in." As David Johns describes, this shifts the onus from the individual
to the welcoming group, which is responsible for making and holding
space for anyone who needs it.[12] And whether students are active members of the organization or not, it helps to have queer Black friends, who
are often sources of Black queertidian comfort and joy.

BLACK QUEER MUNDANE JOY

Researchers have repeatedly documented the power and importance of
friendship for LGBTQ+ people.[13] LGBTQ+ people who are not welcome
in the homes of their birth families move away, often to cities, and form
chosen families, or what Didier Ebron calls "concentric circles of friendships," to support each other and build new lives.[14] The common social
experience within these friendship circles is living as someone who is
stigmatized because of their sexual identity and/or gender expression.
But the pleasure and joy of these friendships extends beyond the realm
of gender expression and sexual intimacy. Friendship networks are
indispensable for queer people's mundane day-to-day needs, emotional
well-being, and economic sufficiency.

Drawing on the work of Judith Stacey, Anthony Giddens, and others, Sasha Roseneil argues that these new models of friendship queer
the very idea of the family and change the assumptions and aspirations
of friendship for people at all gender and sexuality locations. Roseneil's
interview-based study of care, friendship, and nonconventional partnership reveals that people across the sexuality and gender-identity
spectrum were often closer with their friends than they were with their
parents or siblings. Friends, rather than long-term romantic partners,
were the most crucial reservoir of emotional support. In addition, Roseneil echoes findings in other studies suggesting that the line between
friend and lover among people who do not identify as straight is often
blurry, as friends become romantic partners and then return to the

friend zone, often remaining on good terms and continuing to provide at least some of the support described above.

This challenges assumptions about the centrality of long-term, monogamous, coresidential romantic partnership as the basis of intimacy and secret to happiness. Roseneil's respondents frequently reject these beliefs and aspirations. She writes, "Very few expressed a conscious yearning to be part of a conventional co-habiting couple or family. In not conforming to the dominant heteronormative relationship teleology, which posits that a relationship should be 'going somewhere'—that somewhere being shared residence and long-term commitment— sexual/love relationships were described instead as being about the construction of mutual pleasure in the present."[15] Marriage equality has been a central site of the battle for LGBTQ+ rights in the United States and elsewhere, and more radical critics of patriarchy and heteronormativity have long observed that aspiring to the heteronormative model of legally bound partnership is not freedom. It seems that even straight people do not like marriage much (the divorce rate in the United States is roughly 50 percent), which is not surprising, since the institution was created and practiced in Western societies in order to cement men's control of women, rather than make people happy. So the lessons queer folk have learned about the value of friendship and new possibilities of intimacy extend beyond LGBTQ+ communities. Roseneil and others argue that LGBTQ+ people stand at the vanguard of a new wave of friendship that washes over us all, regardless of our gender customs and sexual practices.

Queer friendship is imbued with a sense of vitality and urgency, not only because the life cycle of the heteronormative, reproduction-obsessed couple is not a chief concern but because the people who build queer friendships live life under attack, and the future is not guaranteed. Jack Halberstam writes, "Queer uses of time and space develop, at least in part, in opposition to the institutions of family, heterosexuality, and reproduction. They also develop according to other logics of location, movement and identification. . . . The constantly diminishing future creates a new emphasis on the here, the present, the now, and while the threat of no future hovers overhead like a storm cloud, the urgency of being also expands the potential of the moment."[16] There is a need to seize the moment and make friends in the here and now, because LGBTQ+ people cannot take the future for granted or count on the people they have known the longest. Halberstam's analysis of logics of movement and identification is helpful. Indeed, if the logic of coming out is a heterosexist and linear imposition, as suggested above, then the continuousness of coming out and the fluid negotiation of coming into the life *is* a queer location and movement. And the "constantly diminishing future" is, for many respondents, real. As I will describe in the conclusion, many of the students are pessimistic about the future for queer Black people in America. But the constantly diminishing future is not endemic to the students' reflections on the importance of queer friendship. They revel in what they believe will be lasting bonds. There is a durable sustaining queerness that gives regularity, solidity, and hope to their days on campus. They take great satisfaction in the present-day joy of queer closeness, support, and pride, while cultivating a lasting sense of their friendships that orients them towards the future. Two HBCU students, Sydney and Abraham, spoke about friendship, and their faith in the lasting power of their college friendships was clear when I asked them, "What do you think are some of your strongest memories of college so far?"

> Definitely my friends. They say the people you meet in college, like your friends in college, they're going to stick with you forever. And I really feel like the friendships that I've built in such a short amount of time is something that has never happened before. (Sydney)

> Genuine bonds. When you get older and you hear people tell you, "Oh, this is my college friend and we've been friends for this amount of years," I actually see what they mean. Because now we've formed these type of bonds with people that actually can last a lifetime. Because to be honest, after high school, I do not even talk to any of my high school friends. I socialize with them every now and then but it's not the same as my college friends. (Abraham)

In addition to their faith in the future of their college friendships, Sydney and Abraham speak to the intensity of the bonds. For each student the kind of friendship they have in college is unprecedented. It does not compare with the friendship they experienced in high school, and they are struck by how quickly the bonds have grown. This leads me to wonder which specific qualities of the friendship are so striking as to distinguish these bonds from the previous social connections that students have experienced. For Abraham, loyalty is key.

> ABRAHAM: My first memory and the first reason why I stayed at this campus, it was one member's birthday and he invited all of us out to the club in [a nearby city]. I had work at the time but I wanted to go. It was my first time going out. It was my first time making bonds with people to where it was like, okay, now I want to stay [at college]. Even afterwards that was my real first group of friends. We started hanging out to where we spent all our time together. We went to dinner, lunch, breakfast. I even spent a night at their house sometime because we formed that type of bond. Our organization became like a family. If we felt like someone in this family was being attacked by someone on this campus we jumped in and said, "Yo, that's not going to happen on our watch."
>
> MICHAEL: I don't want to use the word "attack," but what are some of the things that people have to deal with?
>
> ABRAHAM: We have to deal with the fact that we always have to have a guard up. We have to deal with the fact that at any moment of the day we have that fear of someone saying something or being physical with you, and then how can you handle it without being the one to get in trouble. So as a community, it's always living in that fear. It's even to the point where some people would rather disguise themselves and hide who they are because they don't want to get attacked. Whether it's verbal or physical it's something that plays on the mind heavily.

Friendship is the essence of Abraham's college experience, and the force that made him want to stay at Juniper. The blossoming of friendship was made possible by the space carved out by the student organization, which reinforces the fact that Black queer student organizations engender both community and safety for their constituencies. And safety looms large here, because of the danger implied in Halberstam's reflections on queer time and the fear of being attacked that Abraham and his friends have to deal with. This dangerous reality makes intense loyalty a requirement for Abraham and his friends. They do not believe their potential conflicts will be justly mitigated and/or prevented by their university, so they must be each other's protection.

An ordinary and queer intensity in close friendships emerges in this setting. There is the collegiate experience of going to lunch, then dinner, and then meeting up for breakfast the next day with the same group of friends. There is a comfort and closeness to the shared adventures, embarrassments, and recuperations that define so many people's college years. But having this ordinary fun as a group of Black LGBTQ+ friends, openly but with the risk of attack perhaps lurking in the back of one's mind, is a queer injustice. The protection of queer company is thus transformed from friendship to "family," as Abraham says. Several students echoed the importance of loyalty and affirmation of chosen family without the ominous threats Abraham worries about. When I asked Trent about the things at college that brought him joy, he said,

> Not really a deep answer, but sometimes just seeing a nice movie whenever you can is enough for me to be like, "I'm happy." Like, "I'm content." I also would say my friends. I've had friends that I've known since freshman year, have kind of just had my back no matter what. And college can be a very tough time, especially with, like, relationships and things like that. And just having those people that you know will always be behind you no matter what is like, really important. So I would say that. Going to movies with my friends is like, that's it. That's, like, the top tier right there.

Again, the power and comfort of the Black queertidian is on display. This is an ordinary and heartfelt reflection on the indulgence of treating oneself to a movie, or visiting with friends who have been with you through thick and thin. For Trent, these comforts, rather than enactments of Black queer fabulousness, are the pinnacle of Black queer joy. He celebrates friendships that steady him through failed relationships, reinforcing Roseneil's argument about the ascension of friendship, rather than monogamous romantic partnership, as a defining feature of queer social life in the twenty-first century. Of course, romantic relationships are deep sources of happiness as well, and several students suggested they would not have found the sort of intimacy they did with their partners if they had not grown into their LGBTQ+ identity at college. Earlier in the chapter, Mitchell described how close he had grown with this boyfriend, to the point where he was eager to start bringing his partner around his birth family, whether his parents were ready or not. Patricia discusses her romantic relationship as a breakthrough that has changed her life in ways she could not have imagined in high school.

> In high school, relationships is just kind of "Eh." It was like an "Eh" subject for me, like it's something that never really got explored as much. I guess I didn't really feel comfortable in who I was, my sexuality, like even realized what I truly liked, until I came to college freshman year. I fell in love for the first time. I didn't really know what falling in love was, and I fell in love for the first time, and had my first real relationship, and it happened to be with another woman. And since then, life has been great.

One of the themes that emerges in students' reflections on their friends is a sense of novelty. They may have had friendships before, but not like this, in an environment away from home, with space to affirm their identities in ways they previously had not. A key reason for the feeling of newness is that during college, students meet and spend time with so many more Black and openly queer people than they ever have before. The diversity and depth of Black queer social life on campus helps them take risks and opens them up to new forms of connection and mutual recognition. Deron describes the exhilaration of connecting across Black queer difference on campus at Douglas University.

> It's so funny now, like being an older gay on the campus, I came in with a group of gay boys. And we wasn't like flaming gays, but we were all different. Like we owned our differences. And we just used to vibe together, but over the years we went separate ways. But like this year, I was introduced to a group of gay boys that were completely different than how I came in. Like, these boys wear makeup. These boys damn near wear wigs, and stuff like that. And at first I was like [disapprovingly], "Oh my god!" And I used to talk about it with my other gay friends, like, "They doing too much, I don't like that." And I used to like, hate on them. But it was in a sense because I wanted to be wearing a dress. Just like, that's who they are. But dealing with them, like through that, I learned how to deal with them differently because I got to know them. Like I was afraid,

more afraid to speak to them than anything. I never interacted with, like, super-gay people. Like I just never thought to do that. I always told myself that I would stay away from gays like that. And this one guy in particular, his name is Louis, and he's, like, one of the older guys. How he is, even though he does the major in dancing, and he wears the wigs, he does his thing. Like, he owns his stuff. Can't nobody take that away from him. And he taught me just how to be confident. And I haven't even been friends with him that long. Like, I've had probably less than ten conversations with him within the semester, and we went out to eat last night with some of our other friends, and me and him were just like, in our own world. We wasn't flirting or anything like that, but we were just connecting on some gay-to-gay stuff. He was like, telepathic. It was so cool.

Sadie Hale and Thomàs Ojeda argue that gay men's misogyny and the policing of queer femininities cannot be discounted simply because gay men are oppressed.[17] Their explanation draws on Stephen Maddison and others, who suggest that misogyny is a form of male bonding for all men. The bonding takes on added significance for gay men because hostility towards femininity and women can be an affirmation of their manhood, and manhood is essential to their gay identity.[18] Hale and Ojeda locate this phenomenon mainly within white gay male culture, which produces specific codes and expectations of male privilege and other forms of exclusion, including racism. Deron's account of his own prejudice towards more feminine gay students does not exactly mirror these values and patterns of exclusion, but he does introduce the story by aligning himself with the "group of gay boys" he arrived on campus with. This alignment suggests that misogyny and policing of queer femininities within his original friendship group functions as precisely the sort of bonding practice identified by the scholarship.

The narrative turns when Deron reflects on the true reasons for his prejudice. Useful though it may have been for forming bonds with his initial friends, his misogyny was motivated by his own regret that he has not been able to embrace femininity the way he wants to. He identifies his own fear and lack of self-assuredness, and admires those traits in Louis, whom he is inspired by and now friends with. There was no single event or extraordinary force that brought Deron and Louis together. There may be attraction, but Deron insists that they were not flirting. Their connection is deep, queer, and mundane. Cultivating the company of other Black gay men allows Deron to see himself in others, and see qualities and courage that he aspires to. Parker, a trans student at Weddell College (a large, public PWI), weaves together threads of mutual recognition, validation, and the formation of chosen families. They explained,

> PARKER: But I know in meeting each other, we were both kind of like, "Wow, another one!" And we're always like, so excited. And then Toni had met another like Black queer person, and their name is Megan. It's like whenever Black queer people like get around each other, I feel like we get strong in our personalities, 'cause it's like, oh, we're maybe not comfortable in wearing this, but I'm like, "I know Toni would love it if I wore this or I did my hair styled like this." Or I know those people who would. I know that there's support around me. And it's like these networks keep growing and growing. It's like, do you watch *Pose*?
>
> MICHAEL: I haven't watched every episode, but I've seen some of it.
>
> PARKER: It's like when Blanca sees Damon on the street, and she's like, "You're in my house now." It's basically these little chosen families, these communities starting. It's like, we may grow up and grow apart, but then it starts all over again with these networks of queer people and trans people. 'Cause it's just what happens. We're always going to find each other and, like, build communities, no matter where we are. Because we exist everywhere.

One of the challenges of writing about the mundane, and writing about something as cliché as the power of friendship, is that it becomes difficult to pin down the substance of the bond between two people. Parker's description is immensely helpful in the struggle to avoid vagueness. They tell us how it feels to meet another Black queer person, or for a group of Black queer friends to grow in number. It is thrilling because it makes Parker feel stronger and more confident in their personality. It allows someone to present oneself with the faith that whatever gender signifiers and/or identities are chosen, they will find support. The friendship contains a feeling of momentum, which is itself an orientation towards the future, rather than the desperate present. There is a sense that one connection leads to the next, and queer family building is historical and repeating. Friendship gives Parker and their clique a sense of omnipresence despite their experience on campus, which is frequently characterized by disrespect and marginalization. Black queertidian friendship is inevitable and expansive.

Friendship is not the only source of ordinary joy for the students. Several students spoke about the joy of learning and their passion for the specific subject or major they specialized in. On occasion their enjoyment was driven by a sense that their work in class was moving them closer to their postcollege goals, like medical school or a career as a filmmaker. But some students, like Peter, focused on the experience of the class itself. "My greatest sources of joy, as a college student, I love being in class. I love being in class. I love being able to participate. I feel really happy when I say, when I answer a question and it's right, 'cause sometimes I'm like, I don't know if this is correct. I think my favorite thing is being in my English classes. I love learning. I love looking up words when the teacher's saying just a word that I've never heard before nonchalantly and have to look it up really quick. I like those moments."

Peter is a student at Evergreen, which is a private HBCU. Several students on campus talked about the individual attention they received from their professors, and a sense that the faculty were invested not only in the subjects they taught but the overall well-being of the campus community and the mission of the college. Though Peter did not explicitly connect his joyful learning experience to his majority-Black learning environment, other students did. Rae, a nonbinary student at Douglas University, offers a reflection that combines several themes of the HBCU experience, and foregrounds their gender identity and sexuality.

HBCU culture, it's like no other. I really like networking. I like the different styles. Black is beautiful. With me being a queer, no label. I love looking at the ladies here. I love complimenting them and things like that. I knew that my professors would go in deeper with me, pushing me more, being a double minority in society. They were pushing me more to reach what I needed to do, and you know, just seeing people that might come from the same background as myself, and just being comfortable in the environment I am in. 'Cause some of the schools I went back home, like history class, I remember being the only Black person while we was talking about slavery, and everybody was like, "How do you feel about this?" And now that I'm here, I had American history, and we can talk about Africana studies and things like that, I don't feel like I'm like outed.

The educational benefits of being in a majority-Black learning environment are plain to see. Several students across HBCU campuses believed they were getting a more genuine and committed form of education because they were learning Black history from Black professors at a Black college. Rae was far from the only student to contrast their HBCU learning experience with their learning experience in high school, where students frequently reported that they were both ignored as thinkers and singled out when it was time to talk about race or Black history. The next chapter contains testimony from HBCU students who felt that they were marginalized by their professors because of their queerness. Rae reports the opposite, and says that they felt professors supporting them even more strongly because they are a "double minority." It is striking that Rae uses the language of the closet to describe the absence of stigma they feel in this learning environment, where they can live without feeling "outed."

Another key dimension of Rae's joy in college is the social life of the Black campus. There is an indulgence in the diversity and different styles of Blackness and an explicit appreciation for Black women's beauty. Again, HBCUs were not universally described as places where queer students felt free to express their sexuality publicly, whether through words or displays of affection with their partners. Such acts were not strictly forbidden, but they were not common. It is also worth noting that Rae is nonbinary and on the masc side of the queer gender spectrum. Their public appreciation for more feminine Black women stays within the expected gender roles of masculine and feminine courtship. A queer and femme Black man expressing similar desire toward other men would likely find a dramatically different reception, given the testimony of other students and the histories of these colleges. Still, Rae's description of the joy they take in everyday people watching and the gift of sharing space with so many beautiful Black women—Rae says that their Blackness is intrinsic to their beauty—is noteworthy. This is an ordinary queer Black sexual joy that cannot happen in the same way on PWI campuses.

Finally, several students celebrated the role of queer Black student organizations as either direct sources of joy or indirect factors in their realization of happiness. Elizabeth gives an example that illustrates how a Black queer student organization can be an indirect facilitator of joy and satisfaction. When asked to reflect on a strong memory from her time at college, she told me,

> One really positive thing was that when I was going through the process of joining the org, I decided to conquer one of my fears, which is talking to people first. And I asked this young lady, 'cause she's a model, and I've always seen her work with other people. I was like, okay, I want to do that for myself. And it was just her that I wanted to do that with. So I conquered that fear that day, and I asked her if she could do a photo shoot with me, like free of charge, of course. And she said yes, and when I did that, I was, that like made my entire week, 'cause I am the type of person who, like I don't like to talk to other people first. And so, yeah, I did that.

Queer desire suffuses this mundane and triumphant memory. Though Elizabeth does not say that she desires the woman in the photo shoot, she does say, "It was just her that I wanted to do that with." She connects her reluctance to speak to this person with a broader sense of social anxiety, as she is uncomfortable initiating conversation with others. Elizabeth does not specifically describe which experiences or activities from the student organization gave her the confidence to take the social risk. But there is something about the experience of joining the group that prepares her to put herself out there in ways she had not previously. The social acclimation and confidence building that originate at meetings and social events sponsored by the student organization extend beyond those settings.

The connection between the student organization and Elizabeth's happiness is indirect, but several students gave specific examples of the ways organizational activities helped them find joy and empowerment through helping others. Trent, a gay student at Barents University, told me that his strongest memory at college was his role as one of the chief planners of a huge social gathering for LGBTQ+ students of all backgrounds on his PWI campus.

And just having that space of such a huge event for so many students to like be free and be themselves was new for me. I didn't really have that platform ever in my life to be like, I'm doing this for someone else, and like have that funding and be able to create something that everyone loved. So that being my first experience with doing something, that definitely is going to resonate with me for the rest of my life. And it kind of just brought out that passion I have for like, helping other people and things like that.

The university setting provides Trent with resources he never had access to. He took the resources and acted on his authority as a leader of the student organization to contribute to an event that everyone loved. This was a transformative experience that brought out Trent's passion for helping others and imparted new confidence that if he has the platform, he is capable of doing great things. It is also decidedly queer, in that the event he planned was specifically designed to create a school-sponsored space where LGBTQ+ students could celebrate and mark their time on campus in ways that they could not in high school. Easton, a student at Evergreen, shared a similar reflection on the satisfaction of accomplishment, while emphasizing that his joy in helping others allowed him to conceive of himself beyond his sexuality.

> The things that I really love about being on campus, kind of the freedom as a student to create a space that you feel safe in. I do a lot of things and I like to stay busy. I work for the school as well, I'm a health education specialist. But being a student and being able to lead a organization, help plan events are my joy. I love doing those things because it shows that I'm more than my sexuality, I'm a person that can get stuff done. But stressors would be adult-ing. It can be stressful, but I can say with those around me as you struggle together and lift each other up, I see joy in that as well.

It is not necessary to transcend sexuality to experience joy, but this statement shows that making space for queer joy on campus allows students to experience multiple forms of mundane happiness. Easton is drawn to health education specifically because of his experience as a gay Black man. Like Trent, he is afforded resources by the school to plan events and help others, and when he is successful in these endeavors, his confidence grows and his self-image as someone "who gets stuff done" is enhanced. When he takes a moment to think about the parts of his life that are challenging or stressful, he talks about "adult-ing," which I understood as taking care of all the responsibilities one has to manage when living away from parents or guardians for the first time. But he is able to turn these challenges into joy when he deals with them in partnership with his peers, and they lift each other up.

This chapter began by examining commonplace ideas about LGTBQ+ identity development and the process of coming out. It is well established that coming into the life as a queer Black person is not linear, and coming out is not a one-time, liberating experience that leads to a joyful embrace of consistent and public queerness. Instead of these assumptions about the prerequisites for queer Black contentedness, the interviewees offered ordinary examples of the things that made them happy. Chief among these examples is their indulgence in friendship with their peers. The bonds they forge with their queer Black siblings seem deeper and more meaningful than the friendships in high school. The love and support they feel boost their confidence and provide hope for the future. Everyday indulgence in friendship fits into the rhythm of their college lives, as they build community and carve out space that makes them comfortable on campus. The next chapter, however, catalogs the significant threats and impediments to happiness and safety at college, as students encounter persistent racism and homophobia.

[5]

EVERYDAY OPPRESSION

Trent is a twenty-one-year-old senior at Barents University, a large, public PWI in a midsized southern city. On the whole, he has enjoyed his time in college. He will likely finish his career as an English or writing major, though he began school thinking he would major in business or marketing. He is not sure what he will do after college, but he is confident in his abilities as a leader and team member, largely thanks to the roles he played in LGBTQ+ organizations at Barents. In the previous chapter, he described the mundane pleasures he finds in college: hanging out with his friends and going to the movies. He exuded a reflective, grateful, and comfortable presence as we spoke about his life before, during, and after college. But several times during the interview it became clear that Trent's time at Barents was often difficult, and he was straightforward in his criticism of his peers and his university. When I asked him an open-ended question about his biggest disappointment during his time on campus, he described a particularly arresting incident: "I was walking down the street and someone threw a beer bottle at me and called me the n-word, and, like, just moments like that just remind me, like whoa, I really do have to watch my back. Like, I can't even walk down the street without someone trying to assault me, basically. So it's like, moments like that really remind me of who I am, like, remind me of my skin color and things like that."

Trent came to Barents from a mostly white public high school in a rural part of the state. He and the other Black students at his school were well aware of the racism they faced, as he told me they were watched and disciplined by teachers and administrators far more than their white peers. So he entered college without assuming that he would be treated the same as white students, or that the racism he experienced would suddenly disappear. But what strikes me about this incident is Trent's emphasis on the public and bold nature of this attack. The slur was shouted and the bottle was thrown in a public space, for all to see. The assault was not perpetrated by an authority figure but by a civilian who could very well have been one of his classmates. Trent has found happiness at Barents, but he also feels unwelcome and unlike his neighbors because of their racism. He explained,

> A lot of times, I'm reaffirmed that I go to a primarily white institution, in the ways that they act, in the ways that they vote, in the ways that they express themselves. There's definitely a lot, especially with the election happening while I've been in college, like, the day after the election was like tense. Everyone here, the campus was so divided. You know, you have a big population of people who were like, "Oh, I support Trump." You have people who were like, "Well, Trump wants all these communities out of the country." Like, how can you support that person? And just seeing that divide really made it apparent to me that not everyone here believes the same things or cares about the same things as me.

Much of this book focuses on the Black queertidian as a space for either unremarkable self-making or ordinary Black queer joy. But the opening sentence of this excerpt from Trent alludes to the regularity of Black queer distress and danger. "A lot of times," he says, he is reminded of the whiteness of the space and the divide between himself and others in his community. This divide was exacerbated by the presidential election of 2016 and Donald Trump's implicit and explicit deployment of white-supremacist rhetoric and policy. For Trent and many of his Black peers at PWIs, these feelings of being outcast in a predominantly white community were commonplace. They did their best to build their own communities as shelter from and means to navigate racism, but they could not escape it.

This chapter details the ways racism and homophobia shape students' lives. It begins with my attempt to capture the most common challenges faced by Black LGBTQ+ students at each type of college. One of the tropes driving this book is the stereotype that white spaces may be racist, but they are more welcoming of queer people than Black spaces. The complementary stereotype is that Black spaces are safe from racism, but deeply homophobic. The conversations with students did not exactly reflect these stereotypes, but there were clear differences along these lines.

The second section of the chapter focuses on racism and homophobia through a different lens: students' experiences with racism and homophobia in sex and dating. This is an arena that is somewhat dependent on the type of school each student attends. In some cases, students consider their campus community to be their primary dating market, and in others the campus was part of a larger dating scene with more opportunities, but many of the same challenges. It is important not to exaggerate or generalize from the conversations. There is no single dating market for all Black LGBTQ+ students, but there are common experiences that are shaped by racism and homophobia. Before I outline the commonalities in this realm of college student life, it is important to establish what "racism" and "homophobia" actually mean in contemporary America.

RACISM AT PWIS

Racism is more than just prejudice. It is a combination of hatred, discrimination, violence, and institutions that sustain inequality and injustice, regardless of institutional workers' intent. The phrase "institutional racism" means that schools, neighborhoods, and criminal-punishment and other systems actively benefit white people at the expense of people of color, even when the rules governing these systems are racially neutral. The institutional basis is important because it explains how inequities in health and wellness, criminal punishment, and economic resources between Black and white people in the United States sustain themselves regardless of the "racial climate" of the country or public-opinion data about Black aptitude.[1] For instance, discriminatory mortgage lending and insurance practices enacted by banks and American government in the 1930s institutionalized the Black-white wealth gap through home ownership, property values, and generational wealth. While discriminatory lending practices are no longer legal, the racist outcomes remain because of these established patterns of wealth and residential segregation. Educational attainment is one such outcome. As long as public-school funding is institutionalized by laws pertaining to neighborhood boundaries and property taxes, the racist disparities of our public education system will persist, regardless of the attitudes of teachers and public-education administrators.

Much of the research on racism in the late twentieth and early twenty-first centuries addresses not only how institutional racism is sustained and updated but how racist ideologies are transmitted through American culture. In other words, how do racist belief systems and prejudice survive in a society with a stronger cultural condemnation of public racist expression and action than it offered in previous historical eras? Tali Mendelberg explains that explicit racist appeals in political campaigns, such as endorsements of segregation and insistence on Black inferiority, diminished as social norms of equality and color blindness shaped political rhetoric after the civil rights movement. Those explicit appeals were replaced by implicit and coded appeals, such as the specter of urban crime, that are devoid of explicit racial labels but specifically designed to trigger white fear and disdain for Black people.[2] Eduardo Bonilla-Silva details the phenomenon of "racism without racists," as white people disavow personal culpability and theories of nonwhite biological inferiority, but uphold narratives of Black cultural pathology as an inconvenient "truth" that explains social inequality and their own (racist) personal preferences.[3]

Joe Feagin describes the durability of the "white racial frame," an amalgamation of often subconscious, and sometimes even inarticulable, preferences and assumptions that are disseminated by white elites through structural (for example, criminal punishment) and cultural (for example, media) apparatuses. Among these assumptions are the fallacies that white-dominated societies are civilized and all others are not, white experiences are normative, and racism no longer exists.[4] Feagin and Leslie Picca also document the "two-faced" nature of white racism in America, as white people often profess and feign racial tolerance in public spaces, while maintaining the exclusion and degradation of people of color in "backstage" social spaces, where these behaviors are completely normal and often crucial to white social bonding.[5] And of course, all of these efforts to describe racism in the early twenty-first century are compatible with theories of intersectionality. As explained in the introduction, racism combines with other social forces, like gender and class, to render its meaning and impact. Intersectionality allows for the possibility that oppressed people may be subject to discrimination along a single axis of power in some circumstances, while also subject to discrimination at intersecting axes of power in others.

Donald Trump's 2016 presidential campaign and subsequent presidency upended the assumptions about how comfortable white people are embracing explicit racism in public life. As Mendelberg and others demonstrated, racism was strategically embraced by the Republican Party long before Trump rose to prominence. But Trump was willing to combine implicit appeals with explicit and degrading language, for example, suggesting that the people Mexico was "sending" across the United States border were "rapists," and referring to Haiti as a "shithole country." This combination of implicit and explicit racism is intended to justify racist oppression and cement the belief that America is a country for white people. Trump repeatedly embraced neo-Nazis and white-supremacist militias, whom he called "very fine people" after the 2017 Charlottesville attacks and commanded to "stand down and stand by" during the 2020 presidential campaign. Research shows that this rhetorical turn influences white people's behavior, as racial resentment was the key reason Trump captured white people's votes in 2016, despite the desperate myth that Trump's success could be attributed to populist economic anxiety.[6] According to the Southern Poverty Law Center, the number of white-nationalist, anti-LGBTQ+, and anti-immigrant hate groups in America rose to an all-time high of 1,020 in 2018,[7] and FBI records showed that hate crimes in 2019 reached records not seen since 2008. Black people were targeted more than any other group.[8]

Not surprisingly, racism on predominantly white colleges is commonplace and well documented. Much of the early-twenty-first-century research on this topic reckons with the more covert forms of racism described above. Feagin and Picca's book on backstage racism, for example, is based on the experiences of college students, and myriad studies document the microaggressions students of color are regularly subjected to on white campuses. Microaggressions are "commonplace racial indignities, whether intentional or unintentional, which communicate hostile, derogatory, or negative racial slights and insults."[9] Derald Wang Sue, who developed the term, has repeatedly demonstrated that while microaggressions often go unnoticed or seem innocuous to those who do not experience them, they have ill effects on the academic performance and well-being of college students.[10] Examples of these more subtle, not explicitly hateful provocations might include assumptions that a student is part of a specialized underprivileged or urban cohort because they are Black and/or Hispanic, or being ignored or questioned by campus transportation providers who do not recognize students of color as typical students because they are not white. Somewhere between innocuous racism and explicit hatred are those instances of white backlash to Black progress. Such campus demonstrations and incidents may not directly attack people of color, instead taking the form of affirmations of white "free speech," protests against affirmative action, and other concerns about encroachment on white rights.[11] And finally, plenty of research documents more explicit and undeniable racism directed towards students of color on white campuses, such as the racial epithets and threat of violence described by Trent at the outset of this chapter.[12] As mentioned above, hate crimes spiked during the Trump era nationwide, and FBI data confirm that hate crimes on college campuses followed the same trend.[13] This is the environment Black students at PWIs live in, and my conversations with them contained numerous examples of each of these different forms of racism at locations across this spectrum.

Perhaps most urgently, the students feared for their physical safety and attributed this fear directly to the racism stoked by Trump's campaign and electoral success. Here are examples from two campuses other than Barents, where Trent's n-word and bottle-throwing incident occurred.

When Trump won, there was a moment where I was walking down the street and there is some folks in a big pickup truck, massive wheels, and there's a massive Confederate flag. I've never seen a flag bigger. Just, they were waving it, and there was somebody in front of me who looked Latinx, and they were like, "Go back to your country. This is Trump nation!" And that's not something you can really ignore. Like, people feel safe enough to do that on a campus like this and not get reprimanded at all. (Tamika, Caspian)

I think that there's a lot of polarization here, like specifically on this campus. I think that that's super unhealthy. And it creates a really bad environment. As soon as I stepped on campus, at least, it just, you know that something bad could happen at any time, like, an incident could happen. So I really want to make this place like, more safe and peaceful for all people, not even just people like me, and have less tension. (Kerry, Adriatic)

Two elements of these stories are worth highlighting. First, there is Tamika's observation that the perpetrator carried out the affront without any fear of punishment from authorities at Caspian. This theme was repeated by students on other campuses, especially at Barents, where students told me that two of the most frustrating things about the school's diversity and equity efforts were that the administration repeatedly asked students of color to solve their problems, and interviewees could not recall a time when an incident was reported and the perpetrator faced serious consequences. This brings me to the second point, articulated by Kerry, which is that students often take on the primary responsibility for creating a better campus climate. When she says "people like me," she opens up the possibility that she is foregrounding her intersectional experience as a queer Black woman. But the "polarization" she refers to was invoked as part of our discussion about racism specifically, and students saw political polarization through a primarily racial lens, rather than an explicitly intersectional lens, or one that illuminated divisions along gender or class lines. Chief among students' coping strategies at Adriatic and elsewhere is the creation of student organizations or affinity groups where they can build community and rely upon each other for safety.

On the opposite side of the spectrum, there were students who never expressed any concern for their personal safety but struggled with the anxiety and doubt that grow from repeated racial microaggressions. Two students in different class years and different social circles at Timor University, a large, public PWI, provided poignant examples when I asked them, "What are some of your disappointments or frustrations in college?"

I'm on my predominantly white floor, I think it's only me and this other boy, that is Black on my floor. Every time I walk down the hallway, or every time I just do regular things that they do, I get stares. Like, we had a floor meeting, I think it was on like, the first official day, and we met the RA [resident assistant] and all that. And we all had to go around the room and introduce ourselves, and I had to introduce myself, and everybody was staring at me like I was crazy. Like I was saying my name, what I'm majoring in, and all that like everybody else was doing, but everyone was staring at me like I lost my mind. So that makes me feel uncomfortable. Like that's really, just being the minority. It's hard sometimes. (Ian)

I think when I speak up in class, and the way many of my peers react. It's sort of disappointing. And even some professors. I don't even think they realize they're doing it, at least I hope so, I hope they don't. But yeah, just like sort of like, what you're saying may be an amazing idea, but it doesn't resonate with me, so I'm just going to like, push that idea to the side. So that kind of feeling is just really frustrating, and I just can't imagine what someone who maybe doesn't understand why their reaction might be that way, how they might feel. I'm able to deflect it, because I understand, because I've grown up with that mindset. (Nick)

These are classic examples of microaggressions, where social norms practiced by Black people are treated as social violations not because the action is out of place but because the person is out of place. Ian's example is especially instructive because he describes being stared at, which illuminates the reality of white surveillance of Black people whose deviance is self-evident. The knowledge that you are being watched the whole time is even more salient in light of Snorton's analysis of the hypervisible "glass closet" in which queer Black people reside. Someone like Ian cannot access the premise of privacy that animates the closet/coming-out metaphor when he is treated as an exotic object from the very first day in his residence hall because he is Black and queer. Not surprisingly, Ian reports that these interactions have a damaging effect on his mental state.

While Ian did not tell me that he struggled with mental health issues, during our interview Nick reported that he suffered from anxiety and imposter syndrome. It is not difficult to explain these outcomes based on Nick's account of his time in class, where he makes what he thinks are valuable contributions that are ignored. During our conversation he explicitly attributed this experience to his Blackness, rather than a combination of race, sexuality, and gender expression. He frames these incidents in exactly the way the literature on microaggressions suggests, in that Nick gives grace to those who mistreat him and says, "I don't even think they realize they're doing it, at least I hope so, I hope they don't." The inability to place responsibility for the aggression upon those who commit the act is one of the things that turns the pain back inward and results in self-doubt. Nick had to learn to "deflect it," as he faced different versions of this mistreatment long before he arrived on campus. It is difficult to continually ignore the idea that your college was not founded for you and does not function in ways that support your success. Students described this sense of being an outsider in different ways.

Trent's description at the start of this chapter about the political tension on his campus is not of a sense of complete alienation from the college but of a gap between him and many of his peers that is simply too large to bridge. Trump's rise brought this social and political distance into stark relief, and it is a harsh realization that "not everyone believes or cares about the same things as me." Especially troubling is a further reflection he offered that "there's nothing I can really do about it." The divide is not a temporary rift but something that Trent is constantly reminded of and feels powerless to change. In looking for explanations as to why the possibility of changing the culture seems so unlikely, Naima, a student at Tasman University, called it an institutional problem: "The school is like, it almost functions like a corporation, like a business. So in many senses, like you can tell that the interest is disingenuous, and they're mainly concerned about their bottom line being money. And the way that these institutions function, they're interwoven with white supremacy. This is not a space that's meant for people like me to thrive. It's not built to be conducive to us having great lives. So you have to kind of like, carve out your place in this space."

Naima described her university as one that caters to wealthy white people and treats the finances of their professional schools with more care than they do their undergraduate students. She did not specifically elaborate on her description of the college as interwoven with white supremacy, though over the course of our interview it became clear that she viewed the capitalist pursuit of profit as inherently tied to racism.

The final line of her description was echoed almost exactly by Bruce, who replied in the following way when I asked him in a very open-ended fashion to describe his time at Adriatic: "I was at this play last night called ——, and they were saying, you know, something a lot of students of color feel here, where like you're trying to find yourself against this white background [gestures at the buildings on campus]. . . . 'Cause, like, this space wasn't meant for me."

Students feel like outsiders because the economic mandates of the institutions do not support their well-being and because the culture of the place and physical space is undeniably white. This notion is not only implicit in the functioning of the university, but thanks in part to white supremacists' newfound boldness, students seem to be making it explicit more often. Candace is Bruce's classmate at Adriatic, and she told me about an incident that he did not mention.

> One of the Black sororities here like posted, like painted a wall on our, like, "It's okay to be white," which is like a tagline of like, I think like [white] supremacists. Like there's a certain group, like an alt-right group here that like uses that. And so whenever somebody brought it up in the [sorority's] group chat, people were like, "Whoa, you know, like relax. You know, we don't always have to be talking about politics." . . . You had the choice to decide if you want your life politicized. Which is not true because consistently, Black people, Black women, like even Black students have had their lives politicized.

This harassment exhibits several of the themes contained in the spectrum of racism described above. It is a classic example of the imagined victimization of white people, as the "reclamation" of white cultural pride and freedom of speech are driven by the sense that white people are somehow harmed by the sorority's capacity to engender Black pride and solidarity. The response to the vandalism also exemplifies a type of denialism that Bonilla-Silva and others call attention to. When Black students object to the affront, the logic of color blindness suggests that they, the Black students defending themselves, are somehow guilty of "politicizing" the harassment, or that Black people are the real racists because they are always "playing the race card." Candace, of course, sees right through this sort of gaslighting, noting that only white people could conceive of "politicizing" race as a choice because whiteness is normative. The mere survival of people of color within the American polity is a political act, because the history of the country was predicated upon the genocide, enslavement, criminalization, and legal erasure of Black, brown, Asian, and indigenous people.

Another topic that students discussed in their interviews is the fallacy of the college campus as a "liberal" safe haven for Black people. When I asked Luke, a student at Weddell University, about one key message he would want people to take away from reading the book he would be part of, he said, "I guess college is seen as sort of like an open space, but how for Black queer people, it's not going to be that. It might not be that." The fallacy of liberal white safety was evident in the residential segregation of the geographic area the colleges are located in, not to mention the social lives of students on campus. Queer white student networks and formal organizations might be assumed to be liberal and more welcoming than broader white society, but the students I spoke with had a long list of frustrations with queer white spaces and people. Luke described the feeling of being gawked at by their white LGBTQ+ students, just as Ian and Nick described being stared at in their residence hall and in classes at Wedell. "There are a lot of queer people here but a lot of them are white," Luke said. "And so their sort of attitude towards you, you can sort of sense it, the way they speak, the way they look at you and stuff, it's just, it's weird." When Black LGBTQ+ students try to ignore these microaggressions and take the initiative to keep company with white LGBTQ+ students and join their organizations, their effort often ends in frustration. Ada describes the almost comical missteps that occurred when she challenged the majority-white LGBTQ+ student organization on her campus to commit to antiracism.

That's something I brought to the table with them, was like how to be an ally within the LGBT community to your, you know, people who are people of color in the LGBT community. But they thought that we were supposed to tell them, like we were supposed to represent the people of color within the LGBT community. Well that wasn't the case. I was just like, "Look, like here are some things you all can do to help us out." And then like, it went off topic, and then someone was just like, "Oh, well I said something before and people got offended." And I'm just like, "What?"

And it was just, and they weren't listening, and then like one person just kept saying, like, "Oh, am I being offensive?"

First, the white students in the organization seemed to turn the responsibility for learning about allyship around to Ada and her friends, when it should be their responsibility. When Ada provided suggestions, the conversation seemed to unravel, at least until one of the white students recalled an incident when he offended a group of students, presumably people of color. So Ada's efforts to introduce white antiracism resulted in calls for her to represent her people. Then one of the members explained that their reticence to practice allyship and resulting inaction stemmed from a previous failed attempt when they were accused of saying something offensive. Their white fragility and need for reassurance hijacked the rest of the discussion. This incident is indicative of a broader phenomenon in which Black LGBTQ+ people may be included in white queer spaces, but there are specific expectations placed upon them. Tamika, a student at Caspian University, explained what went wrong between white and nonwhite students at her school: "But there's not a lot of collaboration . . . stemmed from that because of an incident, a racist incident, that ensued, and queer people were just tired, queer Black people were tired of being treated like they were zoo animals. And it was like, 'Oh, can you share your experiences as a queer person of color?' Like, 'I don't feel like it. No.' So they diverged into, and created their own community, and are probably better for it, because racism is everywhere, and that's something else we have to endure."

Racism is everywhere, and it is exhausting to constantly react and adjust oneself to the surveillance, harassment, and prodding. It is especially tiresome for the students when they are repeatedly asked to educate their white peers and share traumatic experiences. But even when Black queer students are not being unfairly put on the spot by their white peers, there is a profound sense of cultural distance. In addition to advocacy, recall that Black student organizations are places where friendships are forged and bonds are made. The glue of those friendships is more than just sexuality or gender preference; it is culture and play. Before Ada described the folly of her introducing the white student to allyship, she told me about the cultural disconnect she felt at meetings of the white LGBTQ+ student organization. It was not just that they were not addressing racism; it was that the things they were talking about did not appeal to her. "It was conversations about anime, cats, and everything in between. So I was just like, 'What in the world?' But then again, I'm like, this is majority white."

Albert, a student at Tasman University, described similar disappointment. "They [the white student organization] would have like, like *RuPaul's Drag Race* events. They were like, obsessed with it. And I'm just like, I don't—I'm not a fan of the show. I just don't like the show." Then there were times when they discussed other topics that might be of more interest to Albert, but once again, there was a racial disconnect. "They would talk about, it would be like, just like really random topics, like dating in the gay community, or something like that. And I'm just like, they don't really date Black people, so there's that." Racism in dating was a powerful theme in the interviews, which I address more fully in the second half of this chapter. But I include Albert's comments here just to emphasize the point that racism touches multiple dimensions of Black queer students' lives at PWIs, even in spaces that one might assume to be more liberal and welcoming.

Overall, students at PWIs are subject to consistent and diverse forms of racism at college, some of which are intersectional, and others of which fall solely upon the racial axis of power. Similar patterns emerged in our conversations about homophobia, which takes on a different character depending on the racial composition of the campus.

HOMOPHOBIA AT PWIS AND HBCUS

It is worth pausing here to unpack the idea of "homophobia," a term that is inadequate to describe the oppression that LGBTQ+ people face, but remains perhaps the most common. The basic definition of homophobia is hostility toward gay and lesbian people. This limits the usefulness of the term in several ways, as it does not directly address hostility towards people who claim bisexual, transgender, and other gender-queer identities, who are often assumed to be included in the targeted group, but have dramatically different experiences. The suffix "phobia" is also misleading in that it connotes fear of gay people, which is not the same as hostility or systemic oppression, and is not an accurate understanding of the phenomenon. In addition to these problems, the word "homophobia" suggests an individual psychological disposition or prejudice, which does not fully explain LGBTQ+ oppression. Like racism, LGBTQ+ oppression is systemic and institutionalized. It cannot be understood, for example, without reference to the medicalization of homosexuality as illness, which continued well into the late twentieth century in the United States; religious condemnation of nonstraight sexualities, which bars publicly nonstraight people from positions of authority in religious organizations; religious and secular laws against sodomy and same-sex marriage, which criminalize the people who engage in "deviant" sexualities and exclude them from the benefits of legally recognized partnership; and the intentional omission of LGBTQ+ people from civil rights legislation for the vast majority of American history. The cultural and psychological habits and prejudices of homophobia grow from, and are complemented by, its institutional base. The "cure" for homophobia and transphobia is not reduction of personal fear or hatred of queer and trans people; it is institutional and legal change in partnership with cultural embrace of diverse expressions of gender and sexuality.

To address these weaknesses, several scholars augment or replace the notion of homophobia with heterosexism, which foregrounds power relations in ways that the word "homophobia" does not. Analyses of heterosexism alert us to the hierarchy of sexualities and the ways their institutionalization concretely disadvantages sexual minorities. This institutionalization takes at least two pernicious forms. In the first case, institutions operate without naming any sexualities other than straightness, in effect erasing people with other sexual identities from existence and/or rendering them socially and politically irrelevant and vulnerable to exploitation and attack. In the second case, sexual and gender minorities are recognized, but are treated as ill, unnatural, and deviant, in need of surveillance and correction. In addition to the material effects, these institutional practices have psychological effects, namely, sexual stigma, which is expressed in outright attacks of sexual minorities by the dominant group, and "self-stigma" felt by those who are marginalized and targeted because of their sexual identity.[14]

Another problem with the thoughtless deployment of "homophobia" as a descriptor of LGBTQ+ oppression is that it distorts the social and psychological *purposes* of anti-LGBTQ+ bigotry. For example, we know that physical and verbal homophobic attacks perpetrated by men on other men are often undertaken in order to assert and legitimize the masculinity of the attacker.[15] Such attacks are not driven by an illogical fear of gay people. In a patriarchal and heterosexist society where manliness is materially rewarded, it is quite logical to assert one's masculinity. When hegemonic masculinity is rooted in domination, there is an expectation that "real" men compulsively prove themselves by denigrating and harming others.[16]

Given the gendered specificity of homosexual bigotry within a patriarchal and heterosexist society, it is no surprise that homophobia plays out differently in social spaces that are not dominated by men. In some respects, women's socialization is less violently homophobic than men's because hegemonic femininity is not dependent on domination, and women are therefore not incentivized to enact and enforce the hierarchy of sexualities in the same ways. Unlike men's empowerment, women's empowerment is often ideologically linked to the rejection of patriarchy, which opens up space for a reconsideration of gender roles and the politics of traditionally heterosexist institutions like marriage. However, women are not guaranteed to be allies in the struggle for LGBTQ+ liberation, and are often willing participants in the institutionalization of heterosexism. At the microsocial level, performances of femininity by cisgender women are often positioned in opposition to queer self-determination. For example, Laura Hamilton's work on college fraternity partygoers shows that straight women enact same-gender eroticism for the pleasure of male onlookers in straight social spaces. These tactics assign lower social value to actual lesbians who do not participate in such performances and further reduce the social spaces where queer women are comfortable on campus.[17] Again, the point here is that such harmful behavior is not driven by irrational fear, as the term "homophobia" might suggest, but by a rational (and unjust) set of social rewards that is stable, predictable, and reflected in institutional life.

Despite these shortcomings, "homophobia" remains the most widely used term for describing the oppression of LGBTQ+ people, even among those who understand its complexity, including the students I spoke with. Black LGBTQ+ students at PWIs did not discuss homophobia with the same frequency or intensity with which they discussed racism on their campuses. When they talked about their experiences with antiqueer bigotry, they often described it in tandem with racism.

Administration, [university president], he is very like, conservative. And when things do happen on campus—I've been in many protests with students from like, the [Black student union], issues about dealing with queer people, and there's not really much addressed. There's a letter sent through email, and it's like, okay, but you never come out personally to talk to the students to hear what it is that they have to say. And so that really bugs me, the fact that he's saying that we're all about inclusion, we're all about this, we're all about that, but there's no action to back that up. (Summer, Caspian)

I do attend a PWI, and so sometimes it's really frustrating to have re-peated incidences of like, blatant racism, and like, blatant homophobia, and no one, at least none of our school board will do anything. It feels like a lot of the times the responsibilities are placed onto the [students] to come up with a solution, when at the end of the day, it's not our jobs, 'cause we're a student first. And where yes, we love making spaces, and yes, we love advocating for the rights of our people, like, it's not our jobs. (Jewel, Barents)

Summer refers to protests that are organized by two distinct groups, Black students and queer students, and Jewel refers to "blatant racism, blatant homophobia." These two forms of oppression can be conceptual-ized and experienced discretely for the groups in question, though still attributed to problems with a single power structure. There are at least two dimensions to the problems they identify. First, there is the fact that instances of blatant homophobia occur. Jewel is not specific about the perpetrators of these transgressions, but it is clear that her PWI campus is not a safe haven for LGBTQ+ people. The second dimension of the problem is that when these incidents happen, the university administra-tion abdicates responsibility, often leaving the students who are most concerned to address the issues themselves or propose solutions to the problem. Research, in fact, supports the notion that authority figures at universities actually do understand that homophobia is a problem on their campuses, but have not created the programs and structures needed to address it.[18] There is a sense among students that the university offers platitudes about tolerance and even fashions itself as a white liberal safe space for people with many different identities, but does not take the action required to support that image. The professed and assumed white liberal ideology of tolerance, both on campus and in the white and supposedly liberal "college town," functions as an excuse for inaction and as cover for recurring instances of anti-LGBTQ+ bigotry. As a whole, the group of students at PWIs did not frequently discuss experiences of direct homophobic harassment or discrimination by students and professors. The overall setting of the university and the inaction of PWI administrators were the primary targets of their frustration.

Students at HBCUs shared many of these concerns. In the introduction, I introduced Remy, a trans student at Aspen, who believes that college administration is on their side but is handcuffed by the traditions, expectations, and alumni of their HBCU. Remy explains, "I can't be in the pageant. I can't be in the Divine Nine. I can't do none of that. And it's all because they have this thing where you have to be, you know, legally female, I guess, sexually female, for like, Miss Aspen. I just had an issue with Miss NAACP, because I was being told by the administration and everybody that I could do it, but the advisor was like, 'You can't do it.'"

The "Divine Nine" are the nine historically Black Greek fraternities and sororities recognized by their umbrella organization, the National Pan-Hellenic Council. There are numerous accounts, both in my interviews and elsewhere, of LGBTQ+ students at HBCUs joining these organizations.[19] So as a matter of legislation, it is necessarily not true that Remy cannot join one. Still, it may be true that the chapters of these organizations on Remy's campus have written or unwritten rules that prevent Remy from joining. Many HBCU students discussed their sense of widely understood, even if unwritten, limitations around the gender-specific social events and organizations they could partake in, such as Homecoming or campus king and queen elections. Patricia, a student at Fieldrose, described an instance when the organization charged with running a pageant added a rule so that a transgender student could not participate and left a threatening note on that person's car. At Cedar, Zoe, who is masc-of-center, explains, "If I wanted to be Miss Cedar, I probably couldn't, because look at me. And it's hard, because you know why it's like that. HBCUs were built on very strong religious structure."

Remy also refers to the Miss NAACP competition as an organization with a formal rule stating that competitors must be legally female to qualify. Remy and Zoe do not lay the blame for this discrimination squarely at the feet of the university administration, preferring to cite historical factors, including the religious roots and traditions of many HBCUs and the bylaws of nonuniversity groups on campus.

Other HBCU students are not so quick to let administrators off the hook. Victor talks about the institutional discrimination that he believes LGBTQ+ people are subject to on his campus and implores his university leaders to do something about it.

> But when you ain't got nothing, you don't know where to start. So programming and creating a space in an organization for them to flourish is the most immediate thing. Also in updating our Title IX policy, because discrimination on this campus is more than just rape. Let's be clear. Like that's something. They need to go ahead, and there's no discrimination policy for LGBT, and no protection for LGBT students, specifically trans folks. . . . If I identify as "Danisha," I should be able to live where I want to live, and where I'm comfortable. It's just that simple. The Black folks make it so much harder than that.

When Victor says, "you ain't got nothing," he means that there is no institutional infrastructure at his college to support the needs and aspirations of LGBTQ+ students. Programming and safe spaces are the bare minimum, but he would also like to see a forward-thinking commitment to legal equity for transgender students. What is striking about this description is that Victor attributes the problem to "Black folks," rather than the individual shortcomings of university leadership or the historically grounded sexually conservative culture of the university. Again, it is clear from the excerpts earlier in the chapter that white liberal culture fosters an environment where homophobia can thrive. The fact that it is often called "liberal culture," rather than "white liberal culture," is testament to the power of whiteness to render itself invisible and assumed. There is no question that white supremacy and homophobia are bedfellows. Having said this, we cannot ignore the cultural attribution—attribution to shared beliefs, practices, and identities of those in the Black community—of homophobia that is present in this excerpt from Victor. He explicitly links the institutional, legislatively constricted oppression to cultural Blackness in ways that are not echoed in conversations about whiteness and racism at PWIs. He did this later in the interview as well, describing a "moment on my first day of classes, even just the way one of my professors was just talking about a young man and how he was dressed was just so [trails off in frustration]. I was like, 'Oh lord, I'm back at an HBCU.'" On-campus homophobia was frequently described in these more personal and cultural terms by students at HBCUs.

> We have a lot of gay students. We have a lot of DL [down low] students who just don't even want to come out because they're afraid of the perception others will have of them. And then there's just a lot of incidences, really prejudiced incidences that I've witnessed here. So being that it is [religious], being that it's Black, being that we're in the South. Even though we're in one of the more liberal cities, you got to also remember a lot of people come from all over to attend this school, and they all have their own perceptions. (Patricia, Fieldrose)

> This being an HBCU, of course there's a lot of Black people here, and a lot of them still haven't got out of that like, "We don't mess with gay people." (Sonia, Aspen)

> There are so many queer people at Birch that I just didn't even know. And I think part of that comes from the culture, sort of forces us out into the margins and forces us to be silent about that part of ourselves. (Ava, Birch)

> I understand being in the closet, but I don't appreciate those that are in the closet but act as if they're disrespectful to LGBTQ+, when in actuality they are the LGBTQ+. I understand it, like especially here at a traditional school so of course they would keep that under wraps. (Cara, Douglas)

Again, these things happen at all colleges, not just HBCUs. Ava's description of LGBTQ+ people being silenced and forced to the margins is not a cultural pattern that is unique to Black campuses. But these students explicitly interpret their occurrence at an HBCU as something that is related to the culture and traditions on a Black campus. Another difference that presents itself in the interviews is the frequency with which HBCU students mention homophobic incidents that took place in class. Students at both types of colleges discussed feeling like outsiders and having trouble connecting with professors and staff. Research shows that LGBTQ+ college students of all backgrounds and at all types of schools suffer mistreatment in class. They may feel silenced during class discussion, rendered invisible by the material covered in their courses, and have trouble forming strong relationships with their instructors.[20] Trent told me, "I don't see myself in my professors and my classes. Like they're mostly like cis straight people, and like, I don't know, I just, I don't ever feel like I connect with them, besides going to class and leaving and doing my homework and things like that." But he and the PWI students did not describe specific incidents where they were targeted, excluded, or discriminated against by professors because of their LGBTQ+ identity. Though such descriptions were not commonplace among students at HBCUs, they were more frequent.

> One of the administrators of student government, like a staff member, not a student, felt threatened by her [another queer student], because they were interacting with his niece, and he was like, "I don't want her to be interacting with a lesbian or anything like that." And so was like, threatening her career in student government, and trying everything to get her kicked out. And at one point did get her kicked out, but then she joined again. And just like, the blatant, blatant homophobia just surprised me a lot. (Jayla, Cedar)

> There should be more acceptance when it comes to gay kids on campus. Like, a lot of people don't feel as accepted as they want to be. And I've realized that, definitely. That's what I'm trying to tell everybody, because there's a lot of discrimination when they go to classes, and you know, a lot of their professors are international, so their culture is different. We definitely need to come to that bridge, definitely, and get this safe zone thing on a roll. (Mitchell, Hickory)

> I had a professor like basically talk me down in front of everybody, and was like, "You know, why are you thinking about this this way?" And

saying, like "Whoa, whoa, whoa! Why are you saying 'bisexual'? Let's not get graphic here." And then he was like, "Well as a heterosexual man . . ." And so me and that professor don't like each other, and it shows that we don't like each other. Then I had another professor who, in this class, it was just some [slides]. And so I'm looking through the PowerPoint, and it says this particular disease is caused by homosexual sexual practices. So I was like, "No, we can't have that in this slide." And so, I went and told the dean about it, and he removed it and he apologized to me. (Maya, Birch)

Taken together, these experiences illustrate several different enactments of homophobia. Jayla and Mitchell report that LGBTQ+ students are prevented from maximizing their potential curricular and cocurricular spaces because of the prejudice of faculty and staff. Jayla reports the fear of a staff member, who is concerned that a student's sexual orientation might somehow corrupt his niece. Mitchell says plainly that gay students are treated differently in class. He does not attribute this to Black culture specifically but implies that some of his professors come from countries that are not as tolerant of LGBTQ+ people as the United States, not that the United States is especially tolerant. Maya's account adds new layers to these issues, as her example illustrates how minority sexualities are imbued with a sense of danger and therefore dangerous to even speak about. In contrast, her straight professor not only speaks about his sexuality but has the privilege to personalize it and claim it as his own. The second example Maya gives speaks to the continued effect of the medicalization of homosexuality as an illness, and the politicization of sexuality as a matter of public health. These dimensions are especially poignant within Black communities and on Black campuses because of the media and political history of HIV/AIDS in the United States, which positioned gay men, and specifically gay Black men, as scapegoats and pariahs responsible for their own destruction.

Importantly, Maya notes that she mentioned the problems she encountered in class to an administrator who was able to correct them, and Jayla says that the student who was initially robbed of her position in student government was allowed back in. So in both cases, it appears there is some administrative force behind the inclusion and protection of LGBTQ+ students at HBCUs. This extends through faculty as well. Though students do not describe overwhelming support from faculty members, there were a handful of stories about specific professors who were indispensable to students because they introduced them to LGBTQ+ organizations on campus, taught material that reflected students' experiences, and became confidants and mentors. Most HBCU students had few regrets about the college they decided to attend, and several students talked specifically about how the different components of their lives on campus combined and resulted in an affirming experience. Eric, a student at Evergreen, told me, "I don't think it's been that difficult. Like, I've actually been really lucky to have very supportive friends, even when I didn't really know myself what I would end up identifying as or whatever, or identified as at the time. Yeah. I feel like the people that, not even intentionally that I surround myself with, like, they've sort of been supportive and helped me even to challenge my own thinking about things. And especially my professors like [a gender studies professor and mentor], like, it's been a pretty transformative, in a good way, journey."

Eric describes circumstances where he does not have to engineer a specific type of social circle to carve out a life for himself at Evergreen. The people he needs in his life just seem to find him without his intent. There is a spontaneity and naturalness to his identity development on campus that simply could not occur if the atmosphere were ceaselessly hostile. So despite the differences between the PWIs and HBCUs that are revealed in the interviews, the LGBTQ+ experience at HBCUs cannot be reduced to stereotypes. There are moments of affirmation, comfort, and joy for queer Black students, and there are moments of fear and rejection. One of the issues that complicates life on campus no matter what sort of college the students attend is dating and sex—dimensions of students' lives that administrators, staff, and faculty do not have a clear understanding of, and certainly lack the power to directly control. But sexual and romantic experiences are a key channel through which racism and homophobia exert their power.

DATING AND SEX

Patricia talked about her rural, southern hometown in chapter 3. She was eager to get away from what she described as a homophobic culture, and she had little experience with romantic relationships until she arrived at college. She explained, "In high school, relationships is just kind of something that never really got explored as much. I guess I didn't really feel comfortable in who I was, my sexuality, like even realized what I truly liked, until I came to college freshman year. I fell in love for the first time. I didn't really know what falling in love was, and I fell in love for the first time, and had my first real relationship, and it happened to be with another woman. And since then, life has been great."

This is an expression of newfound freedom, and exactly the sort of description we might expect from a young person out from under the constraints of a conservative community for the first time, regardless of sexual preference. But it is far from guaranteed that the transition will play out as described by Patricia, who moved quickly from high school hesitance to an affirming and fulfilling loving relationship in college. Queer students in high school navigate intimate relationships differently from their straight peers for several reasons, not the least of which is the stigma of "not feeling comfortable in [one's] sexuality," as Patricia explains. Mitchell adds another layer to the story, describing how difficult the transition from high school to college can be for LGBTQ+ students who do not have the same opportunity to publicly court and be intimate with their peers.

> Someone said that the reason why a lot of homosexuals ghost each other in their twenties and things of that nature, and don't know how to communicate or how a relationship works, is because we've been hiding who we really were when we were in elementary and middle school and high school. And everybody else who were in heterosexual relationships were dating, getting to know themselves and getting to know the other person, and getting to know that opposite sex. But we didn't get the chance to know the same sex who was within the gay community. We didn't get the chance to openly date this person. Some people have, but a lot of us didn't get that opportunity of openly dating our boyfriends in high school or middle school.

I am not suggesting that all queer relationships for people Mitchell's age are fraught or somehow defective. It is not as if straight couples are immune to the sort of communication problems and patterns, like "ghosting," that he describes. The point, however, is that for Mitchell and his queer peers, courtship and trust building are complicated by questions of public disclosure. On the whole, Black LGBTQ+ students are presented with far more opportunities to be the kinds of sexual and romantic beings they want to be once they arrive at college. But their experiences of finding romantic partners and building relationships are shaped by dating markets that are extremely difficult to navigate, whether they attend a PWI or an HBCU. The first problem, according to the students, is that there simply are not enough queer people on campus, which leads to an awkward social and dating scene. Sonia, a student at Aspen, says, "A lot of gay girls, they just really start coming out in college, so they want experience, just like a guy. They want to experience every girl they can. And I think for me, especially at this school, there's not a lot. So it's like, everyone shares."

Naima, a student at Tasman, expands on these ideas, as she discusses the pressure that builds up in such small social and dating circles. In describing the challenges she faces, Naima moves from Sonia's basic description of scarcity to several other problems.

> I've never actually like had sex with anybody here on this campus. But what I hear from other people, it's small. So when you have drama or issues, it's very like, there's a microscope on it. And for queer people especially, you will probably have to date your friends, which is difficult. I don't really want to date my friends, so I just don't date here. But yeah, I think one of the difficult parts is like, I think seeing other people who are, you can't tell if they're queer or if they're straight. And it's like, I don't want to just ask somebody. That's just rude to me. But like, people don't read flirting here well, probably 'cause they lack social skills. Plus, a lot of girls here are like, homophobic. Like, there are some really beautiful Black women here. I think Black women are the most beautiful women on this campus. But unfortunately, you'll meet some people, like, "Oh, you're so cool." You find out they're like a "Hotep," or they're homophobic. And it's like, "damn."

It is worth moving slowly through this passage from Naima, as she describes a plethora of pitfalls. First, there simply are not enough queer women on campus. Second, even if she found someone she wanted to date, Naima would have to weigh the benefits of that relationship with the potential costs of disrupting friendships and being the center of her peers' attention. Again, we get a sense of the hypervisibility of the queer Black experience. Third, she is uncomfortable asking people she does not know about their sexuality. As we will hear from another student, part of this discomfort may stem from the fact that she is a Black woman at a PWI, and the costs of approaching strangers are considerably higher on campuses where Black students are viewed as anomalies and suspects. Perhaps Naima could solve this problem by gently flirting, or picking up on and sending out subtle cues that eliminate the need for awkward conversational introductions. But Naima's description of her classmates' poor social skills makes this impossible, and later in the interview she clarifies that she feels their social awkwardness grows from a troubling shortage of empathy, especially when it comes to racial and gender-identity issues. Finally, Naima prefers Black women, but even those classmates who might share some common ground based on racial identity are viewed with skepticism because of a streak of homophobia among her Black peers; "Hotep" is a derisive term applied to Black people whose Afrocentrism includes an affinity for Black patriarchy and either thinly veiled or blatant sexism, homophobia, and/or transphobia.

Another complication in the market for partners is the fact that many of the folks that students date or hook up with are not comfortable publicly disclosing their sexuality. Jeffrey McCune's *Sexual Discretion: Black Masculinity and the Politics of Passing* (2014) is essential work for understanding the phenomenon of the "Down Low." McCune focuses specifically on examining this trope as it is applied to Black men, who are the most frequent subjects of discussion. Like Snorton, McCune notes that this obsession with queer Black sexuality, and the mass-mediated construction of the Down Low in particular, is part of a long history of surveilling, condemning, and pathologizing Black people and Black sex as dangerous and corruptive. The moral panic about the Down Low is occasionally activated in the name of Black communal self-defense, as a means to demonize Black men for destroying themselves and the Black community through reckless sex and the transmission of HIV/AIDS to men and unsuspecting Black women. Like Snorton, McCune argues that Black men adopt alternative modes of sexual being, namely, "discretion," which is not the same as the culturally loaded caricature of life on the Down Low but serves as an adaptation to oppressive hypervisibilty and a rejection of "the closet," which they see as racist and inapplicable to their lives. Discretion involves verbal and nonverbal cues that move beyond yes/no, gay/straight, opening up queer possibilities for romantic temporality and sex/gender identity.

McCune's work focuses on men's experience in general and the politics of masculinity in particular, as these are essential to the predatory stereotypes that animate the moral panic embedded in Down Low narratives. But both men and women I spoke to discussed the difficulty of navigating this reality in the market for partners.

> They'll have me come to their room, but they'll have me come to their room at certain times of night so where nobody could see. 'Cause like, who's in the dorms [then]? So nobody could see me walking into their room. I was basically, like, hidden, which hurt my feelings, 'cause like at the time, like I said, I [just got out of a] relationship. . . . And it's just like, why am I here? (Taylor, Linden)

> If people aren't at the same point, that's fine, but then that can make it difficult to be in a relationship . . . I'm not much of a social media person, but I do know people who are like, big social media people. They want their significant others to have, just have a picture of us on your social media [and the partner refuses]. . . . So you're not out to your friends. Your friends don't even know you have like, a significant other. That's just difficult, 'cause some people are out and just welcome to that. But if you're not, if you kind of feel like you're like a dirty little secret, or like you're not a real partner. You're just kind of like a shadow. And especially if it's just like, being physical, because you can't go out in public together. (Jonelle, Timor)

Again, students describe the stigma that grows from being "hidden," or "living like a shadow," when queer people live their sexual and romantic lives as secrets. Black queer discretion may open up possibilities for love, sex, and intimacy that would not otherwise exist. But as described here, it is not a romanticized phenomenon or one that is described as indisputably liberating, and it negatively impacts the experience of navigating the dating market. Note Jonelle's nonjudgmental interpretation of these challenges, specifically when one partner wants to keep the relationship at least partially hidden because they "aren't at the same point." Jonelle makes allowances for this reality, because she knows that the cost of public affirmation of one's LGBTQ+ identity varies. Abraham, who spoke about the sense of physical danger he feels on campus because he is gay, also talked about the sense of surveillance and disdain he feels when he is in public with his partner off campus. "I still get looked at for being gay or being with my partner. I mean we rode the bus one time and everyone turned and looked at me and him like, 'Why are y'all on this bus?' Only one person told us, 'Y'all are cute, I'm happy for y'all.' Everyone looked at us so harshly. And the funny thing is, one of the managers from a restaurant from a sister location of my job, he looked at me harshly. We work at the same company!"

Whether we categorize these commonplace slights as microaggressions, insults, or threats, they are a regular feature of life for many Black queer folks who practice public displays of affection. Jonelle knows this truth, so she does not blame her peers who choose not to be as public as Abraham and his boyfriend. But her grace and empathy are not universal within her circle of queer peers on campus. At another point in the interview, Jonelle described examples of her bisexuality being dismissed by gay and lesbian acquaintances who view bisexuality as a form of cowardice or self-deception practiced by people who are afraid to admit that they're actually gay or lesbian. This is treacherous terrain to navigate. There is pressure to be "out" in a homophobic and heterosexist society, but there is also acceptance of discretion. There is grace given by queer folks to queer folks who are uncertain about how they describe their sexuality, but also disdain for specific labels and choices within queer social circles. All these considerations make it impossible to say exactly how these issues affect dating markets; obviously, there is no single dating market that applies to all Black LGBTQ+ people. But one thing we do know is that those who practice discretion, or uphold clear social boundaries between themselves and queer communities, are not simply eliminated or rejected as potential partners. Here is Chris's description of his experience navigating these complexities, excerpted at length. He explains,

> There's gay people on campus, okay. But then there's more than the gay people. There's the people that don't know if they're gay. And then there's

the people that know they're not gay, but they still choose to do what they want to with men. So you're looking at everything as a whole. You're looking at, there's always going to be those men that have that question, have that, "Oh, how is this with a man?" And they contract stuff because of the fact that they're doing both, women and men. So in order to stop that, we need to let the gay community know that, just be aware.

It is worth pausing here to note that all of this exists within the "whole" of Chris's queer dating experience. He does not foreclose the possibility of partnering with folks who affirm an identity other than publicly gay, nor does he pretend that these identifications do not matter at all. To the contrary, he emphasizes the health concerns that may arise because of the culture of secrecy, somewhat in the same vein as the moral panic about the Down Low, but without the demonization of men who live their lives this way. The conversation continued.

MICHAEL: The way you described those different groups, right, so there are gay men who know they're gay and are living as gay men. Then there may be—

CHRIS: Those that are curious.

MICHAEL: Right, curious or questioning, don't quite know where they fall. And then there are others who—I'm going to try and say what you said, so tell me if I'm wrong.

CHRIS: That know they're straight.

MICHAEL: They live as straight, but they have—

CHRIS: Gay tendencies.

MICHAEL: They're intimate with other men.

CHRIS: Mmm-hmm.

MICHAEL: How do you, not you personally, but how does one manage those different kinds of relationships? Is it like, do you treat everyone the same if you see them at a party? If you're talking to someone, you don't ask those questions? Or how do you know, "Oh, he's gay, he's probably gay, but he's not really there yet" or, "He'll never call himself 'gay' but he's still someone that I would talk to or hang out with." How do you manage those relationships?

CHRIS: I feel like it's everybody's preference. And with the men that know that they are not as such, they're going to let you know.

MICHAEL: They'll tell you, "I'm not gay"?

CHRIS: Yeah. Like, "Don't get your hopes up." They may want to [be intimate], but like, don't get your hopes up. "Oh, I'm not gay. I'm not going to be your boyfriend," that kind of thing.

There is no rule book for Chris and his classmates to follow as they navigate the queer dating market. He emphasizes that "it's everybody's preference," once again making a nonjudgmental statement when asked about how queer Black men should manage those relationships. Another striking piece of this exchange is that Chris does not question the labels that men on the Down Low apply to themselves. He could simply label those men as "gay" no matter what they call themselves, and one could also imagine some disappointment creeping into his description of their choices or his interactions with them. But none of this occurred during our conversation, as Chris accepts that those men are straight; they just happen to have "gay tendencies." Another dimension of Chris's and his peers' relationships with men on the Down Low is that openly gay men are approached by people with questions about gay identity and gay sex. Ben, another student at Linden, described how he handles these instances,

BEN: I know a lot of DL people, 'cause like they'll come up to me and ask stuff, and stuff like that, and try to like help them out.

MICHAEL: So what is that like, when that happens? What is that process like?

BEN: I don't know. They always come up to me and like ask me certain stuff, and I just let them know like the honest truth. Like, there's no reason to like hide it or anything like that. Just like, come out. It's 2018.

MICHAEL: So what kind of questions do they ask?

BEN: It's usually like—let me see. 'Cause this happened recently too. They usually ask about like, the sex. "How do you know you're gay? Who's gay on campus?" Usually their main question is usually about the sex.

MICHAEL: What about it?

BEN: Like, "What do you do? How does it happen?" Like, "What's the top and what's the bottom?" Stuff like that.

Again, there is an openness and absence of judgement described by Ben as he talks about interacting with people who are at different points in their exploration of queerness. He endeavors to help them in multiple ways, and one of those ways is having the courage to "come out," which I take to mean publicly disclosing his queer identity. Even though Ben and his peers understand that coming out alone will not offer protection or guarantee happiness, he still views it as a step forward for men who approach him with curiosity about his identity and life. The other way he tries to help folks who approach him is by demystifying and speaking frankly about gay sex. Engaging in these conversations with people that Ben may not know especially well combats the stigma associated with gay sex and may also produce public health benefits alluded to by Chris. Raising awareness about gay men's health is a communal process, one that is often explicitly adopted by LGBTQ+ student organizations, but also by individual members of the gay community in casual conversation.

Many of these challenges with dating and sex described above apply to LGBTQ+ people across all racial backgrounds. Homophobia and heterosexism produce stigma and fear that imbue the dating market with uncertainty and unsteadiness. There are hints of the ways Blackness and racism intersect with homophobia as the students make their way as sexual beings looking for partnership and company. The Down Low is primarily thought of as a Black social phenomenon. As noted above, it became a mass-mediated trope because it prescribed a racial politics that blames Black people for the dangers they confront in their lives. Chris and Ben are not shocked by men who stay on the Down Low or practice other forms of discretion; they just see this collection of folks as a feature of their lives as gay Black men embedded in broader Black communities. Race is an explanatory factor in their patterns of social and romantic life, though they do not call it out as such, because Blackness is the default. Naima invokes race in a slightly different way when she speaks to the homophobia within the Black community at her college. In her case, race is more explicitly part of the description of the dating market, as she implies that the Black community on her campus produces a strain of homophobia. But race exerts an even more powerful force on the dating market than it is described or implicated as exerting by Naima, Chris, and Ben, who primarily touch upon Black behaviors and practices. White racism is a powerful and injurious force that severely limits opportunities and shapes the dating and sexual experiences of the students.

First, Black queer students are frequently tokenized by their white peers. Candace describes the experiences of a friend of hers at Adriatic, who is accepted by white LGBTQ+ students as a political symbol or form of entertainment, but not as someone they would seriously consider dating. "Like sometimes my [gay] friend will be like, 'Yo, like I feel like I'm really unwanted. Like am I really that unattractive?' And the thing is, he's not unattractive at all. Like, he's so smart. He's so kind. Like, he has like great skin and things like that. And the thing is, he's always like, 'I feel like Black queers are there for the entertainment of white queers, and to be able to feel like they're woke, or like they're part of this group that like, you know, really accepts people.'"

In addition to instances where Black people are tokenized and excluded, there are cases where Black people are tokenized and included as exotic objects or dating experiments. Jonelle makes this link clear: "You get the feeling that you're a token within white LGBT communities. So like, I don't like to be in those circles even as like, a dating option, just because I've had some experience now with dating. 'Cause like, the people I know that may have become a romantic partner, or like hearing stories from other Black LGBT people how like dating a white person was like, not necessarily real. Not a fake relationship, but they're really just doing it 'cause you're Black and they wanted to know what it was like."

At this point it is necessary to name the substance of such curiosity. What, specifically is so exotic about Black people that non-Black people often view us as an adventure or experiment in dating and sex? Perhaps it is a more sympathetic form of racist tokenism, where the intrigue and adventure are drawn from the stereotypical radicalism of Black politics or the celebrated style of Black culture. Perhaps for some non-Black partners, the possibility of achieving cultural clout or bolstering one's political resumé attracts them to Black partners. But more likely, the essence of the curiosity is an obsession with Black danger and a sign of the link between stereotypes of Black deviance and sexual power. As Peter, a student at Evergreen, explains,

> I'm concerned about the gay community, because there's racism within already a marginalized group. It's just upsetting. Like I've had moments

where I was on Grindr [a gay social media dating service], and one guy messaged me, and he said, "Let me see your nigger cock." And of course I was like, "Excuse me?" He's like, "You heard me." So like that kind of culture is crazy. Like, this caricature of Black men by white gay men, and how it continues to exist because there's gay Black men who don't value themselves enough. And they play with them, with that entire gross imagery of like this animal-like man, like ravaging someone.

Peter's analysis is especially disturbing because he attributes the preservation of this stereotype to Black men who are willing to play the role of the sexual beast for white pursuers. Of course, Black men are not to blame for the stereotype itself or the white-supremacist ideology that birthed the specter of the Black rapist in order to justify the murder, mauling, and rape of Black people. But Peter hits on something here: attraction and revulsion are two sides of the same coin when it comes to the white-supremacist sexualization of Black people, because they are both produced by the biologically immutable "truth" of Black beastliness. It is no surprise, therefore, that several of the students I spoke with discussed the opposite experience. They were not fetishized by white people looking for partners, but utterly erased and denigrated by them.

I don't know how to explain it really without sounding vain, I guess. But I'm seen as ugly. And the people who see me as ugly are always like lighter-skinned people, more physically fit people, white people. And I know it's coming from a space of like, ignorance. They don't really understand why they're doing that or what they're doing. And so just the way I'm treated, it's really, people don't really see me for like my inner, like for my personality. Or even like, on campus, if there are like other gay men, the way they treat me is sort of weird. 'Cause I remember I held a door for somebody, and he just scowled at me, and I was like, what the hell? Like, what did I do? It's weird. (Luke)

There is blatant racism in the gay dating market beyond campus, which Luke connects to the racism he is subject to from gay white men on campus. He also seems reluctant to blame the perpetrators, much in the same way that his colleagues at other PWIs are willing to brush off the microaggressions they deal with in their dorms and classrooms.

Luke experiences stigma as an intersection of fat phobia and white supremacy, and when he specifies that it can either be white people or
"lighter-skinned people," he indicates that people of color practice similar discrimination. These stereotypes are applied by people of all racial
identities in queer dating markets, which raises an important and often
debated question: Are Black people with these prejudices "racist"? If
racism requires alignment between institutional power and the social
position of the person with the prejudice, then Black folks with these
prejudices cannot be racist. But Black people can hold white-supremacist
views, which manifest here as colorism: an expressed preference for
lighter skin tones that is reflected in racial and ethnic hierarchies in societies across the globe. Black people at all gender locations are subject to
these prejudices. Femininity is associated with softness and whiteness.
Thea reports that darker-skinned women are assumed to be more aggressive, and are therefore stereotyped and viewed as more legible partners within queer dating markets if they perform aggression or adopt
a more masc-of-center style. "Okay, so like when you have like femme
people and like butch people or whatever, they just associate being
femme with like lighter skin. And like, they're supposed to be more soft
and more feminine or whatever they think femininity is. And then when
you have someone who's more aggressive or more butch or whatever,
there's always an expectation of them to be like darker-skinned, and
whatever they associate being more dominant or aggressive with, which
is, I guess, just an overall thing in the Black community too."

Gendered colorism exists throughout Black communities, including
Black LGBTQ+ communities and dating markets. Managing these prejudices in addition to the commonplace exclusion and denigration Black
students experience on PWI campuses is stressful, to say the least. This
final word from Candace gives a more nuanced sense of all the things
running through her mind as she considers her dating and courtship
options.

> At times, like, I wouldn't even know how to come at people. Like, I don't
> know, because of the high population of white women here, I'm like, okay,
> I'm going to stay out of that [dating white women]. But also because I feel
> like not a lot of Black women aren't too open about things like that, and
> it's like, you don't even know who's actually interested. . . . People look at

you like, "Oh, I'm not going to step up to her 'cause she might like, come at me crazy." And it's like, look, I'm in an educational space. I'm not going to act like that. You know? But yeah, with those stereotypes, I feel like a lot of times it's also internalized within Black women to where we feel like we're not wanted. Like, we don't even feel like we want our own selves, so it's like, let me just stay off to the side.

Highly educated Black women find themselves at a disadvantage no matter what dating market they are in.[21] Moya Bailey and Trudy coined and developed the term "misogynoir" to capture the specific forms of violence Black women are subjected to at the intersection of racism and sexism, which cannot be subsumed into the experiences of women, people of color, or women of color.[22] Candace speaks to the devastating power of misogynoir as a force that causes many Black women to feel as though they are unwanted by others and by themselves. While she does not say that she feels this way about her own desirability, she does explain how the stigma and stereotypes of Black womanhood constrain her ability to approach and date other people. Like Naima, who is featured earlier in the chapter and attends a different PWI, Candace has difficulty identifying potential partners and little desire to approach women who are not Black. But even if she were to find someone she is interested in, Candace is afraid that she will be rejected by other Black women who will take offense and be angry that she approached them, which may be read as fear of Black women's homophobia. Finally, Candace feels pressure to perform a politics of respectability because she is in an "educational setting." For most of the students I spoke with, college was precisely the opportunity they needed to explore their sexuality and identity, despite the racism and homophobia they faced on campus. But like Candace, they also reported real costs to being unapologetically queer inside and outside the classroom, and it is perfectly understandable that she does not want to jeopardize her standing in the eyes of her professors or other community members.

The awkwardness and frustration of dating as a young adult are not unique to Black LGBTQ+ people. But the Black queertidian experiences described here elucidate awkwardness and frustration inflected by possibilities, gaps, and excesses of meaning produced by intersectional sexism, racism, and homophobia. Possibilities like partners who practice discretion and may not be able to have public relationships, but are dating prospects nevertheless. Gaps like the racism that separates Black LGBTQ+ people from non-Black queers who tokenize and disparage them as potential partners. And excesses of meaning where racism and sexism combine to produce distinct experiences like misogynoir, which hovers over Black women in straight and queer spaces.

In the first part of the chapter, students reveal just how frequently they are confronted with both blatant and subtle bigotry, even in "liberal" spaces that one might assume would provide a safe haven from such concerns. These confrontations are tragically mundane, and the students believe they are intensified by the election of Donald Trump. While I provided brief descriptions of racism and homophobia as they manifest in our current political era, there are so many beliefs and definitions of these concepts that it would be foolish to think the students see the world in exactly the same way. In the next chapter, students analyze and interpret their experiences.

[6]

CONFRONTING RACISM AND HOMOPHOBIA

On March 26, 2021, pop star Lil Nas X released the video for his single, "Montero (Call Me by Your Name)." X's escapist, family-friendly smash hit "Old Town Road" catapulted him to stardom years before, and when he revealed/confirmed that he was gay after the song's release, the backlash was relatively meek. But "Montero" is a song about gay sex, and answering a lover's call at a moment's notice. It begins with a voiceover: "In life, we hide the parts of ourselves we don't want the world to see. We lock them away. We tell them no. We banish them. But here [Montero] we don't."

The video is a spectacular, subversive, and unapologetic performance from the opening scene, which depicts X sitting under a tree in a fluorescent, psychedelic Garden of Eden. He gives into a different form of temptation than Adam, as he embraces one of the androgynous and not-quite-human creatures of the Garden, which leads to a new scene where X is shackled and judged by gender-bending Marie Antoinette–inspired versions of himself. His sentence sends him upward, toward the heavens, but he grabs a stripper pole and slides down to hell while dancing and performing tricks in nothing but his underwear. Upon arrival down below, he strolls up to Satan and gives him a lap dance, looking seductively into the camera as he grinds on the Devil. The video ends when X steps behind Satan's chair, snaps the Devil's neck, grabs his crown, and places it on his own head. As the cherry on top, X paired the video with the release of a limited-edition customized sneaker, of which 666 pairs were made, each featuring red paint that is purported to contain "one drop of human blood."

Condemnation from antigay religious figures and conservative commentators was swift. South Dakota governor Kristi Noem retweeted the tweet announcing the shoes' release with the statement, "Our kids are being told that this kind of product is, not only okay, it's 'exclusive.' But do you know what's more exclusive? Their God-given eternal soul." X tweeted back, "ur a whole governor an u on here tweeting about some damn shoes. do ur job!"[1] In response to Fox News broadcasters, pastors, and celebrity athletes who criticized him for corrupting young fans, X retorted, "I spent my entire teenage years hating myself because of the shit y'all preached would happen to me because i was gay. so i hope u are mad, stay mad, feel the same anger you teach us to have towards ourselves." *Billboard* praised X for his brilliant marketing strategy, as the song and video exploded across platforms like Spotify, YouTube, Tik Tok, and Twitter in the days after its release.[2] X knew it would trigger blowback from conservative detractors, and he was all too happy to publicly revel in the fact that their criticism was gasoline on his flaming success. But the song and shrewd promotion were not simply fun and games, as X realized the gravity of his project and reflected upon it in a statement he addressed to his fourteen-year-old self on Instagram. The closing sentences of his post are, "You see this is very scary for me, people will be angry, they will say I'm pushing an agenda. But the truth is, I am. The agenda to make people stay the fuck out of other people's lives and stop dictating who they should be. Sending you love from the future."[3]

In the introduction, I noted the unprecedented visibility and acceptance of Black queer celebrities in American popular culture. X did not introduce himself as queer when "Old Town Road" first became a success, but once he publicly announced that he was gay, he did not hesitate to celebrate his own Black queer fabulousness through his style and self-promotion. His visibility and brashness were perfectly acceptable, or at least received without remark by many conservatives, until he fused his fabulous Black queer style with an explicit narrative about gay lust and sex. This is why it is a mistake to observe the rise of Black queer celebrities and interpret it as signifying total, rather than conditional, acceptance; as soon as folks like X explicitly affirm their sexual desires and criticize moralistic anti-LGBTQ+ ideology, they become targets. The controversy swirling around "Montero" is significant not only because it exposes the tenuous acceptance of Black queer fabulousness but also because X is more than suggestive about the roots of queer oppression and the needed response. He is critical of Christian mythology and those who use religion to shame and punish LGBTQ+ people. His agenda is not only to claim and reimagine biblical characters and iconography but to deliver the clear message that others should "stay the fuck out of other people's lives and stop dictating who they should be."

The previous chapter focuses mainly on college students' regular experiences with homophobia and racism, as it details the daily struggle to overcome those social forces and the impact they have on Black queer lives. This chapter, like X's video, moves beyond experience to examine ideology, interpretation, and responses to transphobia, homophobia, and racism. Like X, the students have theories about what homophobia, transphobia, and racism are and where they come from; colonialism and religion are prominently featured. Toward the end of the chapter, their attention turns to solutions and adaptations to these problems, and as with all of the topics we discussed, there is tremendous diversity in the students' approaches and points of emphasis. They do not share a unified theory, and despite the institutional and systemic nature of these problems, there is a persistent call for person-to-person empathy and education as means to address them.

DEFINITIONS AND ROOTS OF HOMOPHOBIA

In the last chapter, I explained the weakness of "homophobia" as a word for the systemic oppression of LGBTQ+ people. First, it erases transgender experiences and diminishes the differences between transphobia and other forms of bigotry. Second, antiqueer hostility is not a purely psychological phenomenon rooted in fear; as the term suggests, it is a behavioral manifestation of institutionalized patriarchy and heterosexism. My conversations with students illuminated each of these dimensions, and when I asked them to reflect on the roots of homophobia and antiqueer bigotry and oppression (including trans oppression), they emphasized both the individual, psychological elements and the institutional and historical roots. One of the strongest themes of the interviews is that homophobia is rooted in perpetrators' insecurity and revulsion at their own sexual desires and/or gender identity. As Paige says, "I just think people who are homophobic are insecure, maybe. Because if you are confident in yourself, you would know that this person can't change you, or this person can't do anything to make me feel like I'm uncomfortable." And when I asked Cara to explain homophobia, she rejected the concept entirely. The idea of "homophobia" is a fallacy, she says. "I don't think homophobia is a real thing. That shit does not exist. What about me is making you scared? I feel like that whole thing with homophobia is you're not comfortable with your sexuality, and that's not my problem. I don't believe in homophobia. It's the fear of something. That doesn't make sense. You have a fear of gays? It doesn't make sense."

One of the powerful elements of Cara's definition is that she reframes oppression of LGBTQ+ people as the oppressors' problem rather than the victims'. This is not only a clear-eyed diagnosis of the trouble and those responsible for it; it may also provide queer folks with protection from stigma and the sense that they have to fight the battle every single day. Another point worth noting is that when Cara says "gays," she refers to both men and women, as she did not make a distinction between antigay bigotry practiced by people at different locations on the gender spectrum. Some students, however, clearly associated homophobia primarily with men, which echoes several of the points raised in chapter 5 about the compulsive and abusive demands of hegemonic masculinity. Jafar and Brandon offer strikingly similar explanations.

> I think that definitely comes from insecurity. I feel like there are a lot of people, like men specifically, who aren't comfortable with themselves or their gender expression, identity, sexuality, whatever. I know a lot of men who maybe want to wear certain things, but they're afraid of how they're going to be judged, or maybe men who are interested in trying something else, and they may feel judged. (Jafar)

> I feel like the guys that speak more about it or are more homophobic, they try to like, bash the gay community, they don't want those who are in that

community to out them, or whatever. You know what I mean? I just think they're scared. And there's nothing to be scared of. It's your life. You only live once. (Brandon)

Recall that Brandon recounted his experience with men who were interested in gay sex but did not claim any sort of queer identity. During that part of our conversation, he expressed no resentment and little judgement of people, and the absence of resentment is significant here as well. It might seem like a natural response to meet hatred with hatred, that is, to express anger toward those who might degrade and attack you. Several of the gay men I spoke with made it clear that they would stand up for themselves and their friends and physically defend themselves if threatened, but this is a posture of self-defense, not resentment. In the examples from Jafar and Brandon, manhood is embedded in the definition and experience of homophobia because they most frequently encounter it through their interactions with men. But Cat places patriarchy at the center in a slightly different way, as her explanation for homophobia is not about what men think and feel but about men's social and political control over women. Homophobia is not simply practiced by insecure men; it is produced by masculinity and patriarchy. She says, "Homophobia and all these problems also goes back to a dislike of women and femininity, and extending control that patriarchal societies . . . have over women to individual people and women. And then moving into specifically a gay identity, just seeing something that you're not used to seeing, and you're not used to seeing it because society makes it that way."

Toward the end of this analysis, Cat alerts us not only to the mandates of political and social control but to the ways those mandates are experienced as customs, or things people are "used to seeing." Homophobia, therefore, becomes a social comfort that is endemic to the socially constructed man/woman binary. Albert foregrounds that binary in his explanation for homophobia, which he says is a disgust caused by the destruction of the binary and the undeniable reality of queerness. "I would explain it in terms of like, symmetry with men, women, men like women. It's very like, how do you call it, like matching pairs? That's kind of like how the world is framed in matching pairs. . . . Queer-phobia or transphobia kind of like arises from a disgust with like not exactly having those things aligned, or being like, you are breaking the societal rules, therefore you are deviant, therefore you are bad."

Homophobia is not just an individual prejudice; it is a society's response to its rules being challenged and disproven. To disguise the *sociopolitical* nature of the queer threat, patriarchal and heterosexist societies respond to threats by insisting that queerness is an *individual* sickness that must be controlled, punished, or rehabilitated. Albert's analysis raises questions about which "societal rules" he is talking about, and where they come from. At this point, as Thea tells us, we can no longer ignore the racial and religious roots of American homophobia. She insists, "Homophobia came from like European and white communities, and there was nothing wrong with that in our communities until colonization happened. But I don't think a lot of people realize that. . . . I don't know what it's rooted in, but I feel like in the Black community, it's just like, rooted in a lot of Christianity and religious stuff that was also fed to us by white people."

In order to unpack this explanation, we have to establish what is known about the relationship between religion and heterosexism.

RELIGION AND HETEROSEXISM

A 2019 study based on survey data from fifty-five countries around the world found that "every dimension of religiosity has a positive relationship with rejection of homosexuality." People who identify as religious and adhere to a specific denomination reject homosexuality more strongly than those who do not, and high frequency of attendance at religious services is also linked to stronger rejection of homosexuality. Those who believe their religion is the only true religion also hold more negative views about homosexuality than those who do not.[4] It is important to note, once again, that homophobia and transphobia are not the same phenomenon. But a different 2019 study found "consistent evidence that self-identifying as either being 'religious' or as Christian (and to a lesser extent, being Muslim) was associated with increased transprejudice relative to being nonreligious." That study also found that specific forms of religiosity, such as fundamentalism, religious service attendance, and literal interpretations of the Bible, were linked to stronger prejudice directed toward transgender people.[5]

These effects are not limited to straight people. In support of the evidence that one of the results of institutionalized homophobia is pernicious self-stigma among LGBTQ people, research suggests that embeddedness within nonaffirming religious cultures and institutions is associated with higher internalized homophobia for LGBTQ people of all backgrounds.[6] Consistency across racial difference is important because it challenges the stereotype that Black churches are unique in this regard, and numerous studies suggest that white evangelical churches are the most antiqueer worship settings in the American political landscape.[7] But the students interviewed for this book do not have experiences in white evangelical churches, as most of their time spent in organized religious settings occurred within "the Black church." In the United States, "the Black church" is understood as Protestant churches with mostly Black American congregations. The Black church serves as an incubator for Black liberation in thought and practice, as it institutionalized the Black American prophetic Christian tradition, trained many of the most prominent organizers and soldiers of the civil rights movement, and served as a "counterpublic" space for developing political ideas and strategies outside the white gaze.[8]

Several elements of the Black church experience distinguish it from white American Christian institutions, most notably its grounding in Black oral traditions, which reverberate from the pulpits to the pews via the cadence, music, calls, and responses of the church leaders and their congregation. Black churches are distinguished not only by the sound, style, and rhythm of their congregations but by the substance of their speech and beliefs. A 2021 Pew survey found that Black Protestant churchgoers are more likely than any other group of churchgoers to say they have heard sermons about politics and race. Furthermore, opposing racism is "an essential religious issue for most Black believers," as 75 percent of Black Protestants and 77 percent of Black Catholics affirm that rejecting racism is essential to their Christian identity. This is not surprising, given that 71 percent of Black people without any religious affiliation say opposing racism is necessary in order to be a moral person, but it is noteworthy that church attendance seems to intensify that commitment. The Pew survey reveals similar findings when it comes to gender politics, as roughly 70 percent of all Black Americans affirm that opposing sexism is essential to being either a moral or a faithful person.

However, Black Americans who attend church "at least a few times a year" are far less likely to hear sermons on sexism than on racism.[9]

These gendered cracks in the moral authority of the Black church are consistent with Snorton's argument that the Black church has served as "the primary location for the maintenance and perpetuation of Black respectability politics."[10] As one student, Mitchell, told me, "We always had the choir directors that we knew was gay in the church. But guess what? They never was in the pulpit preaching, and they never will be, because that's not what the Black church wants." Homophobia within the church springs not only from interpretations of the Bible and religious customs but from a moral panic about the destruction of the Black family. The violence enacted against Black people in America to this point in the country's history ensures that Black family structures will not mirror white family structures. This does not mean, however, that Black people do not value, build, and protect their families. The notion that Black people are too irresponsible to uphold family values is a racist trope and explanation for Black cultural pathology that has long shaped both religious and secular analyses of Black suffering. Restoration of Black manhood, and Black womanhood in the service of Black men, is often cast as the solution to Black pathology,[11] and it is therefore no surprise that the most visible, powerful, and wealthy figureheads of the Black church have been men throughout American history. The virility and necessity of Black manly holy work enables the bombastic style of Black preaching and spiritual performance. If the pastor is flamboyant, it is not because he has gender trouble; it is proof of God's awesome power to move and speak through ordinary men, making them extraordinary in the process. Snorton observes that the spectacular, attention-grabbing style of the Black (male) preacher has the additional consequence of making the Black church look and feel more intensely homophobic than other religious spaces because of how homophobia is expressed.[12]

Joseph Sorett notes that Black church leaders and congregations are not a static bloc, and Black clergy often speak out in support of LGBTQ+ rights and dignity.[13] They may, for example, specifically speak out in favor of marriage equality and implore their congregation to recognize everyone's inherent value as a creation of God, regardless of their sexuality and/or gender expression. Many Black clergy follow these affirmations to their logical end, which is that there is nothing deviant or unholy about being queer. Others, however, affirm LGBTQ+ personhood and rights while explicitly or implicitly condemning queer sexual behavior. For them, the notion that gay sex is a sin and that gay people should be reformed is not incompatible with other gestures toward gay people's dignity and divinity.

While homophobia in the Black church may be misinterpreted and wrongly cast as exceptionally severe in comparison with other religious traditions, its intensity, when expressed, cannot be denied. Keith Boykin writes that the Black church is both the most homophobic and the most "homo-tolerant" institution in the Black community, with a "don't ask, don't tell" policy that is "killing us as a people." Without its LGBTQ+ congregants, Boykin argues, the Black church could not function, and "that's why nobody ever asks them to leave. Instead they beat them down in the hopes that the gay members will not become strong enough to challenge their own oppression."[14] Snorton, Mignon Moore, and others note that the conditional acceptance of LGBTQ+ churchgoers requires a form of sexual passing that is cemented by exhortations that we "Love the Sinner, Hate the Sin."[15] This disingenuous dogma does not convince or protect Black LGBTQ+ congregants. Research shows that they understand the links between homophobic religious rhetoric and the violence directed toward queer people in everyday life.[16]

For the students I spoke with, religion is the dominant explanation for homophobia more generally and Black homophobia specifically. Homophobia is intersectional, and the students are embedded in Black communities. On one hand, students describe specific, personal experiences with Black religious homophobia, as Trent says, "When it comes to homophobia in the Black community, I feel like it's definitely backed in kind of like religion and upraising. I know I come from a family that's very Baptist. My mom took me to church every Sunday for like fourteen years, sat in the front row, you know, all that stuff, talk about how being gay is a sin. . . . And growing up, that's kind of what made me like hesitant to ever come out."

On the other hand, several students communicated a more abstract sense of the white-supremacist roots of homophobia more broadly. For students like Jace, American homophobia across racial groups is a product of colonization and institutionalized racism.

I think it comes from religion. I hate religion. No. I don't hate religion. I hate the people who created it. I think that people have historically used religion to manipulate the stupid. They've taken advantage of the uneducated. I think that it's weird. I think Black Christians are weird. I don't get it. I would be more religious if Christ or Jesus was Black, if he was believed or perceived to be Black. But as it stands, Christianity by default is a white religion. And I think that through that, so many negative values involving queer phobia and racism and tyranny and, you know, dominating the minority, all those ideas, are forced and shoved into our mindset through religion.

These are long and short histories of homophobia. In the short history of his life, Trent identifies his time in church as the root of his family's homophobia and his own self-stigma. In the longer history of human civilization, Jace describes a pattern of manipulation and ignorance that is intensified by the whitewashing of Jesus Christ. He is particularly incensed that Black people adopt religious homophobia so frequently, given how obvious it is to him that Christianity is a tool to control Black people. Kelly Brown Douglas further develops this argument in *Sexuality and the Black Church* (1999), where she explains that white people continually define and denigrate Black sexuality because doing so is essential to white economic and political domination. Douglas laments that too often, Black religious resistance to racism includes the adoption of white-supremacist repression and condemnation. A more sensuous understanding of the body, beginning with the body of Christ, is needed in order to advance Black sexual and religious liberation.[17]

Both Jace and Trent affirm that religion is used as a weapon to attack queer people. They have personally experienced these attacks, but it does not take someone who is LGBTQ+ to confirm their frequency or how harmful they are. Famed gospel singer Kirk Franklin laments, "They do not understand, sometimes maybe the biology of homosexuality, and so they want to find a scripture to try to justify their own homophobic views . . . you can't abuse people from a platform, because that ain't love, that's not the gospel, to take a microphone and weaponize it to hurt people and to condemn people."[18] The students echo this analysis with specific reference to the role of the Bible in the weaponization of Christianity against queer folks.

It's people trying to use religion as a weapon against other people, honestly. I just feel like a lot of people that I know that are anti-LGBTQ+ or something, they always have a kind of religious aspect to them. They always quote specific verses and stuff from the Bible that just help their cause, but they don't think about every other thing that says, like the Bible says not to do. (Roland)

Religion is more legitimized. That's why more people believe that "this is fact," and "this is not right," and "I know it's not right because of this Scripture right here." So I think we also have to remind people that this is made from humans. Like, this is not like the word of God per se, even though it's what you believe is. (Camila)

The preceding statements affirm religion as foundational to respondents' experiences with homophobia. They also identify the historical roots of the problem, and point to human beings' role as manipulators and interpreters of sacred texts and teachings. It is not simply the religious institution that produces homophobia; it is the human behavior and social construction of religious life that does so. Though they experienced homophobia throughout their childhood, at the time of the interviews the students were young adults. They analyzed these root causes and reflected on how their individual experiences were part of a larger and more complex social tapestry. They also reflected on the specific forms religious homophobia had taken in their lives, and the ways they had reacted and adapted to it. Madison understands her family's homophobia beneath the umbrella of its patriarchal rules and conservative aspirations.

My family is Haitian. And so it's a very conservative, patriarchal, conforming sort of culture. And religion is a big thing, so it's the very strict version of religion, of man with woman, of woman serves their husband, and has children and all this stuff. Yeah, so they're very stuck in their traditional, old-fashioned beliefs. Like it's an issue just to not be married, let alone to be in a relationship with someone of the same gender as you. And I have sort of seen people be, in my family, be homophobic, and they did try to raise me that way as well, which I think also is why it took me so long to be open and comfortable with my sexuality.

This sounds like the "family values" espoused by many conservative American politicians and white evangelical proselytizers. It is vital to understand that religious homophobia retains its value and usefulness not only because it is a compelling ideology with a mythic and spiritual history but because it attaches itself to forms of individual and collective identity that people hold dear. It is one thing to rebel against one's religion, which, for some, resides mostly in the realm of otherworldly belief and fate, somewhat separate from day-to-day life in the here and now. But for Madison and others, faith is a daily family matter, not just an abstract debate about our ultimate end. Embracing her queerness is a challenge to faith, national and ethnic identity, the family unit, and the actual people in her family. Doing so has the potential to ignite a generational crisis among those who raised, love, and care for her, as Sonia makes clear.

> The religious part of it is another thing that kind of steered me away from being 100 percent honest with myself. I even tried to date guys to try to, you know, change that. But being a preacher's granddaughter, not so much the school, but just that part, the family part, kept me from expressing it. . . . When I got here, I talked to a guy, kind of forcibly, because I was trying to change myself, and I was like, thinking like, the religious part would be like, "Okay, I'm not going to get to go into heaven. God's not going to accept me if I'm like this."

For Sonia, breaking away from one's parents and grandparents in this way seemed like a more painful choice than pretending to be someone she is not. There is a profound fear not only of familial condemnation but of spiritual condemnation. This is linked to the motivation of the family members, who steer young people away from queerness because they think it might spare them some pain. Several respondents told me that their kin's religious warnings against queer tendencies were intended as a form of care and love. For Mitchell's mother, the world is too racist and hostile a place for a Black man to indulge in the danger of queerness: "And I remember when I came out, my mother actually told me, she said, 'You already Black. You already a Black man. You already got two things going against you. You gonna add gay on top of that, too?' And that really pissed me off."

Recall that the Black church remains a central space in Black communal life because of its protective capacities. It is, in many ways, a safe harbor for "real talk," political education, and the cultivation of Black beauty and joy. The walls of the church sustain and shelter Black people and enable our survival in a worldly sense, setting spiritual implications aside. But the material, political, and protective functions of the church are inseparable from its structural inequalities and limitations. These institutional prejudices are embodied by congregants, who, as part of their pledge to protect each other, warn their children about the real-life dangers of Black queerness. The students' reactions described above are predictable and well documented: they are saddened, ashamed, and, like Mitchell, angry.

But Black queer folk do not just walk away from church or jettison their religious beliefs. Many Black LGBTQ+ people do not just tolerate the Black church; they love it, because it validates spirituality, sensuality, and the expressive and erotic dimensions of their lives. In Darnell Moore's memoir, *Ashes in the Fire*, he recounts attending church with a gay friend the day after a suicide attempt and feeling that he had truly found God. Ten pages later, he describes how that spiritual breakthrough led to a deeply religious and sexual relationship with that friend, whom he prayed with and made love to.[19] Moore, like so many gay men, found a home in the church choir, which, as E. Patrick Johnson notes, "is a space for talented, expressive gay men that validates their religiosity, provides community, and allows them to express the public secret of their sexuality."[20] As Monique Moultrie's research on faith as a site of Black lesbian activism shows, Black queer people do not merely find space within the church; they engage the church and its congregants, pursuing affirmation and liberation through forced collisions of faith, politics, and sexuality.[21] Similarly, Terrell Winder's interviews with young Black gay and bisexual men show that they repurpose religious messaging to justify their sexuality, explain inexplicable and ordinary occurrences in their lives, and create new religious communities.[22]

Sonia and Amir's descriptions of their relationship with God is a good starting point for illustrating how the students navigate conflicting feelings and experiences with their religion.

He knew me before I knew myself, so He know what was going to happen, regardless of what anybody else thinks. So how can I sit here and be like, "I'm going to go to hell," like, "God's not going to love me." He loves you regardless, and that's what I've always been taught and that's what I know. So knowing that, I was just like, "I'm fine." Like, I can be myself, 100 percent. And that's not to say I'm going to go and get married in a church, to a woman. But I don't feel like there's a conflict between my relationship with God and the lifestyle that I live, at all. (Sonia)

I kind of have second thoughts about being someone who likes same sex and goes to church and stay active in church. But in those moments, I remember the stuff that I was told. It's like, God is gonna love you regardless, 'cause he's God. And he wouldn't make you a certain way, and make you feel uncomfortable about it. So when I have those moments, I'll be like, "You know what? God, you made me." I feel like I still leave everything in God's hands. . . . I'm still going to love and serve God regardless. (Amir)

It is important to respect the difficulty of the journey that led these students to this place of relative comfort. Amir, for example, encountered mental health issues as he grew into his identity, and when he tried to address them with his parents, they were unsupportive and reliant on their religious beliefs in their arguments with their son. Instead of completely rejecting religious teachings, however, Amir relies on them. He specifically relies on the beliefs that God made him, that God is in control of his life, and that he remains a loving servant of the Lord. These long-held beliefs about *God* are affirmed in contrast with his relationship to *the church*, as Amir questions his place as someone who attends church and remains active in that setting. Sonia says something similar, when she reflects, "That's not to say I'm going to go and get married in a church." Setting foot in that particular structure is not an affirming experience. But Sonia's issues with the church cannot diminish God's omnipotence and omniscience, as she, like Amir, affirms what she was taught long ago. "He knew me before I knew myself," she says, "so he know what was going to happen, regardless of what anybody else thinks." God's knowledge and power allow Sonia to feel loved and give her license to live the way she wants to. The church does not control her relationship with God.

In discussing their beliefs and relationship with God, Amir and Sonia make it clear that they are rooted in the Christian tradition in which they were raised. They do not describe themselves as leaving their religion or practicing a new one; they are selectively embracing the tenets of their home tradition and distancing themselves from the institution. Other students, however, are not so attached to the faith traditions they were raised in and are more adventurous about finding their own. While they describe a similarly personal relationship with God, they do not understand it as part of what they were always taught by family members and other religious mentors. Deron, for example, specifically describes rejecting the scripture and embracing his own personal spirituality.

> I used to try to like read Bible scriptures and like make myself better. That did not work. . . . I'd say as far as like claiming a religion, I don't have one, but I am very spiritual. I do believe there's a God and stuff like that. But I didn't believe what everybody else was saying about God and how he hates gay people. He loves me. 'Cause if he didn't love me, I wouldn't have survived it from birth, 'cause I was a preemie, three and a half months. Like, I was two pounds and like, five ounces. I was not supposed to make it, and here I am today. I know somebody out there looking out for me.

The Bible is not rehabilitative, and it seems as if everyone who discussed religion with Deron as he grew up had the same homophobic message. Deron's belief in God's protective love is grounded in the odds he overcame as someone born prematurely. He is less focused on explicitly validating his queerness through his relationship with God, as he does not say, "God made me gay, and He doesn't make mistakes." Rather, Deron says, "God made me, and I know I am blessed." He is not quite sure what to call this relationship with God, though Deron knows he is a spiritual person.

Michael Arceneaux, author of *I Can't Date Jesus*, speaks to the turmoil articulated by the students. He was raised by his mother, and he knows she would not have had the strength and persistence she embodied without her investment in Christianity. "Some of us learn sooner than others how vital it is to have something to believe in," he writes. "For that reason alone, I will always have a respect for the purpose of religion. I just wish the religion I was raised in was truly more accepting of queer people."[23] In the absence of such acceptance from the Black Christians he is closest to, Arceneaux reflects on his choice not to engage deeply homophobic believers in discussions and arguments about his status as a gay Black man. He prefers to walk away, and does not feel compelled to return to his faith tradition or the institutions that steward and promote it. Several students describe their departure from their faith traditions and ongoing efforts to find or build something new. Camila and Ava also discuss taking religion into their own hands.

I'm still in a point where I'm trying to figure out everything for myself and myself alone. I just think that because I have that Christian background, I can't ever totally be myself with my family, just because they just automatically have assumptions about who I am, where I belong because of that. So I think that I've had to take religion into my own hands and kind of make it completely my own in order to feel comfortable. (Camila)

I definitely don't believe in the same system of rules, and I don't even think that I believe in the same sort of god that my parents did or do, 'cause my god doesn't have a problem with me. My god doesn't care. My god sort of focuses on who I am as a person and how I am living a godly life. And so for me, I still have issues sort of with identifying as Christian, even though I still pray. (Ava)

The similarities are striking. Camila and Ava cannot reconcile their Christian upbringing, which is tied to their familial relationships. Ava, in particular, has a birth family that is completely devoted to their church, so it is no surprise that when she left for college and distanced herself from them, she stopped attending services as well. She has actively researched and dabbled in other religious practices, including Islam and Buddhism, but does not consider herself to be part of a single established religion. She still prays to God, but it is *her* God, rather than the God she was raised with.[24] Like Madison and Jace, Ava is highly critical of Christianity because she cannot ignore its connections to multiple forms of oppression, such as patriarchy and colonialism. She does not feel pulled toward reconciliation because she does not want to reintegrate herself into a community of believers that cannot come to grips with its own complicity in, or at least relationship to, these injustices. Racism is, of course, part of the fabric of this history, and students bring their analytic lenses to bear on this social problem just as urgently.

DEFINITIONS AND ROOTS OF RACISM

The racial categories we have today were born during the eras of European colonialism and transatlantic slavery. Those projects—colonialism and slave economies—were tied to the expansion of capitalism. Indigenous people were killed so that land could be seized and transformed into a resource for growing the raw materials needed for international trade. Black people were enslaved, sold and treated as property, and used as the asset base for the earliest days of the American credit system. People had long been divided into groups, stigmatized, and exploited as laborers to line the pockets of wealthy landowners in Europe and elsewhere. But race, as a supposedly scientific and immutable biological fact, was theorized by anthropologists and, later, codified by scientists to justify and explain a global social order that placed white Europeans at the top and people of color beneath them. Though the categories have changed and the scientific basis for race has been disproven, contemporary racial hierarchies serve the same purposes. They organize labor markets, provide convenient explanations for dispossession and violence, and legitimize our capitalist social order.

Racism is both institutional and ideological. Though commonplace understandings of racism frequently focus on individual prejudice, that was not the understanding most often invoked by students. Nor were references to the intersections of racism with sexism or homophobia common during these portions of my conversations with students. They describe themselves and the communities they belonged to with frequent reference to gender intersectionality; they are especially attuned to the differences between Black and white LGBTQ+ communities, for example. But when it comes to the definition of racism, they discuss it mostly in isolation from gender oppression, but with far more reference to class and economics. When asked to reflect on what racism is and where it comes from, many students insist that it is connected to capitalism. Victor says,

> Racism is nothing without capitalism. Racism is not this basic ass thing that we do in the South that is just based upon color. No. Racism is embraced by capitalism, which obviously has an economic advancement over another race. . . . America was founded on the basis of capitalism,

they already came here with stuff that we didn't have. We're nothing. And not only that, but we were also a form of their wealth. The more of us they had, the more wealthy they were. . . . That's why when I tell people racism is nothing without capitalism, because I have to be able to capitalize off of somebody. That's why I can't be racist.

This analysis speaks to both historical and contemporary understandings of racism. First, his comment about the trivializing of racism as a form of southern backwardness demonstrates his awareness of how racism is cast as a southern stereotype intended to absolve nonsoutherners of their complicity. Second, he affirms that America was a colonial project that required the bondage and dehumanization of Black people as an economic necessity for white people's freedom and prosperity. This dehumanization and enslavement were not incidental; they were compulsively required for the country's economic development and white people's further accumulation of wealth, so much so that sharecropping and unpaid prison labor continued after the Civil War and the Emancipation Proclamation. The implications of this truth are not just historical but definitional in a contemporary sense. Racism works in similar ways today, and the label of racism cannot be affixed to Black people who "cannot capitalize off of somebody." Albert, too, traces racism back to the slave trade and insists that Black people are at the center of the definition of racism. "Anti-Blackness started from the slave trade, which thereby kind of created symbolic attachments toward Black flesh that were pretty much the antithesis of what it means to be human. And yeah, ever since the slave trade, things have just been different in the world. . . . In America, we would say, I would say that anti-Blackness is the root cause of all racism, because it kind of creates people who are fully human versus people who are like not really human."

Racism is a combination of prejudice, discrimination, violence, and institutions that reproduce racial inequality and injustice, regardless of intent. Our schools, neighborhoods, and criminal-punishment system actively privilege whites at the expense of people of color, even when the rules governing these systems are racially "neutral." Anti-Blackness is not simply about hating or penalizing Black people. It is about the debasement of Black humanity, utter indifference to Black suffering, and the denial of Black people's right to exist.[25] As Albert says, the dehumanizing ideas that are symbolically attached to Black people made the slave trade possible. The rupture between Blackness and humanity was required in order for the institutional economic infrastructure to be built and refined over centuries. Racism, even in a country with a political culture that rhetorically embraces multiculturalism and diversity, is durable because Black dehumanization is its sturdy foundation. So long as Black people remain at the bottom of the hierarchy, non-Black people derive status from Black oppression and can take comfort in the fact that they are not Black, even if they too are discriminated against and exploited. Camila says, "I think it comes from a very human need, like that is across all races, all nationalities, to feel superior. And I think that it's very human to create an 'us' and 'them' mentality, and to oppress. And I think that because it's such a human urge, even if people think that, 'Oh, I'm not racist, da-da-da-da,' they aren't really willing to give up that kind of privilege and that power that they have. So while they're not directly being like, 'I hate Black people,' like, they're also feeding into it."

This makes it hard to imagine a scenario where all people, but especially white people, will give it up, as Parker describes: "I think racism exists because of colonialism, because it's profitable. It's always going to be profitable to oppress people. I don't think anybody who's in these positions of power want equity and equality, because then there would be no profit. It basically like, fell into white people's lap, and they're like, 'Well, we're not giving this up, absolutely not.'"

Charles Mills explains that not all white people have to be signatories of the "racial contract" that enables white-supremacist and capitalist exploitation, but all white people benefit from it.[26] White people may not claim racism, and they may even verbally deny and debunk racist ideas, but that is not enough to change the social order. The social order places this generation of white people at the top of the hierarchy and does not require great effort on their part. Power and wealth "fell into their lap," and they are not going to abandon them. Jasmine offers more thoughts about the propagation of racist ideas and the economic necessity of continued anti-Blackness: "I think it comes from a colonial moment. I think that it comes from a historical site of power and domination based off of greed and resource exploitation. And I think that in order for that goal of greed and resource exploitation to be achieved, the group with the original objective would have to continually, not just in that moment, but continually use bodies to obtain that."

The common thread running through each of these contributions from students is the colonial, capitalist basis of modern racism. The key word in Jasmine's analysis is "continually." Though present-day American racism is not the same as racism during American slavery, Jasmine reminds us that racism remains as material as ever. The lived reality of racism is what happens to Black bodies. As Ta-Nehisi Coates writes, we can lose our bodies at any time, and the challenge of Black survival is to find a way to live in them.[27] Where, in what dwellings and neighborhoods, are Black people allowed and assigned to live? What food do we have access to? What jobs are we hired to perform? How are we physically treated by medical professionals and police officers? White-supremacist resource hoarding provides patterned and predictable answers to these questions, and those answers remain as deadly as ever to Black people in America. For this reason, "reverse racism" is a fallacy, according to the students.

> Black people aren't even in the position to be racist. And this is my thought on it, period. I feel like everyone who's a minority can be prejudiced, but you can't be racist. You can't be racist because you don't have enough power to systematically ensure different things. (Mitchell)

> My definition of racism is like, systemic oppression upon Black people by the majority-white population. And I think that kind of stems from, to me, there's a difference between racism and prejudice, and so there can't be reverse racism. (Olympia)

There were, however, a few other explanations for, and definitions of, racism, though they were not nearly as prominent as this systemic understanding. One such explanation, which I expected to hear more frequently, is that racism is rooted in ignorance. In some cases, students talked about ignorance as a form of media brainwashing, where the only images and stories that white people see about Black people contribute to stereotypes about Black folks being poor, violent, and uncivilized. In other cases, like Nick's, there is little analysis of the specific stereotypes or misinformation about Black people, but a general sense that Black people and experiences are just alien to the rest of the country. "I always go back to is just pure ignorance," Nick says, "'cause like, when people make comments, it's just so obvious that they just honestly have no idea. Like it's usually people who have never experienced even an ounce of oppression, so they just, they just cannot fathom. I've gotten to the point where I really am not mad at anyone who's racist or anyone who treats me as someone who's inferior to them just 'cause of my skin color, because they just don't know. They just have never come in contact with us."

Recall that in the previous chapter, Nick took a similar stance in his unwillingness to blame people responsible for the microaggressions he felt in class. So it may be that he simply views racism as an interpersonal phenomenon, and it is easier for him to believe that people truly do not wish ill upon him than it is to believe that he is systemically targeted and institutionally oppressed. His interactive, knowledge-based understanding of racism does not have deep historical roots. For example, the reason why people "don't come into contact with us" is that we live in a segregated society, so the ignorance is an adaptation to historically engendered inequality. Nick does not go down that path, however, and racism appears as a largely psychological and individual problem.

In students' comments as a whole, however, these individualistic prejudice-driven explanations were not nearly as frequent or well developed as the institutional and historical explanation for racism. The strongest definition of racism that emerges is that racism is a system, born in European colonialism, committed to Black dehumanization, and sustained to justify white power and economic privilege. Homophobia, by contrast, is understood by students more as learned prejudice and religious brainwashing than institutional oppression. Given these patterns, one might expect students' solutions to racism and homophobia to break down along similar lines. I anticipated strong arguments for destroying racist institutions and the capitalist economic system, and relatively little about changing racist hearts and minds. Considering the intimate and relational experiences of homophobia in religious familial spaces, I expected students to deemphasize institutional heterosexism in favor of a more person-to-person strategy for beating back homophobia. But students' ideas about addressing racism and homophobia did not exactly correspond to their diagnoses of the problems.

SOLUTIONS

One of the strongest themes that emerged in students' thoughts about remedying racism is that it is not Black folks' responsibility. Students are exhausted by the Black queertidian experience of racism, and the resilience and work required to keep oneself safe and whole. All of the interviews were finished by the end of the 2019 calendar year, nearly three months before the pandemic took hold and six months before the murder of George Floyd and the summer of activism that followed. Students did not need the additional layers of racial trauma imposed by the uneven occurrences of severe disease and death from COVID-19, nor did they need another video of a police killing to confirm the deathly consequences of anti-Blackness. For these students, white supremacy is caused by white people, so any talk of solutions must begin with white people.

Racism is more of a systematic thing. And the people that control racism are white people. It's not Black people. It's not Hispanics. It's not Indians. It's not Native Americans. It's nobody but white people. I think that the minorities can't really do much about it. I think it's the people with the power. I think it's the white people. That's why, when I get the opportunity to talk to someone that is of the white race, I try to like tell them, I'm like, "Well, racism isn't really going to end until you guys with the power start bringing awareness to it." (Ian)

I don't think Black people should. We didn't create it. I think the people who need to be doing something about it are white people. Because we literally, we didn't do anything to create that. Like, we're just victims of racism, and I don't think the victims of anything should have to fix what they didn't create. (Thea)

I think that primarily people of color have driven a lot of the work behind fighting against racist rhetoric and policy. So I think a big component now is that white people need to figure out ways to fight and eliminate, not only sentiments but also different policies, whether legal or economic or political, that harm primarily people of color. (Morris)

Some students, like Morris, provide more details about what, specifically, white people should do, and the answer is wide ranging. They need to work at the level of individual "sentiments," he says, but also at the level of legal, political, and economic policies. Others, like Thea, were visibly exasperated by the question, and did not see the need to brainstorm remedies for racism any further, since it is not Black folks' responsibility to combat racism. In some respects, Thea's answer is similar to those of students who told me that homophobia really is not their problem, because it is actually a symptom of the insecurity and self-hatred of people who are uncomfortable with their own sexuality and/or queerness.

Ian is willing to engage concerned or sympathetic white people in conversation about racism. Though he lets them know that only they have the power and moral responsibility to make significant change, he exchanges ideas and tries to increase mutual understanding in the hope that white people will come to grips with their own responsibility. He is not especially interested in hearing white people's perspective on racism, and his comments, therefore, are not a full-fledged argument for empathy and mutual understanding as the most important tools we have for dismantling white supremacy. But empathy and education are far and away the strongest themes among responses to my questions about how to address both racism and homophobia. The emphasis on empathy and education aligns with students' ideas about the interpersonal experiences and psychological roots of homophobia. That is, it is unsurprising that they focus on person-to-person educational and emotional remedies to homophobia because they seem to have more close personal relationships with people who are homophobic. In contrast, the students mostly describe racism as an *institutional and economic* problem, so it was surprising to hear so many of them trumpet more interpersonal and educational strategies for countering it. Here are three examples of students prioritizing empathy as a key tool for combating racism and homophobia.

I think . . . the biggest thing that keeps prejudice such as homophobia and racism going is not being able to see out of someone else's eyes. And you can explain all day long, but until someone feels that pain, they don't really understand it. (Jayla)

I think one thing people can do now is access compassion. Access compassion, and compassion comes through consciousness and awareness and consideration. . . . Fanny Lou Hamer said, after she had been brutally beaten by police and was in jail, you can't harbor hate for those people, because it's going to destroy you. You have to love those people as much as you love yourself, enough to change them, and enough to change the course of history. (Jasmine)

I was even having trouble grasping, like, understanding being transgender. 'Cause I remember somebody was talking about it, and I remember when I went back home and with my friend I was like, "You know, I'm really confused about like that whole community, because I don't really understand it, you know." And he was like, "Okay, and that's fine. But the crazy thing is, it's not for you to, like, it's not for you to accept based on you understanding it. It's for you to accept based on just being a human being, being empathetic." And that really helped me. (Candace)

Candace's reflection on her own discomfort with transgender folks is instructive. This is a case where her bias was not reflective of clear resentment toward the transgender community or rejection of all things queer. As a queer Black woman, she understands that discrimination based on race, gender, or sexual orientation is abhorrent. But she did not accept the idea of being transgender as easily as she accepted the idea of being queer, and she offers this reflection as means to imagine how others who are prejudiced against LGBTQ+ people might feel. Thanks to her friend's explanation that acceptance of transgender people does not require complete understanding of transgender experiences, she came to think about the transgender community in a different way. So her sense that empathy is the key to overcoming racism and homophobia is not driven by an unrealistic or romantic view that everyone's heart and mind can be changed, but by her own experience and the change she notices in herself. Similarly, Nick draws on his own experience as evidence for his belief that individuals can change and that interpersonal interactions and calls for empathy are crucial.

I have one conservative friend that I can highlight, very conservative white friend who grew up with a lot of money, and had very like, Donald

Trump views before he came to this school. He studies here now. He has talked to me more because I went to high school with him as well. He has talked to me more now than he ever has, our whole lives, and it's because like, I stopped running away from him. You know, I was like, I'm going to talk to him. You know, I'm going to engage with him. And now he's like, "Oh, okay. I see."

Nick's experience changing someone's mind, and his belief that we cannot run away from people who are prejudiced, is supported by research on political persuasion. In 2016, the *New York Times* ran a series of stories about political polarization, LGBTQ+ issues, and changing voters' minds. Drawing on research by David Broockman and Joshua Kalla on reducing transphobia,[28] the Los Angeles LGBT Center and the SAVE organization in south Florida implemented a door-to-door canvassing strategy, where volunteers spent time in conversation with voters they knew were hostile to LGBTQ+ rights. The canvassers, many of whom are queer, spent time in dialogue, right on the voters' doorsteps, and their discussions focused on personal experiences rather than logical arguments about the moral, political, or economic imperative for LGBTQ+ rights. The volunteers were not dismissive of the voters' prejudiced views; rather, they countered them with stories about how those views personally affected and harmed them. Weeks later, research demonstrated that they had significantly changed the attitudes of the voters they interacted with, and the organizations continued their work with the hope that those attitudinal changes would influence votes as well.[29]

Abraham also believes that people can change their minds and decide to be less racist or homophobic, but he places the onus for this change more on each prejudiced individual than on advocates for LGBTQ+ rights.

The only way you can combat it is look at what you're taught. Examine, think: Is it positive or negative? Realize where it comes from and then make a change to do better. Because the funny thing is when you're an adolescent that's a time in your life where you can decide, are you going to be like your parents, or are you going to be different. You can follow their same morals, or you can say, "Hey, I respect what you went through, I'm going to examine it, take a little bit of information from it, but I'm going to be different."

Abraham's emphasis on individual responsibility for change is also a call to examine how we are educated. He wants us to consider the information we are fed as well as its source, and make individual decisions about its validity and imprint on our lives. And on college campuses, LGBTQ+ student organizations play a vital role in this education; recall that educating and raising awareness is one of the key functions of those groups, according to the students. Advocates like Easton, who are involved in such organizations, strongly believe in the power of education and awareness raising as means to counter racism and homophobia. There are so many people, he says, who truly do not understand that the things they do and say are wrong or, just as importantly, why they are wrong. Telling the history of the LGBTQ+ community, making connections between racism and homophobia, and teaching people the right vocabulary to have these conversations are key. "Just really educating them on the history of the LGBT community. But not even that, educating them on the viewpoints of how the heteronormative community are oppressing the LGBT community. I wouldn't say a comparison of prejudice and racism, but it's almost like that, how the heteronormative community is kind of oppressing the LGBT community in the sense of just being able to freely express themselves. . . . There's things that people can say that they don't know are harmful or unethical, or just wrong. People aren't aware of the history or the terminology."

Easton argues for a specific type of education that focuses on power and oppression, rather than solely misunderstanding. Though it is true that some students seem more willing to give prejudiced people grace as they engage them in these conversations or attempt to empathize with them, none of the students argued that racism and homophobia are inconsequential. These forms of oppression are morally unacceptable, and they have to be condemned, as Camila explains: "We have to stop telling people that it's okay to think like this. I mean, I think you have to get in people's faces and say, like, 'You know, you're wrong. I don't agree with you.' We can't laugh at the jokes that people are saying. Like, if you can find humor in racism, then I think that you are contributing to racism. So I think that just starting with calling people out for what they're doing, what they're saying, and what they're teaching people."

In recent years, conservative politicians and commentators have instigated moral panic around "call out" and "cancel" culture. The claim, especially as it applies to college campuses, is that when liberals shame people in this way and tell people it is not okay to harass women or express prejudiced views, they are trampling on everyone's right to free speech. This is, of course, a racially coded and disingenuous argument, as "woke" and "cancel culture" have become code words and phrases much in the same way that "urban crime" functions as a phrase to prime resentment of Black people. There is a discussion to be had about whether calling people out in the way Camila describes will actually change the minds of people who are prejudiced. As noted above, research suggests that doing so, especially when those people are subject to public shame, is not likely to change their attitudes. But the goal of identifying and publicly condemning racist and homophobic speech and jokes is not to change the minds of people who are prejudiced; it is to create an environment where everyone can live, work, and learn without being discriminated against. The alternative, allowing these "jokes," which are always more than jokes, to pervade workplaces and educational settings, is harmful, to say the least. We need to cultivate conversational norms of dignity and respect for their own sake, because it is the right thing to do, and because it ensures the safety of everyone in our community. Upholding these norms may not change hearts and minds, but it does contribute to institutional and systemic change.

In summary, when asked to consider the tools at our disposal for combating racism and homophobia, students provide a variety of suggestions. Some say that addressing racism is white people's responsibility, because white people created it. The two strongest themes in our discussions are that everyone, not just people who are prejudiced against Black and queer people, needs to practice empathy, and those of us who know better cannot afford to turn away; we have to engage with people who have these views and educate them. This engagement is not the same as taking a deferential stance, as offenders need to learn hard lessons about why things are the way they are, and they need to be condemned for transphobic, racist, and homophobic behavior. Overall, much of my conversation with students about these issues fell within the realm of interpersonal intervention. This is surprising given students' understanding of the institutional and systemic nature of both racism, which they say is rooted in colonialism and capitalism, and LGBTQ+ oppression, which they say is largely driven by religious institutions and traditions.

However, several students focused squarely on the systemic nature of these problems when I asked them to discuss possible solutions. Their comments along these lines were bold and succinct. Albert, for example, told me, "We can get educated and we can live our lives to the fullest, and try to tear down those systems of oppression, which is really, really hard." Ada emphasized politics, arguing that we need to elect people to government who not only look like us but clearly believe racism is wrong and will fight against it. She paired this emphasis on electoral politics with "being an activist and protesting," which is how Parker came into their trans identity at college. The activism Parker took part in with other Black queer and trans folks taught them that "we have to revolt, tear down these institutions, completely abolish them. Oh, and also as an identification of like, where I stand, 'abolitionist' is also, that's a good word." But perhaps the most thorough consideration of these interlocking systems of oppression and our charge to dismantle them came from Luke, who focused on misogyny as the key battlefront in the fight for lasting change. Here is our exchange:

LUKE: It's hard to like, think of a solution. But I know if you fix that, then everything like, trickles down and it will fix everything else.

MICHAEL: Why? What do you mean by that, "Fix that and it will trickle down?"

LUKE: Basically like, okay, say if we solve misogyny in a way, and how feminine beings are seen, and so then homophobia against gay men, that won't be a thing. Because a lot of people, their perception of gay men is that it's very feminine. And it seems to be like, everything feminine in a society is put down. And so that would solve that. Misogyny against Black women, like misogynoir, that will fix misogyny for like all other women, not even just like Black or like POC, but I guess white women as well. Even like, transphobia. I know like a lot of, the way people see trans men is different from the way people see trans women. And I guess that has a lot to do with like misogyny, like trans misogyny as a whole, and the way feminine beings are seen.

And so it'll just trickle down and fix it. Racism as a whole. A lot of things stem from racism and colonialism. So if we just dismantle like white supremacy as a whole, then all these things would be fixed.

Luke's final comments about dismantling white supremacy are somewhat vague. He affirms that it is rooted in colonialism, but does not quite explain how those colonial roots impact the institutional racism we live with today. But we can see strategy for dismantling racism within Luke's discussion of misogyny, which is the root cause of all gender-based oppression, including homophobia and transphobia. The problem, as Luke sees it, is a deep-seated hatred of femininity and women. People hate gay men because they are seen as too feminine. People hate Black women both because they are women and because they are Black, so if you are committed to eliminating misogyny, you must commit to eliminating misogynoir specifically. As the Combahee River Collective wrote, "If Black women were free, it would mean that everyone else would have to be free since our freedom would necessitate the destruction of all the systems of oppression."[30] Racism, sexism, homophobia, and transphobia are inextricably linked to each other and cannot stand on their own. Though I posed questions about racism and the oppression of LGBTQ+ people separately, Luke was one of a handful of students who answered them in reference to each other.

A critical question remains: How, if at all, do these students apply these ideas to the treacherous political environment they find themselves in? The final chapter tries to give a sense of the politics of Black queer college students. The Black queertidian premise of the book is that these students, and Black LGBTQ+ people more broadly, are not magically radical by nature. They are not destined or required to be the vanguard of the Black liberation movement, despite the recent visibility of Black queer celebrities. I asked the students what they think about politics, and whether there are any particular social issues that hold their attention. I also asked them about the Black Lives Matter movement, and their thoughts about the futures of Black people, LGBTQ+ people, and Black LGBTQ+ people.

[7]

BLACK QUEERTIDIAN POLITICS

Being Black and LGBTQ+ in America has never been safe; the Trump administration made life even more hazardous. Trump's 2016 presidential campaign was an assault on women, immigrants, non-Christians, people of color, and LGBTQ+ people. In a departure from the previous presidential administration, Trump refused to acknowledge June as LGBTQ+ Pride Month every year he was in the White House. He passed legislation that removed protections from discrimination for LGBTQ+ people in health care and the health insurance market, and signed an executive order that allowed federal contractors to skirt compliance with policy that prevented discrimination against LGBTQ+ workers. Transgender troops have served openly in the military since June 2016, and a government study found that transgender military service has no negative impact on the armed forces.[1] But in July 2017, Trump proclaimed he would ban transgender people from serving altogether, without any input or support from military leaders. The ban was challenged in court and overruled later that year, but Trump called for a similar ban the following year. The Trump administration's disdain for LGBTQ+ people was clear during his campaign, and the disaster that loomed upon his election did not go unnoticed by young LGBTQ+ people. Just after Trump was elected in 2016, the Human Rights Campaign conducted a survey of fifty thousand LGBTQ+ people thirteen to eighteen years old.

Even before Trump was sworn in, almost half of the young people in the survey said they had taken steps to hide their LGBTQ+ identity, delayed coming out of the closet, or reconsidered their future plans.[2]

That same survey revealed that Black and Hispanic respondents were changing their appearance and routines, and Muslim, Jewish, and Hindu youth were "concealing symbols of their faith to avoid being targeted." Trump owes his political career to white racism, as he first appeared on the political radar as one of the more vocal "birther" conspiracy theorists obsessed with the false notion that President Obama was born outside the United States. During the 2016 campaign, he repeatedly primed white racism by associating Black and Latinx people with criminal gangs. Racially coded appeals to "law and order" such as Trump's have been key to Republican campaign strategy and ideology since the 1960s, as Black progress and civil rights are framed by Republican politicians as incompatible with white safety. Richard Nixon's attack on "Black crime" was part and parcel of his attack on the civil rights movement, where the "good trouble" caused by activists like Senator John Lewis was reframed as criminal trouble requiring a militarized response from the state. Trump's suggestion that Senator Lewis's district in Atlanta was "falling apart" and "crime infested"[3] continues this tradition and the Republican "southern strategy" of using racism to attract white voters to their party.

One of Trump's first acts as president was to ban Muslims from entering the country under the pretense of national security. The policy's bigotry was evident to all who examined it, and was explicitly called a "Muslim ban" by surrogates and members of the Trump administration,[4] but the Supreme Court upheld it in June of 2018. The administration's xenophobia and cruelty toward immigrants were laid bare when the truth about its practices at the southern border was revealed. Trump implemented a new immigration policy that mandated separation of immigrant parents and children and denied asylum seekers at legitimate ports of entry. The government separated the children without plans to reunite them with their parents, and established child detention centers on military bases to accommodate the overflow from border detention facilities. Of the traumatized children, Trump asserted, "They're not innocent."[5] Children as young as three years old were forced to appear in immigration court without representation, the press captured images of mass immigration trials for adults, and reports of psychological and physical abuse of children in detention were gradually revealed to the public.

Through it all, Trump continued his stream of dehumanizing rhetorical attacks on immigrants and Black people, referring to Black professional football players protesting police violence as "sons of bitches," labeling immigration as "infestation," calling Haiti "a shithole country," and implying that Latin American immigrants are "animals." When white supremacists gathered in Charlottesville with torches and weapons and killed an innocent woman by driving a car into a crowd of counterprotestors, Trump suggested there were "good people on both sides" of the confrontation. White supremacists are undoubtedly emboldened by a president who reflects their views, and the incidence of hate crimes in the United States rose in both 2016 and 2017.[6] And of course, the ultimate result of the legitimization of violent white-supremacist ideology was the insurrection at the Capitol on January 6, 2021. The images of the militarized, murderous mob included photographs of people traipsing through the halls of the Capitol carrying the Confederate flag and wearing "Camp Auschwitz" t-shirts.

I have argued that the white pop-cultural embrace of the Black queer fabulous and fly is accompanied by an explosion of Black queer political celebrity. These developments are certainly encouraging in some respects, as respondents repeatedly trumpeted the value of visibility on their campuses and in popular culture. However, the danger in this celebration is that it distorts Black LGBTQ+ politics and places an unjust burden of responsibility on Black queer people as "natural" political savants and warriors. Black queer survival in a racist and heterosexist society is radical. But even in a context where American democracy was sliding toward authoritarianism and the threat of bigoted violence was fueled by the highest office in government, very few of the students describe themselves as *politically* radical. The Black queer political vanguard is real, and it is responsible for the Black Lives Matter (BLM) movement. But being Black and queer does not guarantee a place on the front lines of American political struggle. Many students foreground Black queertidian social concerns as they describe a political realm that they feel disconnected from. Their analysis provides several insights about the most pressing challenges facing their generation.

POLITICAL IDENTITY AND ENGAGEMENT

As students moved through their teenage years, BLM became a global political force thanks in part to hashtag activism, which lowered the barriers to engagement for young people. When I interviewed them, they were living through the Trump administration, so if BLM had not dramatized the political stakes, there was no shortage of additional signs that the country was in political crisis. And still, numerous students told me they simply did not think of themselves as political or care about politics. When I asked, those students responded bluntly.

I don't know. I really don't be caring. (Faith)

I mean, not really. Not that I'm blinded to it, but it's just not something I really feed into. (Chris)

I don't even indulge anymore. I just don't. If it's right, it's right. It's wrong, it's wrong. It's so much, so much going on. I just don't even look at it. (Lauryn)

It was clear from these students' answers and demeanor that they did not feel comfortable talking about politics and did not think of themselves as political. One might wonder whether my relationship with the students and the sequence of the interview questions affected their answers. At the very beginning of the interview, I asked students to describe themselves. They never used words like "political" or "radical" as part of their answers to the opening questions, as they focused on other elements of their personality or things they valued. Later in each interview, I asked them what they thought of politics today and how they would describe themselves politically. If they perceived me as an authority figure or were otherwise reluctant or intimidated to have a discussion about politics with a professor, they might be more likely to dodge these questions or redirect the conversation. But that is not the sense I got from the students quoted above. By this point in the interview, we had built a rapport, and students had discussed plenty of sensitive topics. Every cue these students gave me, verbal or otherwise, suggested that they simply were not interested in politics and did not think of themselves in those terms.

In other cases, however, students' ideas about whether or not they were political hinged on the way the question was framed. Many students were engaged, but not wedded to traditional political labels, and they made the distinction clear. They did not like the word "political."

> I think other people would describe me as political. I think I would describe me as a person who just wants everyone to be happy [laughs]. And to not feel oppression. So I don't identify with any party, necessarily, or any ideology, I guess I would say. Well, not ideology, that's not the right word. But what I'm saying is that if it is for the human, if it is a human right, then I will support it. (Nick)

> I wouldn't say like, Democrat or Republican. I would say liberal, just because like, I just know, the Democratic Party to me just have issues. So I just feel like definitely, I would describe myself more as a liberal, 'cause I feel like I endorse like everything they say, but some of the practices they do, I don't at all. So I just feel like I don't owe them. (Roland)

When these students heard "politics," they thought about elected officials, the two-party system, and political identity as defined by party. As Roland alludes to, neither party has reliably advanced Black interests over the course of their lives, or through all of American history, for that matter. Students may fight to end oppression or advance a recognizable political ideology, but these beliefs did not necessarily lead them to adopt a political identity, whether the identity was party based or not. In many cases, the students' analysis of racism and heterosexism is the factor that leads them to say they are *not* political, as is the case for Albert, Thea, and Jace.

> MICHAEL: How do you think about yourself politically?
> ALBERT: I don't.
> MICHAEL: You don't?
> ALBERT: No. I don't engage with politics, with capital "P" politics.
> MICHAEL: Why? Why is that?

ALBERT: I've really kind of gone back and forth with myself on this, just because I'm kind of a privileged Black person. Like, I'm the upper-middle-class Black person who is deciding to withdraw from politics because they feel like politics doesn't really address the effects of anti-Blackness at a structural level. Because all these institutions like, invariably hurt Black people, disenfranchise Black people. (Albert)

I do believe that voting is harm reduction or whatever, but I don't like the idea of participating in the system, 'cause I don't believe in the system . . . because of the history and how we're literally sitting on stolen land right now. And just the massacres that happened to indigenous people, bringing people over as slaves. Just like, I don't think anything that was created underneath a system that is literally rooted in genocide and slavery will ever be good for brown or Black people or indigenous people. (Thea)

I hate politicians. I think it all comes down to, my main issue in terms of the social climate is the binary, and how it limits us to either pick a side or be nothing at all. And I hate it. I think so many parts of my identity sort of disrupt the binary, and because of that, I have not been able to be myself for a very long time. I think politics is a part of that sort of binary nature. (Jace)

In addition to detesting binary thinking, Jace went on to describe the disingenuous nature of career politicians and scoff at the notion that anyone elected to power would bring substantive change. Jace not only grew up Black and queer; he grew up poor, and he has absolutely no faith that either political party will end poverty. No matter who is elected, he told me, he and his family will still struggle.

Thea is slightly more sympathetic to voting, but she describes it as harm reduction rather than progress. The institutional history of rights and resources in America is rooted in genocide and slavery. Any governmental system built on that foundation, Thea says, can never be good for Black, brown, and indigenous people, so she will not kid herself into thinking that change facilitated by that system is liberating. Albert feels similarly, and describes the crisis as an institutional problem. He recognizes the ways his class position affords him some privilege relative to other Black people, but his class standing does not require him to endorse the institutions that shape his life, political or otherwise. It is important to note that all three of these students have strong opinions about the social ills they face on a daily basis; they are not completely oblivious to the politics of their lives. Thea, in particular, is more than opinionated; she is actively and visibly engaged on her campus as an activist working toward improving conditions for queer Black people. And yet, she sees her efforts as something slightly different from "politics."

A third group of students contrast with this understanding. They not only identify as political; they explicitly tie their politics to their Black queer identities, unbound from narrow, party-based political identity.

> I'm very political. I love politics. I love social justice. . . . I feel like with being any other than like a cis-het white Christian male, straight male, like, your existence is political, whether you like it or not. So being Black, a woman, and queer, all that is political, and I cannot get away from it, 'cause I feel like I can't not be political. (Valerie)

> I'm always an advocate for the rights and the privileges to be given to Black, queer, and trans people. That's always like, in the forefront of what I kind of live for and stand for. If I'm ever in an argument, it's probably about that. If I'm ever in argument with my family, it's probably about checking about them about something that could be somewhat problematic. I'm also a pushback against respectability politics. (Desean)

These students understand "political" in a more generous sense, which is also the sense that suggests that queer Black people have no choice in the matter: they are political because they exist in a society that makes no place for them. This is a perfectly valid assessment of one's political location, and its validity partially explains the recent pop-cultural rise of Black queer political celebrity. It is not, however, the way that every student feels about the nature and significance of their existence. E. Patrick Johnson's reflections on the relationship between queer theory and queer praxis open up space for Black queer diversity when it comes to political identity. Johnson asks how the mediation between "subjectivity and agency" or identity and empowerment "propel[s] material bodies into action."[7] In other words, something between subjectivity and agency, something *beyond* subjectivity/identity, *must happen to or call us* in order for us to be political agents. What does coming into the life of Black queerness and affirming a Black LGBTQ+ identity lead these young people to do? How does it change their actions in the world, explain whether they adopt a subdued or energized political identity, and speak to their understandings of themselves as political beings? Mitchell and Parker provide two striking examples of this calling and coming into politics.

> I love to help people, and I realized that helping people in the role of, you know, surgery and medicine and stuff was not really what I wanted to do. And I would say my calling still is, you know, to help people and things of that nature, but I realized that I can also help people in another way. And that has really been big on what I've been doing. I'm very big on advocacy when it comes to LGBTQ+ community. I'm currently serving as the intern for diversity and inclusion here at the university, and also, last year I went on to go to Washington, DC, at the HRC [Human Rights Coalition] campaign.

Mitchell's engagement in politics is not magically guaranteed by the impulse to help people or by his race, sexuality, and gender expression. Rather, it is developed and enabled on his HBCU campus through his contributions to institutional life and LGBTQ+ advocacy. Parker's account of their political development maps even more neatly onto Johnson's considerations of theory and praxis in "quare" studies.

> My major is philosophy and political science. I took a minor in human rights. And that's the thing I feel the most strongly about, because my second year, there was the uprising in [southern city] because a Black man had been murdered by [police]. I had already joined a group that was like, a radical leftist student organization at the beginning of that year, and that happened. So that completely changed the trajectory of my college experience and life, and what I knew I was about at that point. I went through the trauma of like, being on the streets, being teargassed. It's all the things you learn about. It was like the police, they showed up very physically, and I'm like, "Oh, okay, this is what we've been studying."

Again, Johnson asks, "What propels material bodies into action?" The answer is not "identity" or "identity politics." As Parker explains, the answer is a combination of things. The unique opportunity college life gives people to philosophize—to read, think, and reflect—is part of what moves Parker's body to action. Parker's connections to other organizers, both on campus and off, moves them to action. The physical presence of the police and the violence police inflict not only validate their movement, according to Parker; these threats change "what I knew I was about"; they change students' identities. This confluence of factors, again, not merely the social identity of being Black and trans, is what allows Parker to think of theirself as "political."

ASSESSMENT, ENGAGEMENT, AND KEY ISSUES

So there is diversity in how students think of themselves, as some affirm a far more specific and explicitly political identity than others. But I wanted to know not only how the students built or eschewed political identity but what they thought about the political issues of their time. I asked them to analyze the world around them and give me a sense of what they and their peers are living through. Their assessment is worrying. First, students like Jason explained that they were discouraged and exhausted by recent developments. "I don't know if I can give that much of a response on that question [about politics], because after [the 2016 election], I've just been like, checked out, at least in the grander scheme of things. I wish I could get more, but like literally, I've kind of shut down. 'Cause I used to kind of be really involved, or aware. But literally, I was just like, 'Wow, Donald Trump is president. So fuck it.' I got my own problems to worry about."

Hannah Arendt's *Origins of Totalitarianism* explains the key role that apathy plays in the rise and maintenance of authoritarian societies. Authoritarians strive to create a fictional "reality" that becomes the basis of their social movement and the loyalty of their followers. In order to do this, authoritarians flood the public sphere with claims that are untrue, or, as Trump administration strategist Steve Bannon said, "flood the zone with shit."[8] This forces every member of the public, not just their followers, to discern what is true and what is false. This is easy for those seduced by the authoritarian, because for them, the truth is whatever the leader says, even when the leader contradicts himself. But for skeptics and dissenters, the task is much harder and more discouraging. We must work with evidence to debunk each lie, and carry the frustration of knowing that authoritarian loyalists will not be convinced by evidence that invalidates their claims. Why, then, should people put themselves through the tedium of debunking inane falsehoods and arguing with opponents who cannot be reasoned with? It is so much easier, as Jason describes, to say "fuck it," and "check out," and that is exactly what the authoritarian is counting on. Authoritarian rule depends not on universal support among subjects but on fervent support from a loyal base, and acquiescence and apathy from would-be challengers. As Morris told me, "There's just this general sense of burnout from everything that's happening, and this feeling that like, there's just so many different things that occur in the world of politics today, that it can be really hard to find just one focus."

Other students are not completely burned out, but are learning to live with and manage the stress. Trump's election makes the world less safe and reflects a reality that is difficult to face. Cat explains.

CAT: It's very stressful to do, so I try to take it in doses.
MICHAEL: What makes it stressful?
CAT: Just seeing someone get up on a podium and spew hate and misinformation on a regular basis, and knowing that they were elected by people, and that's how they use that power, and that's what people wanted them to use that power for. And just the people making our decisions right now. It's like, how did y'all get there? It's like, you know how they got there, but then you're losing faith in humanity by acknowledging that.

It is disturbing enough that lies and hate speech are common features of Trump rhetoric. But what is so troubling for Cat is the realization that Trump is not an anomaly. He was elected by millions of people, and he behaves the way his constituents expect him to. This is a crisis of faith not only as it pertains to democratic institutions and government officials but as it pertains to civilians: the neighbors and classmates who empower and support the Trump administration. The threat is not abstract, as the testimony in previous chapters shows; it is present and queertidian. The political situation makes students like Sydney less safe than they were before Trump was elected. "Places that you could go before or you were more comfortable going before, you know, they aren't as comfortable now. People who are for Trump are not necessarily that because Trump is racist. But the ones who are have really exposed themselves. Because they feel they have that sense of comfortability now to say what they want, to do what they want, to think what they want. And I think that now the dynamic of our lives have changed in that sense of, we have to be more aware than we already were of our surroundings now."

The good news is that this sense of danger does not discourage all students from participating or standing up for themselves and others. Plenty of students were awakened by Trump's rise and motivated to change their level of engagement. Camila told me, "Politics just, I absolutely hate them. But I think that where we are now, the only way to make improvements is for me to be involved in politics, even though I don't like them." And Camila has been involved in multiple ways, as she is both a student leader on campus issues and someone who no longer avoids having conversations about national politics. One of the ways she and her peers increased their level of engagement is emphasizing the importance of voting and participating in voter-registration efforts, as Gwen explains: "I just recently started getting really into it. Like I voted in the [2018] midterms. I think that's like the most recent, for like the first time. And I do regret, like I didn't vote in like the big one, the Trump winning stuff. I really wanted to, but like, in the back of my mind, I was like, 'Oh, there's no way that like he's actually going to become president,' and then he did, and I was like, 'Fuck.' Like I'm realizing that like little things, like my single vote, matter."

Again, voting is not the only type of political behavior, and Lessie Branch warns that voting is seductive and insufficient as a political response to the multigenerational crisis of Black oppression in America.[9] But Gwen's comments show a burgeoning sense of efficacy. She understands, crucially, that neither apathy nor faith in others is a sound strategy for avoiding disaster. And even though much uncertainty remains, the act of voting sparked a bit of hope that was not present before. Olympia wrestles with the same issues that Gwen, Cat, and many of her peers do. But she fights through these doubts and embraces a sense of agency that exceeds electoral politics.

There are times where I have to like stop reading the news or like seeing what's happening, because sometimes I felt like all of that responsibility falls on my shoulders. And like, in a figurative way, it kind of does, but not like, literally. A lot of my friends on campus help me to realize like, you can only do what you have the capacity to do at a certain time in your life. Like now, what can I do with the sort of capital that I have? And so, I think that's kind of helping putting into perspective a lot of different issues, especially issues that affected me growing up.

Olympia's analysis illustrates that students are both limited and enabled by their status. Because of their financial and scholarly responsibilities, not to mention geographic limitations (they must live on or near campus), they may feel that they cannot influence off-campus politics—the stories that make national headlines—to the degree they would like. However, with the aid of student organizations, many of the students have a burgeoning sense of the influence they can have on campus, and they can take on many of the same social problems on a scale that is smaller, but no less significant.

Olympia also mentions that her drive to get engaged is based on her personal experience. I asked students about the political and social issues that were most pressing to them, and three main topics rose to the fore: the dehumanization of immigrants; transgender rights and violence; and Black Lives Matter. Clearly, they were attuned to these issues because the Trump administration had addressed them through both rhetoric and policy. Olympia describes her personal connection to recently imposed limitations on immigration and the dehumanization of Black, brown, and yellow immigrants: "Definitely immigration, especially because that's a system that my parents went through twenty, twenty-three years ago. In like 1989, it was definitely easier to get your citizenship than it is now. So then it's kind of thinking like, our country as a whole, what direction it's going into. I'm one of those people that, if there's anything going on in the world, I will like, take that on my shoulders, which is really "bad."

There is a sense that the Trump administration is trying to unmake history and create conditions that make it impossible for Olympia and her parents to feel safe and protected in the United States. She is concerned about what that means for the country as a whole, but also concerned about her ability to take on the burden of worrying about and working against such injustice. In other words, this political issue is deeply personal for her, because it threatens her family's safety and becomes a source of personal stress. These are immediate and legitimate worries for the students I spoke with, as Abraham explains: "Illegal immigrants and just equal rights. Probably those two [issues]. One of our members, he was illegal, and he was deported and no one knew. I kept telling our members, 'We haven't heard from him, is something wrong?' We didn't find out until the end of the semester that he's already been deported, was detained, and he couldn't even tell anyone about it. Something needs to be done. It tears away actual bonds for people."

The Trump administration did not invent the deportation of undocumented immigrants, as more than five million people were deported under President Obama's watch. But President Obama also established the Deferred Action for Childhood Arrivals (DACA) program, which put an end to the deportation of undocumented minors who were brought into the United States without choice. Obama also prioritized specific groups of immigrants for deportation, such as people who had recently entered the United States, and people who were convicted of crimes or engaged in terrorist activity. Trump dramatically expanded the groups who were targeted, including people who could be charged (not necessarily convicted) with a criminal offense, and people who improperly accessed government benefits. In his first year of office, the Trump administration arrested undocumented immigrants who were not convicted of crimes at double the rate of the Obama administration.[10] Over the course of his time in office, Trump empowered Immigration and Customs Enforcement (ICE) to execute dozens of violent raids designed to intimidate immigrants. The Trump Justice Department also instituted a policy of separating children, including toddlers, from their parents as a deterrent to immigration, without any viable plans to reunite immigrant families after detainment. This policy, in addition to explosive reporting about the camps used to house undocumented immigrants, spurred massive protests in the United States and drew the condemnation of human rights advocates across the world. So it was not just the legal roadblocks to citizenship and safety that defined Trump's administration; it was the racialized dehumanization of immigrants, which was not lost on the students.

I think the way that immigration is being handled really, really sucks. Like, just the fact that someone can put their lips together and say, "Separate the children from the parents," or that this race is better than this race, in so many uncertain terms, is kind of like, crazy to me. 'Cause I don't feel like people should be treated as animals. I think about that a lot. (Shannon)

I feel like treating people as objects, I feel like with immigration, that's what it's like. Putting them in cages? I don't even know how it works, but just basically sending them back to wherever they came from and not like even like, thinking about maybe why they're here. (Jafar)

Students' concern for the dehumanization of vulnerable people extends to the second political and social issue that emerged as a major concern: the rights and safety of transgender people. In addition to the legislative and symbolic assault on transgender people detailed at the beginning of this chapter, transgender people face commonplace discrimination as applicants for housing and employment. People who are impoverished and unsheltered often turn to other options, including illegal trades, in order make ends meet, which makes them especially vulnerable to violence. Morris explains this succinctly: "I know the administration, they kind of like have tried to start this thing where they redefine a lot of language in like the government agencies to be strictly like two genders, men and women. And so I think it's just like overall, trans people are super vulnerable, because they can't rely on like the government or private entities. And so they kind of have to figure out ways to live day to day, and that's even thinking about, like in particular Black trans folks, even more a very difficult and dangerous situation to be in."

It is difficult to find reliable statistics on transgender assaults and killings, but the Human Rights Coalition (HRC) has tracked transgender and nonbinary killings since 2013. Their findings suggest not only that such violence is on the rise but that Black and Latinx transgender people are at far greater risk than other transgender folks. In 2019, no fewer than twenty-five transgender or gender-nonconforming people were violently killed, 91 percent of whom were Black and 81 percent of whom were under thirty years old.[11] In 2020, HRC reported that no fewer than forty-four transgender or gender-nonconforming people were killed.[12]

Students are acutely aware not only of the multiple forms of jeopardy Black transgender people face but of the relative lack of attention to their plight relative to other social issues. Unlike the immigration crisis, the crisis of Black transgender suffering and the murders of Black transgender women were not considered worthy of national media attention, and students noticed. When I asked Luke which political issues concern him, he responded, "Trans misogyny, like how a lot of Black trans women have been reported murdered recently, and nobody seems to care. They don't really, I mean, people might say something, but it will be really like, trash." Gwen had a similar response.

> GWEN: Maybe like, violence against trans Black women.
> MICHAEL: Why does that come to mind for you?
> GWEN: Mostly because, like, I only hear about these stories on Twitter, and they never really make the big, big news, which is weird. Because if it was like, anybody else, I think more people would know about it. But it's almost like people don't care.

Luke's analysis is connected to comments he made, quoted in the previous chapter, about the degradation of femininity and the prevalence of misogynoir. He believes that in order to address all forms of oppression, we have to begin with misogynoir, which includes the degradation of Black trans women, because liberating folks who are most vulnerable will result in a trickle-down effect. His comments about the lack of coverage of Black trans women's murders is echoed by Gwen, who learns about these issues mostly through social media. This not only highlights the role of Black queer social media as a counterpublic space for education, networking, and mutual support; it speaks to a major weakness with the choices that major media outlets make about what gets covered. A 2021 study found that ABC, CBS, NBC, MSNBC, Fox News, and CNN spent a combined total of fifty-four minutes covering transgender violence in 2020. MSNBC accounted for more than half of the coverage, and only nine of the twenty-three segments mentioned the name of the transgender victim; this is the reason for the "Say Her/Their Name" hashtag and campaign.[13] The erasure and dehumanization are not abstract concerns for the students; they are pressing issues. Summer's comments weave the multiple forms of Black trans oppression together and reveal the difficulty in figuring out how best to address these issues on campus: "I fear for, under this current administration, LGBTQ+ people in general and our lives, specifically trans women, trans people in general, with like, the military ban that happened. And just the fact that, especially for trans women of color, the life expectancy is like thirty-five or something like that. That really, really worries me. We have trans women of color in our group. . . . I worry about when they get out into the world, and under this current administration, and attitudes have flared up, and people are just like, angry and upset."

Again, many students told me they did not follow politics or consider themselves to be political. But Summer articulates a political analysis of the problem of Black transgender violence. It starts at the institutional level, with the Trump administration and the adoption of discriminatory legislation. It bleeds from legislation and institutions into culture, as Summer echoes the concerns of so many of her classmates that Trump has emboldened bigots and given license to others who wish to express their anger through violence. This is one of the areas of students' lives where they were unable to imagine readily available solutions to the problem. Several students talked about the networks of care enacted through Instagram and other platforms, like Venmo and Cash App, which allow them to financially support vulnerable trans folks who need money for food, medical care, and shelter. But beyond these crowdsourcing band-aids, hope for dramatic improvement in the lives of their transgender siblings seems to be in short supply. This is especially discouraging when we consider the queer politics of the final political and social issue that students are especially focused on: Black Lives Matter.

BLACK LIVES MATTER

In order to understand the significance of Black Lives Matter as a collectivist social movement, it is vital to understand the limits of voting and individualistic political participation for Black people. Especially at the federal level, Black voters have consistently defended themselves from the worst vestiges of government racism by voting for the Democratic Party, a party that is far from radical or pro-Black, but is less likely than the GOP to further entrench white supremacy through legislation and rhetoric. The passage of the Voting Rights Act falsely signaled to Black Americans that they no longer needed to prioritize solidarity and protest politics to improve their lot in America. As many Black folk accepted this narrative and became more invested in individualistic rather than collective political action, the Nixon administration abdicated the War on Poverty and started a racist "War on Crime," which continued at the federal level virtually uninterrupted through the George W. Bush years. In other words, Black Americans remained under attack with weapons just as deadly as those used during Jim Crow, but abandoned their commitment to the politics of radical collective solidarity, opting for electoral politics instead.

Investing in self-defense through elections has proven especially ill considered in light of recent events. The Voting Rights Act of 1965 has been gutted by the Supreme Court of the United States. In *Shelby County v. Holder* (2013) the Court ruled that section 5 of the Voting Rights Act was no longer valid, which meant that southern states previously required to seek federal approval prior to changing their voting laws were allowed to change their rules without federal oversight. Less than one year after the decision, Texas, Alabama, North Carolina, Virginia, Mississippi, and South Carolina put policies in place that damaged the Black electorate, including voter roll purges and voter ID laws.[14] In 2016, a study found that the 2013 voter ID law passed in Wisconsin suppressed the total number of ballots cast by roughly two hundred thousand. The study also found that the effect of the Wisconsin law, as well as similar laws passed in Mississippi and Virginia, was most severe in counties where Black people constituted at least 40 percent of the population.[15] Trump won the state of Wisconsin in 2016 by fewer than 23,000 votes, in no small part thanks to these attacks on Black voting rights.

Black Lives Matter is not only a response to police violence. It is a reignition of the Black collectivist political tradition at a time when it is clear that individualist tactics are insufficient at best. One of the things that makes BLM different from previous Black American liberation movements is its institutional structure. So much of the civil rights movement was built within the hierarchical Black church and in dialogue with college student organizations, labor organizers, and professional legal advocates. It churned forward with key legislative goals: desegregation, antidiscrimination law, and voting rights among them. In contrast, Black Lives Matter began as horizontally organized hashtag activism and moral demands without a clearly established legislative goal: it was #BlackLivesMatter before it was a social movement.

"Hashtag activism" remains a subject of much debate, as detractors worry that social media posting has become a convenient substitute for material political action that demands sacrifice and directly confronts institutional power. Critics also note that the speed of hashtag activism across social media is both enabling and crippling. Social media users can scarcely keep track of the transition from one hashtag to the next, and many hashtags are created deliberately to create social media trends and narratives that drown out factual information. Despite these concerns, the impact of BLM demonstrates just how powerful this new collectivism is and disproves the notion that hashtag activism is guaranteed to weaken traditional politics. Voting, high-profile legal challenges, and direct action have all exploded because of #BlackLivesMatter. As Sarah Jackson, Moya Bailey, and Brooke Welles explain, hashtag activism enables the rapid and democratized development of networks of political dissent and collective action. Even in a public sphere flooded with misinformation and the frames of traditional (and reactionary) news and political speech, hashtag activism is effective political education and infrastructure.[16]

"#BlackLivesMatter" was first tweeted by sociologist Marcus Anthony Hunter in 2012. It was popularized and transformed into a movement by Black-queer-woman organizers Alicia Garza, Patrisse Khan-Cullors, and Opal Tometti. Khan-Cullors used the hashtag in response to a Facebook post by Garza in the wake of George Zimmerman's acquittal for the killing of Trayvon Martin in July of 2013. As Garza explains, "Opal [Tometti], Patrisse, and I created the infrastructure for this movement project—moving the hashtag from social media to the streets. Our team grew through a very successful Black Lives Matter ride, led and designed by Patrisse Cullors and Darnell L. Moore, organized to support the movement that is growing in St. Louis, MO, after 18-year old Mike Brown was killed at the hands of Ferguson Police Officer Darren Wilson." Garza's essay about the origins of the movement lays out the necessity and purpose of BLM. She explicitly defines it is a corrective to previous Black liberation movements, which have stolen and erased the work of Black women and queer Black people. It is not just a response to police and state violence; it is "an affirmation of Black folks' contributions to this society, our humanity, and our resilience in the face of deadly oppression." It is a call to affirm Blackness, rather than shy away from it, or shelter it under universalist "All Lives Matter" rhetoric. And vitally, it is founded and directed by "Black queer and trans folks bearing a unique burden in a hetero-patriarchal society that disposes of us like garbage and simultaneously fetishizes us and profits off of us."[17] Khan-Cullors makes this point doubly clear in her memoir, as she writes, "After Ferguson, when we speak of ourselves, we always lead with this, that not only are we unapologetically Black . . . we are also Queer- and Trans-led and non-patriarchal."[18]

I concluded interviews with students at the end of the 2019 calendar year, long before the murder of George Floyd in May of 2020 and the demonstrations that followed. Because of the impact of that summer on the image and memory of BLM, it may be difficult to recall that the movement was six years old before Floyd was killed, and had long since captured the political imagination of the country and the world. By and large, students understand BLM's origins and goals, and are immensely sympathetic to the work it has achieved and its aims for the future. Alice told me that it started with Trayvon Martin, but "it also has branched into, you know, police brutality and racial discrimination, and I think it's going further and further out as more and more stuff happens." And Jason said, "I go to an HBCU, so it's really hard to escape the fact that we're always talking about Black Lives Matter, police brutality. That's definitely an issue, 'cause as a Black male myself, I have to deal with that shit. . . . I didn't think that would happen to me, but when it actually happens to you, it's like, it's real."

Cathy Cohen describes a path by which marginalization leads to political beliefs and actions.[19] First, lived experience, such as being harassed by police or having one's family torn apart by the criminal punishment system, results in a worldview that challenges dominant narratives. Second, though there may be institutional means to pursue redress for injustices, marginalized people develop their own organizations, information, and leaders outside of established political institutions. This triad of organization, information, and leadership is perfectly illustrated through the story of BLM. The founders came to collaborate with each other thanks to their previous experience as organizers who were not sponsored by political elites. They spread information and grew their ranks through counterpublic social-media and hashtag activism, as described above. The third consequence of marginalization, according to Cohen, is that once the group is mobilized, its actions are consistently framed. We can clearly see the after-the-fact framing of mobilization in Garza's essay, which stipulates that BLM will not apologize and will not play by rules that were not designed to lead to the nonnegotiable outcomes BLM seeks: Black freedom, dignity, justice, and security.

BLM would not have any lasting power if its basis and aims were only affirmed by its leadership. Everyday people, including the students, believe in Black Lives Matter because they experience police violence and discrimination. They also believe in it because they perceive it to be effective. In 2016, 43 percent of Americans supported BLM, but by the summer of 2020, that percentage had grown to 67 percent, according to the Pew Research Center.[20] Data show that in the months after the summer of 2020, support from white people and Republicans in particular decreased.[21] But the fact that BLM could shift public perception roughly 25 percent in two years is proof that it changed the minds of millions of people. As Roland told me, "I definitely think it's getting more recognized, and people are starting to take more notice of it and actually starting—even Black people, just like everybody in general, I'm just seeing more white people wearing the Black Lives Matter shirts and stuff more often." In addition, a 2021 study found that cities with massive BLM protests experienced a significant decline in police violence.[22] So protests not only change minds; they get results. Students did not cite any studies like these when we discussed the value of BLM, but they are convinced BLM makes a difference nevertheless. As Tracey says, "This is the greatest time to have pride with everybody standing up, they're not afraid of their culture, they're proud of their culture. So that's what Black Lives Matter means to me. That movement is powerful, it needs to stay around. And it gets things done. Because the day that we protested, the next day Cyntoia [Brown] was granted clemency. So that was a great feeling to know that I was a part of that, because I been knowing about her case since I was thirteen years old. Almost got arrested, but I made it through, thank God."

Cyntoia Brown was sixteen years old when she was tried and convicted as an adult for admittedly killing a man whom she claimed assaulted her during a sexual encounter in 2004. Brown was granted clemency in 2019, by which point her case had become a frequent topic on social media, where it was often discussed in connection to the other injustices Black women and girls face in the criminal punishment system. Tracey takes pride in raising her voice on Brown's behalf, and she directly connects her advocacy to BLM. Not only does the movement provide her with a sense of personal accomplishment; it fuels her pride and courage. The unapologetic spirit of BLM's founders trickles down to many of the everyday people who participate in such demonstrations. While that spirit is preserved and translated from the leadership to the masses, those who support and participate in BLM actions do not always know who the founders are.

In her prescient 2010 study of Black LGBTQ+ communal life in Los Angeles, Mignon Moore delves into the meaning of Black LGBTQ+ activists at the forefront of racial-justice movements and pro-Black advocacy. These leaders take ownership of the movements not only because they seek racial justice but also because they "saw their activism as paving the way for their own eventual liberation *within the racial community*."[23] Queer Black folk who participate in these movements do not seek the approval of white LGBTQ+ people or white society more broadly. They are invested in building solidarity and power within their racial group and proudly affirming their Black LGBTQ+ identity. This is exactly what Garza affirms in her essay about the origins and purpose of BLM, and Moore also notes that stepping forward in this way makes queer Black activists especially vulnerable. They do not want to be hurt or marginalized in a space that is supposed to be safe for them because it is carved out for Black people. Despite these aims and the statements from Garza, Cullors-Khan, and so many other BLM trailblazers, the work of women and queer and trans Black people continues to be distorted, stolen, and erased. With very few exceptions, students do not associate BLM with Black women, Black LGBTQ+ people, or Black feminist and LGBTQ+ social issues. Those who do make this connection lament that BLM *should* be about queer Black liberation, but its mission changed.

It was started by Black queer people, Black queer women. But nobody really mentioned them as Black Lives Matter. Black Lives Matter who now are straight and Black, they don't really try to showcase the way queer bodies and queer trans bodies are being treated. (Luke)

I didn't know till like, what, last year, that it was actually made by like two women, two queer women that were Black, two Black queer women. And like I didn't know that, 'cause it got took over by cis Black men. So it was just like, what the hell? But I am thankful for them for starting that up and actually realizing that, you know, our lives do matter, and we need to put in work, and we need to be activists. (Ada)

Though Luke and Ada know the truth about the roots of the movement, that knowledge does not change the fact that it has been taken over by "cis Black men." The takeover is even more clear among students who did not know the history of BLM's founding and are upset by what they perceive as disregard for Black LGBTQ+ people within the movement.

I do wonder if it's inclusive, like the whole trans stuff. 'Cause I don't really hear them talk a lot about that. (Gwen)

Black lives do matter, but it should also include the LGBTQ+ community, because these trans women are not even out here being broadcasted or getting recognition for being murdered, literally. I have to see that from other gays on social media like legit saying it, or posting the girls. It's usually never on the news. It's never ever posted when it comes to, you know, Black Lives Matter or any other organizations for that matter. (Mitchell)

This is a case where students' perception of one of their three core issues—violent attacks on Black trans people—informs their perception of another. Again, it is difficult to overstate the importance of social media and hashtag activism as factors that shape students' interpretations and narratives. Katelyn Burns explains the power of the Internet as a tool for increasing trans visibility in American culture.[24] In the first wave during the early 2000s, Burns argues, the Internet allowed trans people to find and connect with each other in unprecedented ways, building digital communities at a scale they could not achieve during the twentieth century. In the second wave, social media, YouTube, and, I would add, hashtag activism transformed visibility and community into political campaigns and policy gains. Burns notes that more recent Internet history includes reactionary political backlash to the progress made through transgender advocacy, as transphobic and otherwise hostile groups have leveraged the same social media platforms and digital tools to achieve their aims. But the point is that students experience the movement for Black transgender visibility and liberation as, in no small part, an Internet movement. They continue to use these applications to share information and uplift and support their siblings. BLM, too, is dependent on the Internet, but students told me that these digital streams do not frequently cross. Despite the wishes and actions of BLM founders, students often experience BLM as a separate conversation from those they are engaged in about Black queer and trans representation, celebration, and advocacy.

Perhaps more discouragingly, a few of the students adopted the conservative and right-wing counternarrative about BLM—that it is a violent movement that uses protest as an excuse for looting. Again, these ideas had taken root long before the 2020 protests, which saw disproportionate news coverage of property destruction despite the fact that the overwhelming majority of demonstrations were peaceful.[25] A gentler version of the narrative that BLM protestors are rioters and criminals is that a few bad apples are ruining the movement for the respectable protestors. The "bad apples" narrative allows police to justify the violence they deploy at demonstrations by suggesting that repressive police tactics are merely defensive. They are not targeting peaceful protestors, police say; they are targeting the criminals and agitators among the protestors in order to defend peaceful bystanders, themselves, and local businesses. This props up a dangerous false equivalency between destroying life, as police do when they kill people, and destroying property. The protection of property is subsequently militarized, which can lead to the sort of vigilante violence enacted by teenager Kyle Rittenhouse during the protests after the Jacob Blake killing in Kenosha, Wisconsin. Remy and Sonia have not completely embraced this line of thinking, and they do offer sympathy for BLM, but they lament the violence that, in their view, mars the movement.

I honestly support Black Lives Matter, and I see the reason for the move-ment. I don't support all their actions though. Like at one Black Lives Matter rally, they was like—I don't know. It was something with the po-lice. They were blocking the police, or they were being violent. I don't know what. It was like blocking or being violent of their nature. I feel like violence is not the answer. (Remy)

Every life matters. So I know it's being pinpointed on Black lives because of the police brutality and stuff. But it's good for that, for sure. But when they take it outside of that, and like, they can't do peaceful protests, the unpeaceful protestors are the problem, to where the BLM whole move-ment is going to always be looked at as . . . still lashing out, still acting up, 'cause certain people don't know how to be peaceful. (Sonia)

The end of Sonia's comments suggests that this is partially a problem of perception. She objects to the violence because she knows that the movement will be "looked at" a certain way. Below, Easton does not offer commentary on undisciplined or violent protestors who ruin the move-ment for the rest, but he is similarly concerned with perception. He sees BLM as poor strategy and framing, because foregrounding unapologetic and angry Blackness leads to a predictable interpretation. News media will cover it using racially coded language and stereotypes,[26] and Black people will be cast as monstrous criminals and separatists. BLM activ-ism is clearly multiracial and multicultural, but for Easton, its unapolo-getic Blackness prevents it from reaching its full potential. "I think that is a continuation of segregation because even though Black lives do mat-ter and they are overlooked, all lives matter. And if we come together in a effort with all ethnic backgrounds, your life matter, my life matter, her life matters, his life matters, that I think would be a better approach to it. Because I think in the world at large they see African Americans as these predators and these monsters, and with the movement in the news, they don't even see the protests that are there to bring awareness, they categorize it as riots."

It is important to reiterate that most of the students support BLM. They believe its key objectives are speaking out against police violence and demanding reform within the police and criminal punishment sys-tem. Even though these aims are widely understood, there is variation in how strongly students support BLM and how effective they believe it can be. There is also a noticeable absence of the belief that BLM is fundamentally a queer Black movement even though its founders repeatedly define it as such. Instead, several students suggest that BLM actually suppresses the concerns of Black LGBTQ+ people, as its dominant message about police violence leaves little room for the other radical arguments made by Garza and her comrades. How can this be? As Jace explains, the very elements that enable and distinguish BLM—hashtag activism and horizontal organization—are also responsible for its shortcomings.

> I kind of slowly realized that Black Lives Matter is no longer a movement. It's more of a phrase. It's a hashtag. It's something that anyone can use to inspire their own movement. Black Lives Matter doesn't have a leader anymore. Like, it was founded by three women, and it grew so much that there are so many factions, there's no concise leader, and therefore there's no real end goal. And because of that, a lot of people don't really know what they're doing, and kind of just use the Black Lives Matter movement or phrase as a means to push their own agenda.

Hashtag activism makes BLM accessible and expansive. It also enables rapid, horizontal organization, which allows for pop-up protests and mass demonstrations at multiple sites all over the country. It eschews a hierarchal, patriarchal structure with a single leader, as those positions are almost never reserved for women in the history of American social movements. As Jace says, this allows opportunists to use BLM in any way they like. Jace is especially frustrated with people who "don't know what they're doing," and later in the interview he criticized privileged Black students at his school, who do not know what it is like to be poor and are not interested in real revolution, but adopt the phrase "Black Lives Matter" because it is fashionable. Jace also notes that BLM "has no real end goal," and this is connected to the movement's origins as an intervention with moral, rather than political or legislative, demands. But as BLM developed, it allowed subchapters to register themselves under a national umbrella. This collection of registered BLM chapters joined with other organizations to create the Movement for Black Lives coalition. The Movement for Black Lives released a highly detailed policy manifesto that includes policy platforms related to environmental and economic justice, among other topics. But BLM never claimed control of Movement for Black Lives, and though the two movements maintain their ties to each other and continue to organize BLM events, the founders of Movement for Black Lives have moved on to other projects. Parker explains the limits of this connection.

> I know a lot of activists, and people are making a distinction between Black Lives Matter and the Movement for Black Lives. And that's been helpful, because it's like, it really just depends on where you are, what your specific organization stands for. 'Cause it can vary place to place. . . . Black Lives Matter was started by Black queer people, but it's like in the news reporting understanding of it, it's almost exclusively talked about, like, "Oh, this is a Black org." It's like, they try so hard to never mention the queerness that it's built on, that it's created from.

This chapter highlights Black LGBTQ+ political diversity through the students' testimony. They agreed to talk to me because they identify as LGBTQ+. But their willingness to include themselves under that umbrella of social identity does not determine their political identities or priorities. Black LGBTQ+ college students do not agree on a single political ideology or a political label (liberal, conservative, radical, socialist, Democrat, Republican) that fits neatly into the matrix of American politics. They are passionate about social issues, including the crisis in democracy/authoritarianism, but they are not all equally engaged in the fight to rectify the problems of their world. Sometimes, the way they talk about the issues they are most passionate about, such as violence against Black trans people, suggests that they do not even see Black queer issues as political, because the political system does not treat them as such. And even BLM, a movement started by queer Black people who explicitly foreground Black queer issues, is subject to different interpretations and levels of support among the students. Black LGBTQ+ people are responsible for the most transformational social movement of these students' lives. Their political impact is radical and indisputable, and some of the students think about the tenets and aims of BLM every day. But others affirm a queertidian reality that holds space for intentional political revolution, but is not consumed by it.

CONCLUSION

BLACK QUEERTIDIAN FUTURES

I can't be a pessimist, because I'm alive. . . . So I'm forced to be an optimist. I'm forced to believe that we can survive whatever we must survive.
—JAMES BALDWIN

I don't think that anything is indicative of the future. That's why it's the future, because it's only made of possibility.
—AVA

This book is a window into the experiences of Black LGBTQ+ college students. They describe how they choose their schools, spend their time on campus, and build community and friendship through Black LGBTQ+ student organizations. They also describe what it is like to live in the United States during the Trump years, a period that saw a steady stream of dehumanizing political rhetoric and policies from the United States government. There was an atmosphere of racism, homophobia, and transphobia that students dealt with, even on days when they did not have personal experiences with bigotry and discrimination. These social forces constrain their lives and, on occasion, motivate social and political engagement. Several of the folks I spoke with are leaders and change makers on their campus and in the communities they belong to. But plenty of students are not consistently engaged in activism or social-justice efforts. Though they have acute understanding and sharp analysis of the injustice they face, they do not consider themselves to be political warriors. Simultaneous with the political and pop-cultural resonance of courageous Black queer fabulousness/flyness, the mundane character of students' lives shines through this book, as the rhythms and possibilities of Black queertidian experience are revealed.

Among the possibilities opened by the Black queer mundane are the connections and affirmations enabled by Black LGBTQ+ student organizations. These collectives are safe spaces on campuses that may otherwise be hostile to queer Black people, and incubators for friendships that students believe will last a lifetime. They provide invaluable service to everyone on campus, as they educate students, faculty, and staff about the basic terms and requirements of Black LGBTQ+ lives. The organizations destigmatize the fraught, liberating, and unpredictable process of "coming out" (a phrase that does not always apply to Black queer experiences), making space for progress, stagnation, questioning, and discretion. And they give students a platform and sense of self-esteem that enable them to contribute to their college communities and push their institutions forward in myriad ways.

It is impossible to make definitive comparative statements about how Black LGBTQ+ students experience HBCUs and PWIs, but much of what these students told me about the challenges they face is not surprising, considering what we already know about college life in the United States. Interviewees at PWIs often feel disrespected by their school's leadership and alienated from their non-Black classmates, including classmates who are LGBTQ+. But it is not always easy to find a haven among Black students on those campuses, as Black students often carve out spaces that are not welcoming to queer folk. Students at HBCUs have to deal with interpersonal racism from white people far less frequently during their day-to-day lives. But according to these students, the HBCU experience is not especially affirming when it comes to queer sexual and gender expressions. The stereotype of virulent, ceaseless homophobia and transphobia within Black communities is not borne out in students' testimony. But there is clear frustration among HBCU students that the institutions and all who contribute to them—staff, faculty, and students—can and must do more to ensure their success and happiness.

And there really is no mystery about what must be done at HBCUs, or PWIs, for that matter, in order for colleges and universities to reach their full potential as learning communities that Black LGBTQ+ students can thrive in. M. Jacqui Alexander and Beverly Guy-Sheftall sketched a blueprint for these changes in their 2011 report on "Facilitating Campus Climates of Pluralism, Inclusivity, and Progressive Change at HBCUs." For starters, they recommend that as part of their recruitment efforts, HBCUs actively endeavor to demonstrate to prospective students that their campuses are welcoming to LGBTQ+ students. As chapter 1 shows, the students I spoke with did not experience that sort of active recruitment while making their college choices.

HBCUs should also be sure to have nondiscrimination policies that explicitly mention gender identity and sexual orientation, and demonstrate clear commitment to eradicating sexual assault throughout the college community. Though students did not discuss it with me in great depth, sexual assault is an especially pressing issue for genderqueer and nonbinary students, as recent research suggests that nearly a quarter of such students report being sexually assaulted while enrolled in college.[1] Colleges and universities should legitimize sexual and gender diversity at the institutional level by creating student resource offices, safe zones, LGBTQ+ alumni groups, and gender-neutral/single-occupancy restrooms. HBCUs must attend to their housing and residence policies, not only ensuring that every student has a safe place to live but educating everyone who lives on campus about the ways LGBTQ+ students may be disadvantaged and targeted by housing and disciplinary policies, and changing those policies accordingly. A dramatic increase in investment in LGBTQ+ counseling and health services is needed. All students should have faith that they will be treated with care and dignity by every member of the health services and counseling staff, and that they will have access to the most basic mental and physical health treatments they need.[2] In cases where colleges cannot provide comprehensive, around-the-clock treatment to all LGBTQ+ students because of the inherent limitations of health and counseling services staffing, they should be sure to partner with off-campus organizations and professionals who can fill in the gaps. And finally, as Roderick Ferguson argues, institutions must change their curricula such that Black feminist studies and Black queer studies are clear and unapologetic strengths of their academic programs. These changes require concentrated efforts to recruit and retain faculty who can do this research and teaching with the full support of the institution, and without fear that their identity will be viewed as a liability or affront by colleagues, administrators, or alumni.[3]

In a sense, the recommendations above are the easy part. It just takes courage and will to leave antiquated traditions and structures behind, and invest in the people and programs that will allow Black LGBTQ+ students to flourish. What colleges and universities cannot control, however, is the broader political environment they exist within. Prior to Trump's election, a majority of Black people were optimistic about race relations,[4] and as Lessie Branch highlights and laments, they believed in the possibility of social mobility even in the face of the multigenerational exacerbation of racial inequality.[5] As described in chapter 7, Trump's ascendance led to serious doubts about personal safety and long-term happiness for LGBTQ+ people of color, including Black LGBTQ+ folk. Optimism about race relations between Black people and white people faded as his presidency progressed,[6] and additional public-opinion research shows that the racial and partisan divide has exploded. Republicans, who are mostly white, do not believe that marginalized groups face a great deal of discrimination, and they also exhibit far higher levels of resentment of Black people and LGBTQ+ people than Democrats do.[7] This was the political party in power, and this is the environment in which I had the conversations described in this book. I ended each interview by asking students what they think the future holds for the communities they belong to.

Surprisingly, there was a fair amount of optimism, but students were optimistic mostly along a single axis: the future for LGBTQ+ people. Trent told me, "I feel like we're steadily always just improving just a little bit," and Alice said that "our generation is different" and "moving towards a more accepting view of everything." Jafar cited antidiscrimination efforts, "like someone makes a homophobic comment or discriminatory comment and they're released from their job. And I feel like that shows like where we're heading, 'cause I feel like earlier times, that probably wouldn't have happened."

Other students found different reasons to be optimistic when considering the question purely through the lens of LGBTQ+ issues. Some noted that it has been a long journey just to get to where we are today, and that any step backward during the Trump era would inspire a larger step forward in response once he was removed. And then there were students like Elizabeth, who approached the question from a more personal perspective, emphasizing how far she personally has come, and affirming that there is no turning back. "You can't tell me what to do anymore because I know who I am and I'm comfortable with it, and I have gained the knowledge and the experience within myself to tell other people that you don't have to be afraid ever in your life. Once you're comfortable telling yourself that, 'This is who I am, and I'm not going to let anyone change it or try to change it,' you will just continue to move forward, and nothing ever will keep you down."

Coming into her sexual and gender identity is liberating for Elizabeth, and she has gained knowledge that nobody can threaten or take away. But it is also worth emphasizing that her individual approach to the question of LGBTQ+ futures has collective implications. She is comfortable with herself and confident enough to "tell other people that you don't have to be afraid ever in your life." These sentiments echo the words of so many students who describe why their student organizations and the bonds they formed with friends are so important. Not only do they provide a safe space for joy and friendship; they provide hope—a way to see oneself in times and places beyond the immediate circumstances of one's life. Students serve as examples for each other as they navigate both the present and the future in all their uncertainty.

Other students, however, expressed significant trepidation about the future for LGBTQ+ people in America. They did not focus on how deeply rooted and institutionalized homophobia and transphobia are. Instead, the students who are most pessimistic quite simply have little faith in *people*, who have to become more accepting in order for LGBTQ+ folks' prospects to improve. Jewel laments, "I currently have five roommates, and we'll get into arguments about using pronouns, and I'm like, 'This is like, Respect 101.' Like, 'How do I convey to you that this is like a matter of basic manners and respect for each other?' And they just, it won't click. And so sometimes I feel like there's only so much you can do to like, educate and explain and talk to people before it just seems hopeless."

This is especially devastating because Jewel is not talking about strangers. She is talking about acquaintances who know and trust her well enough to live in the same space. She cannot even get the most basic message through to them, let alone any more potentially upsetting messages about institutional oppression and the disregard and danger so many LGBTQ+ people deal with on a daily basis. This is not a purely academic matter, or a matter of intellectual respect, because the danger of homophobic and transphobic misunderstanding is intentional and often violent. Jace told me he does not fear for his life all that much because he can pass for cisgender and straight, but many transgender people he knows cannot, and "live in constant fear." So, he continues, "it scares me to even be optimistic, because I feel like that's just like, over-estimating the mental capacity of the people in this country. There are just a lot of dumbasses who just don't understand that homosexuality doesn't affect them."

Another reason students are skeptical about the future for LGBTQ+ people is that they have seen how the struggle for rights and dignity continues to play out for Black people in America. "It's going to be much like how desegregation was," Cara told me. "All of the sadness, all of the triumphs are going to come along with it. It's depressing to think about [but] you have to think about it like that. We're going to get small victories but we're also going to get knocked down a few times. Like with gay marriage being legalized, but we also started seeing more trans women being killed. I don't know how long it's going to take, or if we'll even get there."

Again, we see the emotional toll of this struggle, as Cara describes the process as not only slow but sad. She also notes that legal victories are not bellwethers of full-fledged liberation and protection, as the threat of extralegal violence remains essentially unchecked. As in previous chapters, transgender rights and transgender lives emerge as perhaps the key issue for students mulling over the state of LGBTQ+ politics. As Trent told me, "You know, trans people of color are constantly being killed. I feel like they are the population of like, the queer population that is at most risk, for just existing." Black transgender women, in particular, are the reference point for Black queer safety and possibility. "LGBTQ+" is not a single group or identity; it contains multitudes of people and raises a number of thorny issues when it comes to measuring progress. The diversity of LGBTQ+ people makes it difficult to imagine a single future in which everyone is equally honored and safe from harm. Clouds dimmed the landscape even further when students answered the question about LGBTQ+ futures by stipulating that Black and white queer futures are inescapably different. As Albert explains, "For white gay people specifically, like gay and lesbian people, I think like they got it. They can get married, like check, check, check. They're done. They're done fighting. But I guess for Black LGBTQ+ people, and I guess maybe people of color, maybe not, the future it isn't that bright. I don't know. I'm not really seeing it. There's a lot of like, depression, a lot of drug usage, a lot of drug addiction, just general substance abuse in the Black gay community or the Black queer community."

Albert answers the question by framing white progress primarily as a matter of rights granted. Once they (white gays and lesbians) can get married, "they're done." Note that he specifically highlights the privilege of gays and lesbians, which calls attention to the different challenges transgender folk face. And in the second half of the statement, the problems Albert sees for Black folk are not just about civil rights but about hope and happiness. Again, this is a struggle for mental health, among other necessities. Naima's answer overlaps with Albert's as she talks about how the dual demands of personal and political struggle are affected by the specific nature of the oppression one faces. "As you go along the spectrum, whoever has the most proximity to Blackness, they will deal with more and more violence. And honestly, white people will be okay. White queer people, a lot of times they hold onto that one single bit of oppression that they have. And I think when you have like, one thing to face, it's easy to dedicate your life to that. But a lot of times, when you have to deal with like, literally your entire existence being hunted, it's difficult to have that same joy."

Like Albert, Naima conceives of the Black queer future as a matter of physical and emotional survival, rather than just a quest for rights. The object is not merely survival but joyful survival, which she sees as essentially impossible for Black LGBTQ+ folks in the current moment. Her analysis is intersectional, with an emphasis on anti-Blackness as the essence of racism, and she sees "survival, but no peace" for Black people. Several of her peers agree, and draw direct comparisons between the future for LGBTQ+ people and the future for Black people. Jewel, for instance, says there are "more people who are willing to speak up against homophobia. And I do think that generally, over, or like broadly, we are getting better." But when I specifically asked her about the future for Black people in the United States, she said, "It just seems like the world is getting more and more violent towards brown and Black folks, and it's kind of scary to think about that."

This was reminiscent of several of the discussions we had about racism and politics. Students described themselves as disengaged, but often it was by choice, as a means of self-preservation. Current events were so upsetting, and the people threatening their health and safety were so

obviously violent and unhinged, it seemed more sensible and produc-
tive to focus on other things. Jonelle describes the absolute horror of
the moment. Like Malcolm X, her American dream is a nightmare. "I
had a nightmare . . . , and I called it 'Blackpocalypse.' And essentially in
the dream, white Christians asked God to give them demons to get rid
of Black people. And the dream is all of that playing out. So like, that is
just this immensity of the country that I live in, and essentially who has
power."

In his incisive article about the paradoxes and potential of queer activism, Joshua Gamson writes, "The assumption that collective identities
are necessary for collective action is turned on its head by queerness,
and the question becomes: When and how are stable collective identities
necessary for social action and social change?"[8] Queerness proves that
identity is subject to change, undoing, and overflowing, so mobilizing
around any collective identity is always historically specific. What the
students' testimony shows is that we remain in a specific historical moment when Blackness is real, stable, and mobilizing. They do not believe
that (white) queer politics or progress will eradicate white supremacy.
Though their lives and experiences differ from those of straight cisgender Black folk, their fate remains linked to the fate of all Black people,
and this commitment to linked fate is the basis for Black political identity and ideology.[9] As Mignon Moore's research shows, Black LGBTQ+
activists see their struggle as a matter of liberation and full membership
within the Black community,[10] and similarly, Black lesbians prioritize
building bonds and families embedded in Black social networks.[11] Oppression is intersectional, but racism and anti-Blackness pose unique
threats to Black queer survival. There is no Black queer future where deracialized and/or white queer advancement guarantees Black liberation.

The dangers and injustices of the present lead to realistic projections
of the future and an unflinching appraisal of Black queer pain. But the
future is not certain, because it depends on what we do. Ava, who is unflinching in her criticism of her college, her country, and the institutions
and traditions that make her life so difficult, offers her thoughts about
moving beyond the emotional pain and social injustices of the present
day: "If you dwell in that in the moment, and see that as indicative of
the future, then you are going to be depressed and you're not going to
feel like there's anything to fight for. But I don't think that the present is

ever indicative of the future. I don't think that anything is indicative of the future. That's why it's the future, because it's only made of possibility."

Students are not waiting for the future to arrive; they are making it. They are actively seizing possibilities and fashioning themselves as examples, both as individuals and as part of a legacy and family. Patricia stood out as one of the few students in her hometown to leave the state to pursue her college degree. She speaks quietly and assuredly, affirming that her academic and professional achievements will empower her and help her make a difference. "I know people say a degree doesn't mean anything anymore. But me being 'Dr. Williams,' rather than being 'ol' girl Williams' from down the street, really does make a big difference in how I am viewed, and who will actually listen to what I'm saying. And being that I am a Black queer woman, they're definitely going to listen. They might not want to listen, but when they hear me, I want them to be shocked."

She vows to use her degree and title not just to improve her financial situation or to fit into respectable society but to shake up the world. And when the world shakes, it will change, because it cannot possibly stay the way that it is now. There is too much stirring, too much evidence that the present, with all its decay, isolation, and fear, is untenable. Parker knows this because of their Black queertidian—"every single day"— experience, and the legacy they inherit and build.

> Liberation is inevitable. The progress is inevitable. . . . I feel like every single day I walk around, there's going to be a Black queer person who sees me living my best life, and they're like, "Wow." 'Cause that's how I got into Black queer radical shit. I saw Black queer radical people living their absolute best lives. Like, cussing out the police, teaching other Black baby queers all about like, "Let me tell you who Assata Shakur is. Let me tell you who Frantz Fanon is," all that stuff. And seeing all of that, it's like I know. I know we're good.

Parker and their siblings comfort and mentor each other, and that is what keeps hope alive. They arrive on campus struggling with the transition from high school to college and looking for connection. Though Black LGBTQ+ students are not always as visible as they would like to be, students form their own friendship groups and organizations, educating each other and the broader campus community about the issues most important to them. The bonds they build are at once mundane and revolutionary, as they come to regard each other as friends and family through Black queertidian fun and comfort. They rely on each other for protection and sanity, as the flip side of their daily experience is the reality of feeling unwelcome and sometimes threatened. The United States is a country with a deep well of white-supremacist and antiqueer politics. Defying these forces is exhausting, and though students are brave and incisive in their analysis of these and other social ills, their resistance does not always translate into mobilization. Linked fate is undeniable, but there is no single Black LGBTQ+ political program. There are many queer Black communities flourishing, struggling, and figuring things out day by day. The people who build them are ordinary, fabulous, and fly, and their futures are limitless.

ACKNOWLEDGMENTS

Thanks to the faculty and staff on the campuses I visited, who work with the students described in this book. Thanks to the Provost's Office at Wellesley College for all of the support I received. Much appreciation for my students at Wellesley. I'm immensely grateful for Ilene Kalish's commitment and expertise. Thanks to the colleagues and readers who provided invaluable feedback, and additional reverence for the Black LGBTQ+ writers and researchers whose courageous work is the foundation for this book.

I wrote this book during the first two years of the pandemic. I could not have finished it without Sarah. Words are not enough.

APPENDIX

In order to recruit students for the interviews in this book, I began by making sure that I followed each school's institutional review board (IRB) protocols for working with human subjects and recruiting students on campus. After receiving assurance from the institution's IRB, I sent emails to the faculty or staff person or people most closely affiliated with the publicly listed student organization for Black LGBTQ+ students or queer students of color. I explained that I was conducting research about race, LGBTQ+ student organizations, student activism, and the experiences and beliefs of their students, and asked whether they thought it would be appropriate to reach out to students from the organization. In some cases, the faculty or staff advisor put me directly in touch with one of the student leaders from the organization. In other cases, they recommended one or more students for me to contact via email. The email I sent to students included a recruitment letter explaining the purpose of the interviews and emphasizing that the identity of each respondent and their institution would be kept confidential throughout the process. It also urged students to ask me any additional questions they might have about the study. The student, faculty, and staff leaders of the organizations were immensely gracious and indispensable to my recruitment efforts.

All interviews were conducted in person and all students and their colleges were given pseudonyms. Before beginning each interview, I explained the purpose of the research to each student and told them that they would be paid, that they could decline to answer any question they wished, that they could stop the interview at any time without forfeiting pay, that they could receive a transcript of the interview if they asked, and that each person and their institution would be given pseudonyms. I also administered a written consent form containing this information and told them they could receive a copy of the form if they wished. Though I had an interview schedule to guide me, in practice, the interviews often became semistructured conversations. I was sure to cover each of the topics I prioritized, which included, but were not limited to the following: the places where they had lived and gone to school prior to college, their hobbies and interests, their experiences with LGBTQ+ student organizations, their experiences on campus more broadly, and the social and political issues of most concern to each student. The order in which those topics were addressed and the time spent on each topic varied from conversation to conversation. After the interview was over, I administered a brief written questionnaire in order to collect demographic information, including information about the students' gender identity and socioeconomic background. Again, students were told they could decline to answer any questions they wished to without any consequences.

Here is the list of interviewees who attended historically Black colleges and universities, the dates they were interviewed, and the name and location of their institution:

> Abraham, September 29, 2018, Juniper (urban, public)
> Alice, September 20, 2019, Hickory (urban, private)
> Amir, March 22, 2018, Cedar (urban, public)
> Annette, September 29, 2018, Linden (urban, public)
> Ava, February 20, 2018, Birch (urban, private)
> Ben, January 19, 2018, Aspen (rural/suburban, public)
> Bradley, September 20, 2018, Hickory (urban, private)
> Brandon, January 19, 2018, Aspen (rural, suburban)
> Camila, February 21, 2018, Birch (urban, private)
> Cara, January 15, 2019, Douglas (urban, public)
> Chris, January 19, 2018, Aspen (rural, suburban)
> Deron, April 11, 2018, Douglas (urban, public)

Easton, January 15, 2019, Evergreen (urban, public)

Elizabeth, September 30, 2018, Linden (urban, public)

Eric, April 12, 2018, Evergreen (urban, public)

Ervin, September 28, 2018, Juniper (urban, public)

Faith, January 20, 2018, Aspen (rural, suburban)

Hailey, March 21, 2018, Cedar (urban, public)

Jasmine, February 21, 2018, Birch (urban, private)

Jason, April 12, 2018, Evergreen (urban, public)

Jayla, March 22, 2018, Cedar (urban, public)

Lana, January 16, 2019, Douglas (urban, public)

Lauryn, September 19, 2018, Fieldrose (urban, private)

Layla, January 19, 2018, Aspen (rural/suburban, public)

Madison, February 21, 2018, Birch (urban, private)

Matt, September 19, 2018, Fieldrose (rural/suburban, public)

Maya, February 21, 2018, Birch (urban, private)

Mitchell, September 19, 2018, Hickory (urban, private)

Patricia, September 19, 2018, Fieldrose (urban, private)

Peter, January 16, 2019, Evergreen, (urban, public)

Preston, September 20, 2018, Hickory (urban, private)

Rae, January 16, 2019, Douglas (urban, public)

Remy, January 19, 2018, Aspen (rural/suburban public)

Shannon, September 28, 2018, Juniper (urban, public)

Sonia, January 19, 2018, Aspen (rural/suburban, public)

Sydney, April 11, 2018, Douglas (urban, public)

Taylor, September 30, 2018, Linden (urban, public)

Tracey, January 16, 2019, Evergreen (urban, public)

Victor, September 29, 2018, Linden (urban, public)

Zoe, March 23, 2018, Cedar (urban, public)

Here is the list of interviewees who attended predominantly white institutions, the dates they were interviewed, and the name and location of their institution:

Ada, November 8, 2019, Weddell (suburban, public)

Albert, September 19, 2019, Tasman (urban, private)

Bruce, April 5, 2019, Adriatic (urban, public)

Candace, April 5, 2019, Adriatic (urban, public)

Cat, March 28, 2019, Caspian (urban, public)

Desean, September 21, 2019, Tasman (urban, private)

Gwen, March 29, 2019, Caspian (urban, public)

Ian, November 15, 2019, Timor (urban, public)

Jace, April 19, 2019, Tasman (urban, private)

Jafar, April 19, 2019, Barents (urban, public)

Jewel, April 19, 2019, Barents (urban, public)

Jonelle, November 15, 2019, Timor (urban, public)

Kerry, April 5, 2019, Adriatic (urban, public)

Luke, November 8, 2019, Weddell (suburban, public)

Morris, November 2, 2019, Java (urban, public)

Naima, September 20, 2019, Tasman (urban, private)

Nick, November 15, 2019, Timor (urban, public)

Olympia, April 19, 2019, Barents (urban, public)

Parker, November 8, 2019, Weddell (suburban, public)

Roland, April 4, 2019, Adriatic (urban, public)

Summer, March 29, 2019, Caspian (urban, public)

Tamika, March 29, 2019, Caspian (urban, public)

Thea, November 8, 2019, Weddell (suburban, public)

Trent, April 18, 2019, Barents (urban, public)

Valerie, April 19, 2019, Barents (urban, public)

NOTES

INTRODUCTION

1 Trudy Ring, "Kamala Harris Becomes First Sitting V.P. to March in Pride Event," *Advocate*, June 12, 2021, www.advocate.com.

2 As explained by the National LGBTQ+ Bar Association and Foundation,

The LGBTQ+ "panic" defense strategy is a legal strategy that asks a jury to find that a victim's sexual orientation or gender identity/expression is to blame for a defendant's violent reaction, including murder. It is not a free-standing defense to criminal liability, but rather a legal tactic used to bolster other defenses. When a perpetrator uses an LGBTQ+ "panic" defense, they are claiming that a victim's sexual orientation or gender identity not only explains—but excuses—a loss of self-control and the subsequent assault. By fully or partially acquitting the perpetrators of crimes against LGBTQ+ victims, this defense implies that LGBTQ+ lives are worth less than others. ("LGBTQ+ 'Panic' Defense," The LGBTQ+ Bar, n.d., https://lgbtqbar.org)

3 Tim Fitzsimons, "Kamala Harris Brings Pro-LGBTQ Record to Biden Ticket," *NBC News*, August 12, 2020, www.nbcnews.com.

4 *Black Enterprise*, "Kamala Harris—the Power of an HBCU Education," August 26, 2020, 5:20, https://www.youtube.com/watch?v=a74k9c09_KE.

5 Jafari S. Allen, "On a Black Queer Morehouse Commencement," *Huffington Post*, May 22, 2013, www.huffingtonpost.com.

6 Sarah Willie's *Acting Black: College Identity and the Performance of Race* (New York: Routledge, 2003) uses interviews with Black alumni from Northwestern University and Howard University to highlight code switching and other performances of race. Though *Acting Black* does not focus on queerness or gender and

sexuality, its account of the ways campus climate influences racial identity is an important starting point.

7 Perry Bacon Jr., "Support for Same-Sex Marriage Isn't Unanimous," *FiveThirtyEight*, May 4, 2018, https://fivethirtyeight.com; "The Partisan Divide on Political Values Grows Even Wider," Pew Research Center, October 5, 2017, www.people-press.org.

8 For more on this phenomenon, see Marcus Anthony Hunter, "All the Gays Are White and All the Blacks Are Straight," *Sexuality Research and Social Policy* 7 (2010): 81–92.

9 Madison Moore, *Fabulous: The Rise of the Beautiful Eccentric* (New Haven, CT: Yale University Press, 2018), 8.

10 Seth Davis offers empirical support for the benefits of a fabulous response to oppression in his ethnographic study of "fierce" Black queer literacies among Black femmes and queers. Fierce and subversive literacy and rhetoric are armor and weaponry against the violence confronting Black queer people, and fierce queer speech is often the basis for community building and collective affirmation. Seth Davis, "Fierce: Black Queer Literacies of Survival" (PhD diss., Syracuse University, 2018), available at https://surface.syr.edu.

11 I use the phrase "Black queertidian" to describe the mundane self-concepts, moments, considerations, experiences, challenges, and joys of Black queer life. It is an adaptation of "Black quotidian," which is the title of Matthew Delmont's digital history project, *Black Quotidian: Everyday History in African American Newspapers* (Palo Alto, CA: Stanford University Press, 2019). Delmont's *Black Quotidian* illustrates how Black newspapers shaped African American history and culture by publishing stories about everyday people and cultural practices, rather than solely reporting on well-known events and the Black leaders and celebrities who were intimately involved in them. It does not address the central concerns of this book.

12 Cathy Cohen, "Punks, Bulldaggers, and Welfare Queens: The Radical Potential of Queer Politics?" in *Black Queer Studies: A Critical Anthology*, eds. E. Patrick Johnson and Mae G. Henderson (Durham, NC: Duke University Press, 2005), 21–51.

13 S. K. Goldberg, E. D. Rothblum, S. T. Russell, and I. H. Meyer, "Exploring the Q in LGBTQ+: Demographic Characteristic and Sexuality of Queer People in a U.S. Representative Sample of Sexual Minorities," *Psychology of Sexual Orientation and Gender Diversity* 7 (2020): 101–12.

14 Rhea Ashley Hoskin, "'Femininity? It's the Aesthetic of Subordination': Examining Femmephobia, the Gender Binary, and Experiences of Oppression among Sexual and Gender Minorities," *Archives of Sexual Behavior* 49 (2020): 2319–39.

15 M. Shelly Connor, "Dapper: Fashioning a Queer Aesthetic of Black Womanhood," *Root*, December 2, 2017, https://theglowup.theroot.com.

16 Carly Thomsen, *Visibility Interrupted: Rural Queer Life and the Politics of Unbecoming* (Minneapolis: University of Minnesota Press, 2021), x.

17 Charlene A. Carruthers, *Unapologetic: A Black, Queer, and Feminist Mandate for Radical Movements* (Boston: Beacon Press, 2018), 23.

18 Glendon Francis, "10 Black Queer Artists Get Real about the Intersectionality of Resistance during Pride 2020," *Billboard*, June 24, 2000, www.billboard.com.

19 Eve Kosofsky Sedgwick, "Queer and Now," in *The Routledge Queer Studies Reader*, eds. Donald E. Hall and Annamarie Jagose (New York: Routledge, 2013), 8.

20 Roderick Ferguson, *One-Dimensional Queer* (New York: Polity, 2018).

21 Roderick Ferguson, *We Demand: The University and Student Protest* (Berkeley: University of California Press, 2013).

22 Kristen A. Renn, "LGBT and Queer Research in Higher Education: The State and Status of the Field," *Educational Researcher* 29 (2010): 134.

23 Kristen A. Renn, "LGBT Student Leaders and Queer Activists: Identities of Lesbian, Gay, Bisexual, Transgender, and Queer-Identified College Student Leaders and Activists," *Journal of College Student Development* 48 (2007): 311.

24 Antonio Duran, "Queer *and* of Color: A Systematic Literature Review on Queer Students of Color in Higher Education Scholarship," *Journal of Diversity in Higher Education* 12 (2019): 390–400.

25 See C. Riley Snorton, *Nobody Is Supposed to Know: Black Sexuality on the Down Low* (Minneapolis: University of Minnesota Press, 2014); and Tristan Bridges and Mignon Moore, "Young Women of Color and Shifting Sexual Identities," *Contexts* 17.1 (2018): 86–88, http://journals.sagepub.com.

26 Jason C. Garvey and Susan R. Rankin, "The Influence of Campus Experiences on the Level of Outness among Trans-Spectrum and Queer-Spectrum Students," *Journal of Homosexuality* 62 (2015): 374–93.

27 "Key Events in Black Higher Education," *Journal of Blacks in Higher Education*, 2022, https://www.jbhe.com/chronology. Alan Pifer reports that at the beginning of the Civil War, only twenty-eight Black people were college graduates; *The Higher Education of Blacks in the United States* (New York: Carnegie Corporation, 1973), 29.

28 Carol Anderson, *White Rage: The Unspoken Truth of Our Racial Divide* (New York: Bloomsbury, 2016), 54.

29 Melissa Wooten, *In the Face of Inequality: How Black Colleges Adapt* (Albany: State University of New York Press, 2016), 8.

30 Nathan Grawe, *Demographics and the Demand for Higher Education* (Baltimore, MD: Johns Hopkins University Press, 2017).

31 Monica Anderson, "A Look at Historically Black Colleges and Universities as Howard Turns 150," Pew Research Center, February 28, 2017, www.pewresearch.org.

32 Cleve R. Wootson Jr. and Susan Svrluga, "Trump Questions Whether Key Funding Source for Historically Black College Is Constitutional," *Washington Post*, May 8, 2017, www.washingtonpost.com.

33 Andrew Kreighbaum, "HBCUs and the Trump Administration," *Inside Higher Education*, February 28, 2018, www.insidehighered.com.

34 Tiffany Jones, "DeVos, Trump, and What We're Missing about HBCUs," *CNN*, May 29, 2018, www.cnn.com.

35 Jesse Washington, "Black Economic Gains Reversed in Great Recession," *News Tribune* (Jefferson City, MO), July 10, 2011, www.newstribune.com.

36 Jason Johnson, "The Black Renaissance Is Real: HBCUs See Record Growth in 2017," *Root*, October 25, 2017, www.theroot.com.

37 Casey Dougal, Penjie Gao, William J. Mayew, and Christopher A. Parsons, "What's in a (School) Name? Racial Discrimination in Higher Education Bond Markets," *Journal of Financial Economics* 134.3 (2019): 570–90, https://econpapers. repec.org.

38 Andrew H. Nichols and Denzel Evans, "A Look Back at Success: Identifying Top- and Bottom-Performing Institutions," Education Trust, May 1, 2017, https://edtrust.org.

39 Jones, "DeVos, Trump, and What We're Missing about HBCUs."

40 Sean Seymour and Julie Ray, "Grads of Historically Black Colleges Have Well-Being Edge," Gallup, October 27, 2015, https://news.gallup.com.

41 Johnson, "The Black Renaissance Is Real."

42 As quoted in his interview with Michel Martin, "What's Caused the Increased Enrollment at HBCUs?" NPR, September 17, 2016, www.npr.org.

43 See Shaun R. Harper and Marybeth Gasman, "Consequences of Conservatism: Black Male Undergraduates and the Politics of Historically Black Colleges and Universities," *Journal of Negro Education* 77 (2008): 336–51.

44 For additional reflections on, and solutions to, this challenge, see Elisa S. Abes, "Theoretical Borderlands: Using Multiple Theoretical Perspectives to Challenge Inequitable Power Structures in Student Development Theory," *Journal of College Student Development* 50 (2009): 141–56.

45 The recruitment letter uses the abbreviation "LGBTQ" rather than "LGBTQ+," as I assumed that "LGBTQ" was an inclusive enough abbreviation to draw the students in and worried that adding the "+" might be off-putting or confusing in some way. And importantly, I recruited students through the Black LGBTQ+ student organizations established on campus. I spoke with student leaders and faculty and staff advisors and supporters of those organizations prior to distributing the letter more widely, so everyone connected to the organization understood the inclusivity of the project. Nobody suggested the phrase "LGBTQ+" was not inclusive enough, but I prefer to add the "+" in my writing.

46 Bridges and Moore, "Young Women of Color and Shifting Sexual Identities."

CHAPTER 1. GETTING TO CAMPUS

1 Shoshana Goldberg, Esther Rothblum, Stephen Russell, and Ilan Meyer, "Exploring the Q in LGBTQ: Demographic Characteristic and Sexuality of Queer People in a U.S. Representative Sample of Sexual Minorities," *Psychology of Sexual Orientation and Gender Diversity* 7 (2020): 101–12.

2 William H. Darity Jr., Darrick Hamilton, Mark Paul, Alan Aja, Antonio Moore, and Caerina Chiopris, "What We Get Wrong about Closing the Racial Wealth Gap," Samuel DuBois Cook Center on Social Equity, April 2018, https://socialequity.duke.edu. Also see Tatjana Meschede, Joanna Taylor, Alexis Mann, Thomas

M. Shapiro, Federal Reserve Bank of St. Louis *Review* 99.1 (first quarter 2017), 121–37, http://dx.doi.org/10.20955/r.2017.121-137.

3 Valerie Strauss, "How High School Seniors Really Pick the Colleges They Attend—New Report," *Washington Post*, May 2, 2016, www.washingtonpost.com.

4 Rick Seltzer, "Turning Down Top Choices," *Inside Higher Ed*, March 23, 2017, www.insidehighered.com.

5 Melvin L. Oliver and Thomas Shapiro, "Disrupting the Racial Wealth Gap," *Contexts*, May 7, 2019, https://contexts.org.

6 Don Hossler and Karen S. Gallagher, "Studying Student College Choice: A Three-Phase Model and the Implications for Policymakers," *College and University* 62 (1987): 207–21.

7 Jo Jones and William D. Mosher, "Fathers' Involvement with Their Children in the United States, 2006–2010," *National Health Statistics Reports* 71 (2013), https://www.cdc.gov.

8 See Prudence Carter, *Keepin' It Real: School Success beyond Black and White* (Oxford: Oxford University Press, 2007) and Angel Harris, *Kids Don't Want to Fail: Oppositional Culture and the Black-White Achievement Gap* (Cambridge, MA: Harvard University Press, 2011).

9 Amy Bergerson, *College Choice and Access to College: Moving Policy, Research, and Practice to the 21ˢᵗ Century* (New York: Wiley, 2009).

10 W. Tierney and S. Auerbach, "Toward Developing an Untapped Resource: The Role of Families in College Preparation," in *Preparing for College: Nine Elements of Effective Outreach*, eds. William B. Corwin, Zoe E. Corwin, and Julia E. Colyar (Albany: State University of New York Press, 2005), 29–48.

11 Susan Adams, "White High School Dropouts Are as Likely to Land Jobs as Black College Students," *Forbes*, June 27, 2014, www.forbes.com.

12 Douglas A. Burleson, "Sexual Orientation and College Choice: Considering Campus Climate," *About Campus* 14 (2010): 9–14.

CHAPTER 2. THE BLACK QUEERTIDIAN

1 E. Patrick Johnson, "'Quare' Studies, or (Almost) Everything I Know about Queer Studies I Learned from My Grandmother," in Johnson and Henderson, eds., *Black Queer Studies*, 127.

2 Sedgwick, "Queer and Now," 8.

3 Matt Brim and Amin Ghaziani, "Introduction: Queer Methods," *Women's Studies Quarterly* 44 (2016): 16–17.

4 E. Patrick Johnson, "'Quare' Studies.".

5 This criticism of theory, which has paradoxically become a cornerstone of queer theory, comes from Barbara Christian, "The Race for Theory," *Feminist Studies* 14 (1988): 67–79. It is beyond the scope of this book to offer a comprehensive list of works that are self-described theories of Black queer life and the mutually constitutive properties of Blackness and queerness, but interested readers could begin with Kathryn Bond Stockton, *Beautiful Bottom, Beautiful Shame: Where Black*

Meets Queer (Durham, NC: Duke University Press, 2006); Keguro Macharia, *Frottage: Frictions of Intimacy across the Black Diaspora* (New York: NYU Press, 2019); Jafari Allen, *There's a Disco Ball between Us: A Theory of Black Gay Life* (Durham, NC: Duke University Press, 2021); and Rinaldo Walcott, "Somewhere out There: The New Black Queer Theory," in *Blackness and Sexualities*, eds. Michelle M. Wright and Antje Schuhmann (Berlin: Lit Verlag, 2007), 29–40.

6 Justin Kirkland, "Billy Porter Arrived a Long Time Ago: The World Finally Caught Up," *Esquire*, June 9, 2019, www.esquire.com.

7 Tony Maglio, "Billy Porter Talks about Getting a Sex Scene after a Career of Not Being Anyone's Object of Affection," *Wrap*, August 6, 2019, www.thewrap.com.

8 Miranda Bryant, "*Pose* Star Billy Porter: 'I Should Have Put This Dress On 20 Years Ago,'" *Guardian*, September 15, 2019, www.theguardian.com.

9 Amy Johnson, "Billy Porter Fires Back at Critics Upset That He Will Wear a Dress on 'Sesame Street': 'If You Don't Like It, Don't Watch It,'" *Yahoo! Entertainment*, February 6, 2020, www.yahoo.com.

10 Bryant, "*Pose* Star Billy Porter."

11 Christian Allaire, "Billy Porter Just Made the Most Fabulous Entrance in Met Gala History," *Vogue*, May 6, 2019, www.vogue.com.

12 Raisa Bruner, "Billy Porter Getting Carried into the 2019 Met Gala Is Already One of the Most Glorious Entrances to Behold," *Time*, May 6, 2019, https://time.com.

13 Marianna Cerini, "Billy Porter's Red Carpet Style Transcends Fashion," CNN, February 7, 2020, www.cnn.com.

14 Oprah Winfrey, "Oprah Talks to RuPaul about Life, Liberty, and the Pursuit of Fabulous," *Oprah*, accessed May 4, 2022, www.oprah.com.

15 Evan Real, "'Pose' Stars on Why the FX Show 'Feels like a Form of Activism,'" *Hollywood Reporter*, November 26, 2018, www.hollywoodreporter.com.

16 Danielle Turchiano, "*Pose* Star Indya Moore Reflects on Empathizing with Angel," *Variety*, January 17, 2019, https://variety.com.

17 "Lena Waithe: First Black Woman to Win an Emmy for Outstanding Writing in a Comedy Series," *Time*, 2022, https://time.com.

18 Eliana Dockterman, "Read the Full Transcript of *Master of None* Writer Lena Waithe's Emmys Speech," *Time*, September 17, 2017, https://time.com.

19 Christopher Rosa, "Lena Waithe Wore a Pride Cape to the Met Gala 2018, and Twitter's Loving It," *Glamour*, May 7, 2018, www.glamour.com.

20 Though there was initial speculation that "invented" was misspelled as "inventend," Waithe clarified on social media that the spelling was intentional. The extra "n" before the "d" is meant to add extra emphasis to Black queers' innovation.

21 Jacqueline Woodson, "Lena Waithe Is Changing the Game," *Vanity Fair*, March 22, 2018, www.vanityfair.com.

22 Woodson, "Lena Waithe Is Changing the Game."

23 The couple divorced in January 2020.

24 E. Patrick Johnson, *Sweet Tea: Black Gay Men of the South* (Chapel Hill: University of North Carolina Press, 2008), 2–3.

CHAPTER 3. ADJUSTING TO COLLEGE

1 Jones and Mosher, "Fathers' Involvement with Their Children in the United States, 2006–2010." Also see Roberta L. Coles and Charles Green, *The Myth of the Missing Black Father* (New York: Columbia University Press, 2010).

2 See Tom Mould, *Overthrowing the Queen: Telling Stories of Welfare in America* (Bloomington: Indiana University Press, 2020), and Eric Schnurer, "Just How Wrong Is Conventional Wisdom about Government Fraud?" *Atlantic*, August 15, 2013, www.theatlantic.com.

3 For more on Black kinship see Carol B. Stack, *Strategies for Survival in a Black Community* (New York: Basic Books, 1983), and Katherine S. Newman, *No Shame in My Game: The Working Poor in the Inner City* (New York: Vintage Books, 1999).

4 See Francis A. Pearman, F. Chris Curran, Benjamin Fisher, and Jospeh Gardella, "Are Achievement Gaps Related to Discipline Gaps? Evidence from National Data," *AERA Open* 5 (2019): 1–18; and Victor M. Rios, *Punished: Policing the Lives of Black and Latino Boys* (New York: NYU Press, 2011).

5 Snorton, *Nobody Is Supposed to Know*.

6 See Katie Acosta, *Amigas y Amantes: Sexually Nonconforming Latinas Negotiate Family* (New Brunswick, NJ: Rutgers University Press, 2013).

7 Antonio Pastrana, "It Takes a Family: An Examination of Outness among Black LGBT People in the United States," *Journal of Family Issues* 37 (2016): 765–88.

8 Christopher D. Petsko and Galen V. Bodenhausen, "Racial Stereotyping of Gay Men: Can a Minority Sexual Orientation Erase Race?" *Journal of Experimental Psychology* 83 (2019): 37–54.

9 Mignon Moore, "Articulating a Politics of (Multiple) Identities: Sexuality and Inclusion in Black Community Life," *Du Bois Review* 7 (2010): 3.

10 E. Patrick Johnson, *Sweet Tea*. Thomsen, *Visibility Interrupted*. Though it should be noted that Thomsen's argument is based on interviews with white lesbians who live in the Midwest, rather than Black southerners.

11 Adrian D. Zongrone, Joseph G. Kosciw, and Nhan L. Truong, *Erasure and Resilience: The Experiences of LGBTQ+ Students of Color in U.S. Schools* (New York: GLSEN, 2020).

12 Mignon Moore, *Invisible Families: Gay Identities, Relationships, and Motherhood among Black Women* (Berkeley: University of California Press, 2011), 59.

13 Renn, "LGBT and Queer Research in Higher Education," 134.

14 Thomsen, *Visibility Interrupted*, xiii. Thomsen also notes that foregrounding urban living as the key to LGBTQ+ happiness ignores the differences between gay and lesbian experiences, as there is little evidence that coupled lesbians prefer to live in cities or are happiest in urban spaces.

15 "All Black Lives Matter: Mental Health of Black LGBTQ Youth," The Trevor Project, October 6, 2020, www.thetrevorproject.org.

CHAPTER 4. COMING INTO THE LIFE

1 John D'Emilio, *Sexual Politics, Sexual Communities: The Making of a Homosexual Minority in the United States, 1940–1970* (Chicago: University of Chicago Press, 1983).

2 For a review of this literature and the most influential theories of the late twentieth century, see Heidi Levine and Nancy Evans, "The Development of Gay, Bisexual, and Lesbian Identities," in *Beyond Tolerance: Gays, Lesbians, and Bisexuals on Campus*, eds. Nancy J. Evans and Vernon A. Wall (Alexandria, VA: American College Personnel Association, 1991), 1–24.

3 The stages are outlined in Vivienne C. Cass, "Homosexual Identity Formation: A Theoretical Model," *Journal of Homosexuality* 4 (1979): 219–35; Susan R. McCarn and Ruth E. Fassinger, "Revisioning Sexual Minority Identity Formation: A New Model of Lesbian Identity and Its Implications for Counseling and Research," *Counseling Psychologist* 24 (1996): 508–34; and Ruth E. Fassinger, "Lesbian, Gay, and Bisexual Identity and Student Development Theory," in *Working with Lesbian, Gay, Bisexual, and Transgender College Students: A Handbook for Faculty and Administrators*, ed. Ronni L. Sanlo (Westport, CT: Greenwood Press), 13–22.

4 Duran, "Queer *and* of Color."

5 Moore, *Invisible Families*, 22.

6 Johnetta B. Cole and Beverly Guy-Sheftall, *Gender Talk: The Struggle for Women's Equality in African American Communities* (New York: Ballantine, 2003).

7 Acosta, *Amigas y Amantes*.

8 Moore, "Articulating a Politics of (Multiple) Identities," 8.

9 Marlon B. Ross, "Beyond the Closet as a Raceless Paradigm," in Johnson and Henderson, eds., *Black Queer Studies*, 162–89.

10 Snorton, *Nobody Is Supposed to Know*, 18.

11 "Play brother/sister/cousin" refers to a close friend who is not technically a relative by law or blood but is considered family or kin.

12 David Johns, "We Need to Move beyond Coming Out and Begin Inviting In," *Advocate*, October 11, 2020, www.advocate.com.

13 See Kath Weston, *Families We Choose: Lesbians, Gay Men, and Kinship* (New York: Columbia University Press, 1991); Peter M. Nardi, "That's What Friends Are For: Friends as Family in the Gay and Lesbian Community," in *Modern Homosexualities: Fragments of Lesbian and Gay Experience*, ed. Ken Plummer (London: Routledge, 1992); Peter M. Nardi, *Gay Men's Friendships: Invincible Communities* (Chicago: University of Chicago Press, 1999); John Preston and Michael Lowenthal, *Friends and Lovers: Gay Men Write about the Families They Create* (New York: Plume, 1996); Jeffrey Weeks, Brian Heaphy, and Catherine Donovan, *Same Sex Intimacies: Families of Choice and Other Life Experiments* (London: Routledge, 2001).

14 Didier Eribon, *Insult and the Making of the Gay Self*, translated by Michael Lucey (Durham, NC: Duke University Press, 2004), 26.

15 Sasha Roseneil, "Living and Loving beyond the Heteronorm," *Eurozine*, May 29, 2007, www.eurozine.com.

16 J. Jack Halberstam, *In a Queer Time and Place: Transgender Bodies, Subcultural Lives* (New York: NYU Press, 2005), 1–2.

17 Sadie E. Hale and Tomas Ojeda, "Acceptable Femininity? Gay Male Misogyny and the Policing of Queer Femininity," *European Journal of Women's Studies* 25.3 (2018): 310–24.

18 Stephen Maddison, *Fags, Hags, and Queer Sisters: Gender Dissent and Heterosocial Bonds in Gay Culture* (Basingstoke, UK: Macmillan, 2000).

CHAPTER 5. EVERYDAY OPPRESSION

1 For example, John Dovidio and Samuel Gaertner demonstrated that although white employers held less prejudicial attitudes during the 1990s than they had in the 1980s, discriminatory hiring practices persisted across both decades when candidates had comparable resumes. John Dovidio and Samuel Gaertner, "Aversive Racism and Selection Decisions: 1989 and 1999," *Psychological Science* 11 (2000): 315–19.

2 Tali Mendelberg, *The Race Card: Campaign Strategy, Implicit Messages, and the Norm of Equality* (Princeton, NJ: Princeton University Press, 2001).

3 Eduardo Bonilla-Silva, *Racism without Racists: Color-Blind Racism and the Persistence of Racial Inequality in America* (New York: Rowman & Littlefield, 2003).

4 Joe Feagin, *The White Racial Frame: Centuries of Framing and Counter-Framing* (New York: Routledge, 2013).

5 Leslie Picca and Joe Feagin, *Two-Faced Racism: Whites in the Backstage and Frontstage* (New York: Routledge, 2007).

6 Christopher S. Parker, "Race and Politics in the Age of Obama," *Annual Review of Sociology* 42 (2016): 217–30; Michael Tesler, "Views about Race Mattered More in Electing Trump Than in Electing Obama," *Washington Post*, November 22, 2016, www.washingtonpost.com; Mathew Fowler, Vladimir E. Medenica, and Cathy Cohen, "Why 41 Percent of White Millennials Voted for Trump," *Washington Post*, December 15, 2017, www.washingtonpost.com.

7 "The Year in Hate and Extremism: 2019," Southern Poverty Law Center, 2019, www.splcenter.org.

8 "US Hate Crime Highest in More Than a Decade—FBI," British Broadcasting Company, November 17, 2020, www.bbc.com.

9 This brief definition comes from Julie Minkel-Lecocque, "Racism, College, and the Power of Words: Racial Microaggressions Reconsidered," *American Educational Research Journal* 50 (2013): 436. It is built on the work of Derald Wang Sue et al., "Racial Microaggressions and the Asian American Experience," *Cultural Diversity and Ethnic Minority Psychology* 13 (2007): 72–81; and Derald Wang Sue, *Microaggressions in Everyday Life: Race, Gender, and Sexual Orientation* (Hoboken, NJ: Wiley, 2010).

10 Derald Wang Sue et al., "Racial Microaggressions and the Power to Define Reality," *American Psychologist* 63 (2008): 277–79; Derald Wang Sue et al., "Racial
Microaggressions against Black Americans: Implications for Counseling," *Journal
of Counseling and Development* 86 (2008): 330–38; Von Robertson et al., "Racism
and the Experiences of Latina/o College Students at a PWI (Predominantly White
Institution)," *Critical Sociology* 42 (2016): 715–35; Jennifer Wang et al., "When
the Seemingly Innocuous 'Stings': Racial Microaggressions and Their Emotional
Consequences," *Personality and Social Psychology Bulletin* 37 (2011): 1666–78; Joe
Feagin et al., *The Agony of Education: Black Students at White Colleges and Universities* (New York: Routledge, 1996).

11 David R. Dietrich, "Racially Charged Cookies and White Scholarships: Anti–
Affirmative Action Protests on American College Campuses," *Sociological Focus*
48 (2015): 105–25.

12 Picca and Feagin, *Two-Faced Racism*; Nella Van Dyke and Griff Tester, "Dangerous Climates: Factors Associated with Variation in Racist Hate Crimes on College
Campuses," *Journal of Contemporary Criminal Justice* 30 (2014): 290–309; Rebecca
L. Stotzer and Emily Hossellman, "Hate Crimes on Campus: Racial/Ethnic Diversity and Campus Safety," *Journal of Interpersonal Violence* 27 (2012): 644–61.

13 Dan Bauman, "Hate Crimes on Campuses Are Rising, FBI Data Show," *Chronicle
of Higher Education*, November 14, 2018, www.chronicle.com. For a list of some of
these incidents, see "Campus Racial Incidents," *Journal of Blacks in Higher Education*, www.jbhe.com.

14 For more on self-stigma, see Gregory Herek, Roy Gillis, and Jeanine C. Cogan,
"Internalized Stigma among Sexual Minority Adults: Insights from a Social Psychological Perspective," *Journal of Counseling Psychology* 56 (2009): 32–43.

15 Ken Corbett, "Faggot = Loser," *Studies in Gender and Sexuality* 2 (2001): 3–28; C.
J. Pascoe, *Dude, You're a Fag: Masculinity and Sexuality in High School* (Berkeley:
University of California Press, 2007).

16 R. W. Connell is often cited as the scholar who coined "hegemonic masculinity,"
as her book *Masculinities* (Berkeley: University of California Press, 2005) is a
cornerstone. The idea has been complicated and criticized by many, and Connell responds to some of those criticisms in Connell and James Messerschmidt,
"Hegemonic Masculinity: Rethinking the Concept," *Gender and Society* 19 (2005):
819–59. For a useful summary of these issues and new directions in the field, see
Tristan Bridges and C. J. Pascoe, "Hybrid Masculinities: New Directions in the
Sociology of Men and Masculinities," *Sociology Compass* 8 (2014): 246–58.

17 Laura Hamilton, "Trading on Heterosexuality: College Women's Gender Strategies and Homophobia," *Gender and Society* 21 (2007): 145–72.

18 See Susan R. Rankin, "Campus Climate for Gay, Lesbian, Bisexual, and Transgender People," Policy Institute of the National Gay and Lesbian Task Force, 2003,
www.ngltf.org. The study of campus climate for LGBT people includes over four
hundred academic administrators, roughly three-quarters of whom acknowledge
that homophobia is a problem. The survey also finds that respondents of all types,

including students, staff, and faculty, are evenly divided with respect to the effectiveness of the institutional responses to the problem.

19 Sydney Epps, "Experiences of Transgender Men Who Joined National Pan-Hellenic Council Sororities Pre-Transition" (PhD diss., Louisiana State University and Agricultural and Mechanical College, 2020), available at https://digitalcommons.lsu.edu.

20 Valerie J. Gortmaker and Robert D. Brown, "Out of the College Closet: Differences in Perceptions and Experiences among Out and Closeted Lesbian and Gay Students," *College Student Journal* 40 (2006): 606–19; Rankin, "Campus Climate for Gay, Lesbian, Bisexual, and Transgender People."

21 Brittany Boyd et al., "Exploring Partner Scarcity: Highly Educated Black Women and Dating Compromise," *Sexuality Research and Social Policy* 18 (2021): 702–14, https://doi.org/10.1007/s13178-020-00493-3.

22 Bailey and Trudy explore the growth and development of misogynoir in more detail in Moya Bailey and Trudy, "On Misogynoir: Citation, Erasure, and Plagiarism," *Feminist Media Studies* 18 (2018): 762–68.

CHAPTER 6. CONFRONTING RACISM AND HOMOPHOBIA

1 Jewel Wicker, "Lil Nas X Has Last Word as Controversy Erupts over 'Devil-Worshipping' Video," *Guardian*, March 30, 2021, www.theguardian.com; Graham Hartmann, "Lil Nas X's 'Satan Shoes' Have Sent Conservative Christian Twitter into a Rage Spiral," *Loudwire*, March 29, 2021, https://loudwire.com.

2 Neena Rouhani, "'He's a Genius': How Lil Nas X's 'Montero' Marketing Strategy Pressed All the Right Buttons," *Billboard*, April 6, 2021, www.billboard.com.

3 Raffy Ermac, "Lil Nas X's Emotional Letter to His Younger Self Gives Us All the Hope," *Out*, July 22, 2021, www.out.com.

4 Dirk-Jan Janssen and Peer Scheepers, "How Religiosity Shapes Rejection of Homosexuality across the Globe," *Journal of Homosexuality* 66 (2019): 1974–2001. For similar findings, see Kent Patrick, Wendy Heywood, Judy M. Simpson, Marian K. Pitts, Juliet Richters, Julia M. Shelley, and Anthony M. Smith, "Demographic Predictors of Consistency and Change in Heterosexuals' Attitudes toward Homosexual Behavior over a Two-Year Period," *Journal of Sex Research* 50 (2013): 611–19; and Jeni Loftus, "America's Liberalization in Attitudes toward Homosexuality, 1973 to 1998," *American Sociological Review* 66 (2001): 762–82.

5 Marianne Campbell, Jordan D. X. Hinton, and Joel R. Anderson, "A Systematic Review of the Relationship between Religion and Attitudes toward Transgender and Gender-Variant People," *International Journal of Transgenderism* 20 (2019): 21–38. Another 2019 survey of thirty-four countries by Pew Research found similar results. In all thirty-four countries, religiously unaffiliated people were more accepting of homosexuality than religiously affiliated people. In the United States, the spread was 22 percent; see Aidan Connaughton, "Religiously Unaffiliated People More Likely Than Those with a Religion to Lean Left, Accept Homosexuality," Pew Research Center, September 28, 2020, www.pewresearch.org.

6 David M. Barnes and Ilan H. Meyer, "Religious Affiliation, Internalized Homophobia, and Mental Health in Lesbians, Gay Men, and Bisexuals," *American Journal of Orthopsychiatry* 82 (2102): 505–15.

7 "U.S. Religious Landscape Survey," Pew Research Center, June 1, 2008, www.pewforum.org; see also David Smith, "US Evangelical Christians Accused of Promoting Homophobia in Africa," *Guardian*, July 23, 2012, www.theguardian.com.

8 For more on the church and the Black counterpublic, see Melissa Harris-Perry, *Barbershops, Bibles, and BET: Everyday Talk and Black Political Thought* (Princeton, NJ: Princeton University Press, 2004).

9 Besheer Mohamed, "10 New Findings about Faith among Black Americans," Pew Research Center, February 16, 2021, www.pewresearch.org.

10 Snorton, *Nobody Is Supposed to Know*, 94.

11 Michael Stephens, *Straight Up: The Church's Official Response to the Epidemic of Downlow Living* (Lake Mary, FL: Creation House, 2006).

12 Snorton, *Nobody Is Supposed to Know*, 96.

13 Josef Sorett, "Black Churches, Gay Marriage, and Increasing Nuance," *New York Times*, October 22, 2013, www.nytimes.com. For additional reading on this subject, please see Joseph Sorett, ed., *The Sexual Politics of Black Churches* (New York: Columbia University Press, 2022).

14 Keith Boykin, "Gays in the Village," *New Black Magazine*, May 3, 2022, www.thenewBlackmagazine.com.

15 See Snorton, *Nobody Is Supposed to Know*; Moore, *Invisible Families*, 208–9.

16 Ja'Nina J. Garrett-Walker and Vanessa M. Torres, "Negative Religious Rhetoric in the Lives of Black Cisgender Queer Emerging Adult Men: A Qualitative Analysis," *Journal of Homosexuality* 64 (2016): 1816–31.

17 Kelly Brown Douglas, *Sexuality and the Black Church* (New York: Orbis, 1999). Regulation and denigration of Black sexuality, and Black women's sexuality in particular, is the lynchpin of Patricia Hill Collins's massively influential book, *Black Feminist Thought: Knowledge, Consciousness, and the Politics of Empowerment* (New York: Routledge, 1990).

18 Jared Alexander, "Kirk Franklin Calls Out Homophobia in the Church: 'Nothing to Do with the Bible,'" *Yahoo!*, February 10, 2021, https://currently.att.yahoo.com.

19 Darnell Moore, *No Ashes in the Fire: Coming of Age Black and Free* (New York: Bold Type Books, 2018), 157–68.

20 E. Patrick Johnson, *Sweet Tea: Black Gay Men of the South* (Chapel Hill: University of North Carolina Press, 2008), 184.

21 Monique Moultrie, "Faith as a Site of Black Lesbian Activism," lecture delivered at Harvard Divinity School, March 13, 2020, https://wsrp.hds.harvard.edu.

22 Terrell J. Winder, "'Shouting It Out': Religion and the Development of Black Gay Identities," *Qualitative Sociology* 38 (2015): 375–94.

23 Greg Mania, "Michael Arceneaux on Why He Can't Date Jesus," *Paper*, July 24, 2018, www.papermag.com.

24 Though Ava and Camila are women, Kubicek and colleagues found similar patterns of individualizing one's relationship with God or another higher power in their study of young gay men in Katrina Kubicek et al., "'God Made Me Gay for a Reason': Young Men Who Have Sex with Men's Resiliency in Resolving Internalized Homophobia from Religious Sources," *Journal of Adolescent Research* 24 (2009): 601–33.

25 Michael P. Jeffries, "Ferguson Must Force Us to Face Anti-Blackness," *Boston Globe*, November 28, 2014, www.bostonglobe.com.

26 Charles Mills, *The Racial Contract* (Ithaca, NY: Cornell University Press, 1997).

27 Ta-Nehisi Coates, *Between the World and Me* (New York: Spiegel and Grau, 2015), 12.

28 David Broockman and Joshua Kalla, "Durably Reducing Transphobia: A Field Experiment on Door-to-Door Canvassing," *Science* 352 (2016): 220–24.

29 Benoit Denizet-Lewis, "How Do You Change Voters' Minds? Have a Conversation," *New York Times*, April 7, 2016, www.nytimes.com.

30 Combahee River Collective, *The Combahee River Collective Statement* (Albany, NY: Kitchen Table, 1986).

CHAPTER 7. BLACK QUEERTIDIAN POLITICS

1 Alex Horton, "Trump's Ban on Transgender Troops Hurt the Military, Former Surgeons General Say," *Washington Post*, November 22, 2020, www.washingtonpost.com.

2 Allison Turner, "New Survey of 50,000+ Young People Reveals Troubling Post-Election Spike in Bullying & Harassment," Human Rights Campaign, January 18, 2017, https://www.hrc.org/blog/new-survey-of-50000-young-people-reveals-troubling-post-election-spike-in-b.

3 Christina Walker and Amy La Porte, "Reality Check: Trump Says Atlanta Is 'Falling Apart' and 'Crime Infested,'" *CNN*, January 16, 2017, www.cnn.com.

4 Amy B Wang, "Trump Asked for a 'Muslim Ban,' Giuliani Says, and Ordered a Commission to Do It 'Legally,'" *Washington Post*, January 29, 2017, www.washingtonpost.com.

5 Luke Darby, "Trump on Abused Immigrant Children: 'They're Not Innocent,'" *GQ*, March 24, 2018, www.gq.com.

6 Brian Levin, James J. Nolan, and John David Reitzel, "New Data Showed U.S. Hate Crimes Continued to Rise in 2017," *CBS News*, June 26, 2018, www.cbsnews.com.

7 Johnson, "'Quare' Studies," 135.

8 "Bannon on Trump-Era Technique: 'Flood the Zone with Sh*t,'" CNN, November 1, 2020, /www.cnn.com.

9 In *Optimism at All Costs: Black Attitudes, Activism, and Advancement in Obama's America* (Amherst: University of Massachusetts Press, 2018), Lessie Branch argues that Black Americans are trapped in "paradoxical ebullience," as they harbor hope for economic and political advancement in the United States society despite overwhelming evidence that Black social mobility is essentially nonexistent and racial

inequality is growing more severe. Branch cites Frances Fox Piven and Richard A. Cloward, *Why Americans Don't Vote* (New York: Pantheon, 1988), as she notes the ways voting may limit collective action, which has proven to be a far more effective tool for achieving Black political and economic aims.

10 Anna O. Law, "This Is How Trump's Deportations Differ from Obama's," *Washington Post*, May 3, 2017, www.washingtonpost.com.

11 "A National Epidemic: Fatal Anti-Transgender Violence in the United States in 2019," Human Rights Campaign, accessed May 4, 2022, www.hrc.org.

12 "Fatal Violence against the Transgender and Gender Non-Conforming Community in 2020," Human Rights Campaign, accessed May 4, 2022, www.hrc.org.

13 Alex Paterson, "Broadcast and Cable TV News Spent Only 54 Minutes Covering Anti-trans Violence in 2020," *Media Matters*, February 17, 2021, www.mediamatters.org.

14 Dana Liebelson, "The Supreme Court Gutted the Voting Rights Act: What Happened Next in These Eight States Will Not Shock You," *Mother Jones*, April 8, 2014, www.motherjones.com.

15 Ari Berman, "Wisconsin's Voter-ID Law Suppressed 200,000 Votes in 2016 (Trump Won by 22,748)," *Nation*, May 9, 2017, www.thenation.com.

16 Sarah J. Jackson, Moya Bailey, and Brooke F. Welles, *#HashtagActivism: Networks of Race and Gender Justice* (Cambridge, MA: MIT Press, 2020).

17 Alicia Garza, "A Herstory of the #BlackLivesMatter Movement by Alicia Garza," *Feminist Wire*, October 7, 2014, https://thefeministwire.com.

18 Patrisse Khan-Cullors and Asha Bandele, *When They Call You a Terrorist: A Black Lives Matter Memoir* (New York: St. Martin's Press, 2018), 216.

19 Cathy Cohen, *The Boundaries of Blackness: AIDS and the Breakdown of Black Politics* (Chicago: University of Chicago Press, 1999), 48–53.

20 Juliana Menasce Horowitz and Gretchen Livingston, "How Americans View the Black Lives Matter Movement," Pew Research Center, July 8, 2016, www.pewresearch.org; and Deja Thomas and Juliana Menasce Horowitz, "Support for Black Lives Matter Has Decreased since June but Remains Strong among Black Americans," Pew Research Center, September 16, 2020, www.pewresearch.org.

21 Jennifer Chudy and Hakeem Jefferson, "Support for Black Lives Matter Surged Last Year: Did It Last?" *New York Times*, May 22, 2021, www.nytimes.com.

22 Travis Campbell, "Black Lives Matter's Effect on Police Lethal Use-of-Force," *Social Science Research Network*, May 13, 2021, https://papers.ssrn.com; Jerusalem Demsas, "The Effects of Black Lives Matter Protests," *Vox*, April 9, 2021, www.vox.com.

23 Moore, "Articulating a Politics of (Multiple) Identities," 13.

24 Katelyn Burns, "The Internet Made Trans People More Visible: It Also Left Them More Vulnerable," *Vox*, December 27, 2019, www.vox.com.

25 Roudabeh Kishi and Sam Jones, "Demonstrations and Political Violence in America: New Data for Summer 2020," Armed Conflict Location and Event Data Project, September 3, 2020, https://acleddata.com.

26 Andrew Rojecki and Robert M. Entman, *The Black Image in the White Mind: Media and Race in America* (Chicago: University of Chicago Press, 2001).

CONCLUSION

1 According to the Association of American Universities, 26 percent of women and 6 percent of men experience sexual assault during their time in college. See David Cantor et al., "Report on the AAU Campus Climate Survey on Sexual Assault and Misconduct," Association of American Universities, January 7, 2020, www.aau. edu. Additional studies document the need for improving these outcomes specifically at HBCUs, such as Christine H. Lindquist et al., "The Context and Consequences of Sexual Assault among Undergraduate Women at Historically Black Colleges and Universities (HBCUs)," *Journal of Interpersonal Violence* 12 (2013): 2437–61; and Christine H. Lindquist et al., "Disclosure of Sexual Assault Experiences among Undergraduate Women at Historically Black Colleges and Universities (HBCUs)," *Journal of American College Health* 64 (2016): 469–80.

2 These recommendations are outlined in M. Jacqui Alexander and Beverly Guy-Sheftall, "Introduction," in *Facilitating Campus Climates of Pluralism, Inclusivity, and Progressive Change at HBCUs*, eds. M. Jacqui Alexander and Beverley Guy-Sheftall (Atlanta: Spelman College Women's Resource Center, 2011), 9–48.

3 Roderick Ferguson, "The Past and Future Diversities of HBCUs: Queerness and the Institutional Fulfillment of Black Studies," in Alexander and Guy-Sheftall, *Facilitating Campus Climates of Pluralism, Inclusivity, and Progressive Change at HBCUs*.

4 "Race Relations," Gallup Historical Trends, accessed June 1, 2021, https://news. gallup.com.

5 Branch, *Optimism at All Costs*, 2. A 2021 report from the Brookings Institution shows that "one in five Black Americans are experiencing poverty for the third generation in a row, compared to just one in a hundred white Americans," and "Black families experience higher poverty, less upward mobility, and more downward mobility" than white families. See Scott Winship et al., "Long Shadows: The Black-White Gap in Multigenerational Poverty," Brookings Institution, June 10, 2021, www.brookings.edu.

6 "Race Relations."

7 Meredith Conroy and Perry Bacon Jr., "There's a Huge Gap in How Republicans and Democrats See Discrimination," *FiveThirtyEight*, June 17, 2020, https:// fivethirtyeight.com.

8 Joshua Gamson, "Must Identity Movements Self-Destruct? A Queer Dilemma," *Social Problems* 42 (1995): 403.

9 Michael Dawson, *Black Visions: The Roots of Contemporary African-American Political Ideologies* (Chicago: University of Chicago Press, 2001).

10 Moore, "Articulating a Politics of (Multiple) Identities," 13.

11 Moore, *Invisible Families*.

INDEX

ABOUT THE AUTHOR

Michael P. Jeffries is Dean of Academic Affairs, Class of 1949 Professor in Ethics, and Professor of American Studies at Wellesley College. He holds a PhD from Harvard University and is the author of three previous books on race and American culture: *Thug Life: Race, Gender, and the Meaning of Hip Hop*, *Paint the White House Black: Barack Obama and the Meaning of Race in America*, and *Behind the Laughs: Community and Inequality in Comedy*. He has published dozens of essays and works of criticism in the *New York Times*, the *Atlantic*, the *Guardian*, and the *Boston Globe*, and has been interviewed by the *Washington Post*, the *New York Times*, and NPR.